Routledge Revivals

The Stationary Economy

First published in 1965, this is a reissue of the first volume in Professor Meade's highly influential *Principles of Political Economy,* which aimed to provide an overview of economic analysis in light of contemporary developments in the subject. This volume is based on models of economic systems in which conditions are such as to make possible a state of perfect competition, in which there are no capital goods, in which consumers' tastes, technical knowledge, and the size and composition of the goods are static.

The Stationary Economy

Principles of Political Economy Volume I

J. E. Meade

Routledge
Taylor & Francis Group

First published in 1965
by George Allen & Unwin Ltd

This edition first published in 2012 by Routledge
2 Park Square, Milton Park, Abingdon, Oxon, OX14 4RN

Simultaneously published in the USA and Canada
by Routledge
711 Third Avenue, New York, NY 10017

Routledge is an imprint of the Taylor & Francis Group, an informa business

Publisher's Note
The publisher has gone to great lengths to ensure the quality of this reprint but points out that some imperfections in the original copies may be apparent.

Disclaimer
The publisher has made every effort to trace copyright holders and welcomes correspondence from those they have been unable to contact.

A Library of Congress record exists under ISBN: 76215187

ISBN 13: 978-0-415-52647-0 (hbk)
ISBN 13: 978-0-203-10660-0 (ebk)
ISBN 13: 978-0-415-62174-8 (pbk)

THE STATIONARY ECONOMY

BY

J. E. MEADE

C.B., F.B.A.

Being Volume One of A

PRINCIPLES OF POLITICAL ECONOMY

LONDON

UNWIN UNIVERSITY BOOKS

FIRST PUBLISHED IN 1965

SECOND IMPRESSION 1966

UNWIN UNIVERSITY BOOKS

George Allen & Unwin Ltd.
40 Museum Street, London, W.C.1

PRINTED IN GREAT BRITAIN
in 10 point Times Roman type
BY UNWIN BROTHERS LIMITED
WOKING AND LONDON

PREFACE

When I set to work on my 'Theory of International Economic Policy' (*The Balance of Payments* and *Trade and Welfare*) I was already middle-aged, but still innocent. I thought that with a copious supply of paper and ink, great patience and perseverance, a clear head, goodwill, and a training in the methods of economic analysis one could derive from a few very simple realistic assumptions about men's behaviour a precise theory about the universally correct policy to adopt. In the course of the work it became increasingly clear that the vast number of possible combinations derivable from a very limited number of alternative institutional conditions and modes of human behaviour made it impossible to devise a correct policy without much empirical enquiry into the nature of the surrounding conditions. As my work was not empirical, it inevitably became taxonomic—a classification of the circumstances in which it was best to adopt policy A, of those in which it was best to adopt policy B, and so on. But even so it was bound to remain very incomplete. For the number of possible combinations of relevant conditions was so immense that it was impossible to give a complete classification; one could give only illustrative examples of the principles on which a classification might be made.

In this basic sense the 'Theory of International Economic Policy' must be judged a failure; and I am not now attempting to write on the same lines the 'Theory of Domestic Economic Policy' which at that time I intended to undertake. Nevertheless the 'Theory of International Economic Policy' was not, I venture to suggest, a total waste of time. It could in fact be recast, without any very great change of content, into the form of a series of simple exercises in which one was establishing such propositions as: 'If conditions α, β, γ exist, then policy A will lead to result W and policy B to result X; but if conditions δ, ϵ, ζ exist, then policy A will lead to result Y and policy B to result Z; and so on.' For reasons which are expressed at length in the Introduction to the present work (pp. 22–23 below), this now seems to me to be the better way of presenting the principles of economic policy.

The present work, therefore, makes no claim to universality. It claims only to present a series of 'models'—i.e. of economic systems, each built on greatly simplified assumptions about human motives, technology, and social institutions—and to undertake in each case a series of 'exercises'—i.e. to examine the links of causal relationship in each case. I am convinced that a systematic treatment of the whole field of economic analysis on these lines is worth while for two reasons.

First, while no final decision about policy should ever be taken without adequate empirical enquiry, experience has convinced me that a training in economic principles of the kind given by the examination of these simple models inculcates a way of looking at things which helps greatly in reaching a sensible final decision. The empirical researcher and the policy-maker are much more likely to ask the relevant questions.

Second, there have been very rapid technical advances in economics in recent years in many special fields—in the theory of growth, in dynamic control mechanisms, in applications of the theory of games, in linear programming, and so on. As a result of this in economics, as in practically every other systematic body of study in the modern world, two things have happened: work is increasingly apt to be expressed in highly technical language and often in mathematical form, and workers have become more and more specialized in narrow fields of study. But in the formulation of economic policy, when one is considering any particular decision, it is of basic importance to consider the whole range of economic implications and not merely the effect of the policy in one special part of the field. There is thus a crying need for attempts to translate, as far as this can be done, precise mathematical results into less technical terms and to relate all the branches of economic analysis to each other. There is a place now for the modern equivalent of the old Political Economist, namely the worker who, in the interests of those whose task it is to apply economic theory in policy decisions, specializes in generalization. The present work is designed to make a contribution of this kind.

This first volume, *The Stationary Economy*, covers only a small and preliminary part of the subject. It is based on models of economic systems in which conditions are such as to make possible a state of perfect competition, in which there are no capital goods, and in which consumers' tastes, technical knowledge, and the size and composition of the population are static. It is my present intention to follow it up with a second volume on *Capital, Growth, and Fluctuations* which would allow for the modification of a number of the restrictive assumptions of the present volume, but which would still be based on the assumptions of constant returns to scale, of no external economies or diseconomies, of no objects of communal consumption (such as defence, police, etc.), and of the other conditions which make perfect competition possible. It would need to be followed by a third volume on what happens *Beyond Competition*. There might even be room for two further volumes—the first to relate important acts of economic policy simultaneously to the influences stressed in each of the first three volumes, and the second to consider the 'international' relationships between the independently formed policies of separate 'national' authorities. But how far in fact the work will proceed is a matter of great uncertainty.

There are two main branches of economic analysis on which I have relied in the present volume. On the first of these, namely what may be broadly described as the indifference-curve techniques, there is a vast wealth of literature in the learned journals, much of which stems directly or indirectly from the work of Professors R. G. D. Allen and Sir John Hicks in 'A Reconsideration of the Theory of Value' (*Economica* 1934). For the second, namely the application of linear programming, I have relied largely on Dorfman, Samuelson, and Solow *Linear Programming and Economic Analysis*. But in both cases I have learned a thousand and one things from many other books, articles, and colleagues. I make no claim to basic originality; but it is impossible for me to acknowledge the source of each particular idea. Indeed I do not know precisely whence I have acquired them. But I would like specifically to acknowledge the great help which I have received from my colleague Mr C. J. Bliss who read the whole of this volume in MS. and made a number of helpful suggestions.

J. E. MEADE

Christ's College
Cambridge
June 1964

CONTENTS

INTRODUCTION

Many students of economics come to the subject because they are interested in the possible improvement of society. The author of this work (like many others in the late twenties and early thirties) came to economics because he abhorred mass unemployment and wanted to know why society was failing to avoid the stupidity of idle men and machines combined with crying real needs for the products of those men and machines. The problems of the present age are different. The huge and growing disparities of wealth between the rich developed and the poor underdeveloped countries of the world would be the problem which would be most likely to attract him to economics if he were now starting once more at the beginning.

For tackling any major economic problem of this kind one must be in a position to understand the causal relationships in an economy. For example, would a reduction of the rate of income tax increase or decrease the volume of employment? For this purpose a well-furnished tool-box of instruments of economic analysis is a necessary but by no means a sufficient part of one's equipment. Economic analysis as such is merely a process of logical deduction whereby one says: 'Given certain assumptions about economic and social institutions, about the nature and size of economic resources, and about the way in which individuals react in given situations, then such-and-such a change at such-and-such a point in the system will have such-and-such effects upon other variables in the system.' For example, given certain assumptions about the population, the existing capital equipment, and the available natural resources, about monetary and fiscal institutions, about free enterprise or socially controlled institutions for production and trade, about the psychology of persons in their reactions to changes in prices and incomes, and about many other relevant matters, a change in the rate of income tax—when one has taken into account all the manifold interactions between one section of the economy and another—will have such-and-such effects upon the level and the rate of growth of employment and production, upon the level of money prices and incomes, upon the distribution of incomes, upon the balance of payments with other countries, and upon many other important variables.

To reach conclusions of this kind one must have two rather separate types of skill and knowledge.

First, one must have had practice in the logical analytical processes involved in studying interrelationships between variables in systems of the kind which economic life constitutes.

Second, one must have knowledge about the actual resources, institutions, and behavioural reactions in the actual situation which is under study. Much, but not all, of such knowledge will be quantitative in character and subject to statistical examination.

This work is confined to the first of these two types of investigation. The reader should be warned that it is, therefore, a most incomplete guide to the real world. Before any worth-while decision can be reached about any particular economic policy in the real world, institutional, historical, and statistical investigation of the actual situation is an essential complement to the general education in economic principles which it is the sole purpose of this work to promote. But it is claimed that a general education in general economic principles will in fact help towards a correct interpretation of the facts in any particular situation. For this purpose what is needed is a synthetic view of all the main ways in which various economic policies and institutions may interact on each other; and with the many notable, highly technical, and still rather separate, advances which have been made by economic theorists in different parts of the field of economic analysis in recent years, a restatement in the simplest possible terms of the broad synthetic view is now much needed. This work aims at contributing towards such a restatement.

First principles are helpful; but there remain many reasons why it is impossible to lay down *a priori* from first principles any one economic policy as being the one which it is best to adopt in all conceivable circumstances.

In the first place, the choice between different economic policies must depend upon the relative weights which are placed by the policy-makers upon the various possible (and often conflicting) objectives of policy. The various objectives which it may be hoped to attain by means of economic policy may usefully be grouped under the three general headings of the Efficiency, the Distributional, and the Social aspects of economic life.

(1) An economic system may be said to be inefficient in so far as it would be possible with the given resources of the community to make some citizens at any one point of time better off without making any others at that same or some other point of time worse off. The involuntary mass unemployment of the 1930's was an outstanding example of economic inefficiency, since it would clearly have been possible to use the products of the unemployed men and machines to raise immediately the general standard of living of all consumers and/or to produce capital goods which would enable future generations to be better off.

A less glaring example of economic inefficiency occurs when all resources are employed, but when there is a misallocation of resources between various uses. This occurs when too many of some resources are employed in one occupation or industry and too few in another. Thus there may be an overproduction of one product (say, bread) and an underproduction of another (say, clothing), so that some consumers could be immediately better served without any one being worse off if less bread and more clothing were produced. Or too many ploughs and too few looms may be produced now in the sense that future consumers would be better off if they had less ploughs (and so less bread) but more looms (and so more clothing). A rather more subtle case of misallocation of resources occurs when one industry (say, the food industry) has too much of one resource (say, labour) and too little of another resource (say, land) while some other industry (say, the clothing industry) is suffering from a shortage of labour and a surplus of land. The output of both industries could then be increased simultaneously if labour moved from the food industry (where it is over plentiful) to the clothing industry (where it is scarce) while the use of land was shifted in the opposite direction.

Economic arrangements may also affect the technological efficiency of the production system. Inventions and innovations which lead to the production of a greater volume of output by a given amount of resources are directly the concern, not of the economist, but of the engineer. Nevertheless some economic arrangements may provide strong, and other arrangements only weak, incentives and opportunities for research and development and for the use of newly discovered methods of production. An economic policy which promotes technical progress may itself be said to increase the efficiency of the system.

(2) Economic policies which lead to the full employment of available resources, to the efficient allocation of resources between different uses, and to a high rate of technical progress will all help to raise the general standard of living. But policy-makers are not concerned solely with the general average standard of living. They are also interested in its distribution between individuals. Here problems of equity and of the comparison of one man's welfare with that of another are involved. The basic principles upon which income and wealth would be distributed in an ideal community are not for the economist as such to determine. But it is the economist's concern to consider how any given economic policy is likely to affect the distribution of income and wealth and thus to make it more or less like the pattern which the policy-makers consider desirable.

Distributional issues always involve a clash of interest. Should citizens A, B, and C be made better off at the expense of citizens D, E, and F? The most obvious and direct distributional issue of this kind is the distribution of the community's income and wealth at any one period of time between the existing citizens of the community. Should the standard of living of the poor be raised at the expense of that of the rich? But this is not the only type of distributional issue that arises in society. The distribution of income and wealth between the present generation and future generations presents a similar problem. How far should the present generation cut back its consumption in order to accumulate capital in order to increase production and so the standard of living for future generations? The decision, through the choice of appropriate economic policies, of the 'optimum level of savings', i.e. of the amount of its current output which the present generation will refrain from consuming but will invest in capital available for future use, raises the same sort of problems of comparison of the needs of one set of persons with those of another set of persons.

There may be yet another instance of this same sort of 'distributional' problem. It may be possible by governmental policies of one kind or another to influence the birthrate and so the size and rate of growth of the total population. If full employment is maintained, a change in the size of the population will normally lead to a change in the same direction in the total output of the community. But it may well be that output will not go up in the same proportion as population. If output per head will be lower with a higher population, then there is a 'distributional' issue between the born and the unborn. With the smaller population each citizen will enjoy a high standard of living; with a larger population each citizen will have a lower standard of living but there will be more of them. It is not for the economist as such to determine which is the better state of affairs. But the economist is nevertheless concerned with this question of the 'optimum size of the population'; for it is his concern to consider both what are likely to be the effects of different economic policies on the size of the population and what are likely to be the effects of a given change in the size of the population on the average standard of living.

(3) The main objectives of economic policy are no doubt concerned with either the efficiency (size-of-cake) or distributional (division-of-cake) aspects of the society concerned. But there are a number of other social effects of economic policies which the policy makers will undoubtedly wish to consider in the choice between various policies. Two such social objectives of basic importance are individual freedom of choice and security. An economy in which individuals are free to choose what jobs they will take, where they will live, and what particular goods and services they will consume may—other things being equal—be considered better than one in which these things are determined for them by some superior authority. Similarly, a society in which the individual citizen faces

great risks and uncertainties (that he may lose his job or that his income may be reduced) may—other things being equal—be considered less desirable than one in which economic policies are so devised that he is less uncertain about the future.

It will be a major theme of this work to point out the possible conflicts between different possible objectives when one is choosing between various economic policies. At this stage it is necessary only to give one or two basic examples. A tax-cum-social-security system could be devised which produced absolute equality in the distribution of income; but if it meant taking away all the additional income earned by the exceptionally energetic and making up the deficient incomes of the exceptionally slothful it would clearly blunt most individual incentives for economic efficiency. Or, to take another example, measures which stimulated inventiveness might increase economic efficiency by leading to more effective methods of production; but the individual worker's security in his job might well be reduced, since anyone might at any moment turn out to be the handloom weaver who had to give up his job to the mechanical loom. All that can be done is, in the choice of a policy to deal with any particular evil, carefully to consider its effects upon the other objectives of economic policy. The final weighting of objectives is, however, a political and not an economic decision.

Different societies will no doubt give different weights to these final objectives; and for that reason one cannot say that a policy which is 'right' for one society is necessarily 'right' for another. But even if the weights given to the final objectives of policy were the same in all societies, there would be other reasons why the policy which was appropriate in one society might differ from that which was appropriate in another society. One of the main sources of such differences is variations in the endowment of communities with the basic economic resources for production. As a first broad approximation the basic resources needed for production can be divided into land, labour, and capital, if we mean by land all natural resources, by labour all human productive activity, and by capital all man-made instruments of production or improvements of land and labour. We can then divide economies according to the relative supplies of these basic factors of production into the six main types shown in Table I.

The first three economies shown in this table are all richly endowed with man-made capital equipment, and we may therefore call them all developed economies. On the other hand, the last three are all undeveloped economies because they have little man-made capital. But each of these two broad types of developed and undeveloped economies can be divided into three sub-categories.

Type of economy	Relative factor endowment in Capital	Labour	Natural resources
(1) Simple Developed	+	−	−
(2) Malthusian Developed	+	+	−
(3) Empty Developed	+	−	+
(4) Simple Undeveloped	−	+	+
(5) Malthusian Undeveloped	−	+	−
(6) Empty Undeveloped	−	−	+

+ means richly and − means poorly endowed with the factor in question.

Table I.—*Factor Endowments and Types of Economy*

Thus in economy (1) there is much capital equipment relatively to both the other factors; and this we may call the simple developed economy. In economy (2) capital development is great relatively to the community's natural resources, but there is also a large population pressure on those natural resources; so we may call this the Malthusian type of developed economy. In economy (3) there is much capital per head of the population, but the population is spread over large open spaces; so we may call this the empty type of developed economy. Similarly, economy (4), having little capital relatively to both labour and natural resources, is the simple type of undeveloped economy; economy (5), having little capital but also much population pressure relatively to its natural resources, is the Malthusian type of undeveloped economy; and economy (6), having little capital and little population relatively to its land and other natural resources, is an empty undeveloped economy.

Different types of problem may arise in different types of economy. Here it is sufficient to give only one broad example.

Compare the Simple Developed Economy with the Malthusian Undeveloped Economy (economy 1 with economy 5). In economy 1 there being already much capital equipment relatively to both labour and land a main problem may be to find profitable uses for more capital equipment; every man and every acre may be already fully equipped. If people are saving out of their incomes, it may therefore be difficult to find useful outlets for the expenditure of these savings on new plant, buildings, machinery, tools, and so on. As a result there may be a deficiency of total demand for goods and services; people are not buying enough consumption goods because they are saving a large part of their incomes, but they are not buying enough new capital goods (machines, etc.) because everyone and every place is already fully equipped. This deficiency of demand may lead to unemployment of capital, labour, and land simply because there is an insufficiently high level of demand for goods and services in general. In economy 5, on the other hand, the problem will be to find profitable employment for all the available labour because capital and land both being so scarce there is not enough land or enough machinery and tools to equip everyone for productive work. Here again as in economy 1 there may be unemployed labour.

But the problem of economy 1 is nevertheless totally different from that of economy 5, as can be seen from a consideration of the policies which would be appropriate to cure the unemployment. In the case of economy 1 what is needed is a set of measures which will induce people to spend more money on goods and services in general, whether these be consumption goods or capital goods. An increase in money expenditure in general will bring into productive employment the unemployed capital, the unemployed labour, and the unemployed land in the community. But such a policy for the general expansion of monetary demand would do no good in economy 5; for it could not draw unemployed labour into work in the conditions of that economy where capital and land are already fully employed and where there is no more capital and land to provide the necessary equipment for a larger employed working force. In order to give full employment in economy 5 measures must be designed to decrease the size of the working population or to increase the amount of capital equipment or to induce a shift in the economy from industries and processes of production which use a high ratio of capital and land to labour to those which use a high ratio of labour to land and capital.

But in order to decide what is the best policy to adopt in any circumstances it is not sufficient to know what weight is to be given to the various possible objectives of policy and what are the real resources at the disposal of the community. It is also necessary to know how the community is organized for economic purposes. For the relevant institutions may differ very widely from community to community. One of the most relevant matters in this connection is the method of organization of the various markets in the economy. There may, for example, be (i) completely free competition between a very large number of buyers and sellers in a market, or (ii) only one or two large monopolistic buyers or sellers in the market, or (iii) a single socialized organization producing and rationing supplies to consumers, or (iv) any one of a large number of State controls (like the setting of a maximum price) in an otherwise free market. Thus the community's farming may be carried out by capitalist tenant-landlord farms or by small peasant proprietors or by collective farms; or the wage rate may be fixed by a bargain between a monopoly trade union and a monopoly employers' federation or by individual competition in a completely unorganized market or by some governmental wage-fixing authority.

There are many other possible institutional variations. Thus, in one economy practically all real property may be owned by the State; in another economy it may all be owned by private persons; and in yet a third economy private persons may own not only all the real property of the community but also in addition a large volume of paper debt owed to them by the State (the so-called 'National debt'). Or, to take another example, in one economy social attitudes and educational arrangements may be such as to make the movement of men from one job to another easy and frequent, whereas in another society occupational and geographical movement may be rare and difficult. Finally, in one community the State may be under the necessity of raising a large proportion of the national income in governmental revenue to finance a heavy expenditure on armaments, whereas in another community expenditure on armaments and, as a result, the general level of tax rates may be low.

Clearly some of these differences in institutions may themselves be considered as being the results of conscious acts of economic policy; for example, the setting of a legal maximum price in a market is likely to be an act which can be decided on economic grounds by the government itself. But not all the differences in economic institutions are of this nature; for example, the level of expenditure on armaments cannot be considered to be solely or even primarily an economic decision. And it is difficult to know where to draw the line between institutions which can and those which cannot be altered by the government on economic grounds; for example, to make employers and workers compete for labour in a fully competitive labour market by making trade unions and employers' federations illegal may be a theoretically possible line of economic policy, but in fact it may well be totally impossible politically. In many choices between different economic policies a large range of relevant institutional arrangements must be taken for granted; and the effect of any given economic policy will clearly greatly depend upon the institutional set-up within which it has to operate.

Finally, societies may differ very much in the behaviour and motivation of their citizens. In one society the main motive in life may be to make as large an income as possible; in another it may be to acquire as much power over others as possible; and in a third it may be to carry on with life as before in a traditional manner. One example of this sort of difference might be that in one society businessmen aimed at maximizing the profits which they could earn; in another society they might try, even at the sacrifice of profit, to expand their commercial empires to the greatest possible size; and in a third community they might prefer simply to continue making the products and earning the income which their fathers had done before them. Clearly the effect of any given change in an economic policy is likely to be very greatly affected by the way in which the individual citizens react to a change in their economic environment.

The possible relevant variations of such reactions are almost innumerable. Here, once more, we shall confine ourselves to one or two examples. In deciding how much of their income to save and how much to spend on present enjoyments, are the citizens in the economy under study mainly affected by (i) the size of their current incomes relatively to their needs, (ii) past habits regarding the level of their consumption, (iii) what their neighbours the Jones's are spending on consumption, or (iv) the rate of interest which they could earn on their savings? Within a family budget of any given size do housewives and other consumers (i) have rather fixed habits about what they will buy, (ii) shift quickly and frequently from goods which have become more expensive to goods which have become less expensive, or (iii) determine their purchases from time to time according to changes in outside advertisement campaigns? Do a particular group of wage-earners demand higher pay mainly (i) because their employers have large profits out of which to pay them, (ii) because the pay of other workers has gone up, (iii) because the cost of living has gone up, or (iv) simply because there is a high demand for their particular work? Clearly it will be important in discussing the choice of an economic policy to consider the individual's behavioural patterns in the particular economy in question.

The study of the principles of economic policy is further complicated in the real world because there is more than one independent government determining the choice of policies. Because of differences in their final objectives, in the basic resources of their communities, in their institutional arrangements, and in the behavioural patterns of their citizens, different sovereign governments are likely to adopt different economic policies for their independent communities. But no economy is unaffected by what is happening in the other economies, though some will be more dependent than others upon what is happening elsewhere. Each government in choosing its own economic policy must take into account what is happening elsewhere. Moreover, in various ways it may through its own choice of policy be able to affect the choice of policy by other governments and thus indirectly make the outside conditions more or less favourable for the achievement of its own objectives. Such effects may be achieved by the direct exercise of economic pressure by one government upon another or by the threat of such pressure or by the conclusion of a mutually advantageous bargain or treaty between two or more governments or even by the institution of a super-government endowed with the power to enforce (within certain specified limits) the adoption of particular policies by the subsidiary governments. In any case in the choice of an economic policy any one government must always take into account the facts (i) that it is not operating in a 'closed' vacuum but in an 'open' system in which the results of its policy will in any case be greatly affected by what is going on elsewhere and (ii) that its own choice of policy may directly or indirectly affect the choice of policies by other governments in ways which are of great importance to itself.

It should by now be clear to the reader that any economic system constitutes a very complicated set of relationships. There are a very large number of variables. Incomes, prices, outputs, levels of employment, savings, consumptions of various goods, additions to various forms of capital equipment, imports, exports, wage-rates, rates of interest, the amount of money, and many other quantities are all simultaneously affected by the independent decisions of individuals, business corporations, and governmental bodies. Thus a change in economic policy will set up a whole series of interrelated reactions. Not only are there a large number of variables and of interconnections between them; but there are a very large number of combinations of possible assumptions about policy objectives, endowments in basic resources, institutional arrangements, and behavioural patterns within an economy. It is this complexity which above all constitutes the essential difficulty for economic analysis.

How then can one proceed? The author of this work can think of only one method. One must construct a simple model which isolates one or two features of a possible real world; one must study their implications in this simple setting and then progressively elaborate and expand the model by making the assumptions less and less restrictive. But on each occasion there will soon come a point at which further elaboration will make the model too complicated for it to be of any more use than the real world itself in helping one to comprehend the forces actually at work. Then one must begin again with another simple model which isolates another set of relevant features of the real world and start the whole process of gradual elaborations over again.

In this procedure one should be extremely frank about the assumptions which are being made at each stage for each model. This will unfortunately make many students despair of a discipline which appears so unrealistic. But this risk must be taken. Any other course means that the economist bamboozles himself as well as his students. One should always avoid the risk of claiming more for one's analysis than one can in fact rightfully claim. The art of political economy is to choose models which combine simplicity with relevance to certain important features of the real world. The economist can never be sure that he knows the answer. But if he has built a large number of models which between them incorporate in various ingenious combinations all the main features of the real world which he thinks are likely to be relevant to the issue which he is examining, and if each of these models passes the same verdict upon a given economic policy, then he may have some confidence that this verdict is more likely to be right than wrong. The author of this work is convinced from his own personal experience that, employed in this careful manner, economic analysis can help greatly to illuminate problems of policy in the real world.

CHAPTER I

TEN ASSUMPTIONS

We shall start our model-building by considering the operations of an extremely simple economy in which the two original factors of production, land and labour, are used directly to produce various goods for individual consumption and in which the underlying conditions are unchanging so that a stationary self-perpetuating equilibrium state is reached. The present volume is devoted to the examination of such a society. Such a society is, of course, horribly unrealistic. Nevertheless it is claimed that this investigation is useful on three counts. First, it enables one to isolate and thus examine precisely and carefully certain relationships of first-rate importance of a kind which are at work in the real world. Second, it provides a training in certain tools of analysis which will prove of great use when the strict assumptions of this volume are relaxed and models are made more realistic. Third, the model can provide an example of the basic clash between what is desirable in society on efficiency grounds and what is desirable on distributional grounds; and it provides, therefore, a good introduction to a wide range of problems concerned with the choice of economic policy.

It would be possible to examine this basic model on either of two extreme assumptions about the institutional framework of the economy. One could assume that the economy was a perfectly free competitive *laissez-faire* market system in which any individual citizen was free to buy, sell, and produce anything he wished and in which the organization of production and consumption was carried out by the free play of competition between indivduals each of whom acted in the search of his own maximum advantage. Alternatively, one could assume that all production was socialized and that the State alone was allowed to decide what should be produced and consumed, so that the organization of production and consumption was the result of a central plan. One of the important purposes of this volume is in fact to consider the similarities and the contrasts between these two methods of determining how the scarce resources of the community (land and labour) will be used to produce goods and services for the best satisfaction of the citizens' needs. Our procedure in this volume will be first to discuss the issues at length on the strict assumptions of a perfectly competitive *laissez-faire* market economy and then to conclude the volume by considering how the same problems might be tackled in a completely socialist economy. It would be possible to proceed in exactly the opposite order—to consider at length all the issues in the context of a socialist economy and then on the basis of that discussion to explain how a *laissez-faire* market economy would cope with the same problems. We have chosen to consider the *laissez-faire* economy first and the Socialist economy second simply because that follows the historical sequence of the development of thought on these problems.

We shall accordingly start with the following ten strict and far-reaching assumptions.

(1) We assume that we are dealing with a closed economy in the sense that there are no other economies with which the citizens of our economy have any economic relations.

(2) Second, we shall be assuming that there is no Government expenditure and no Government taxation. This complete absence of a Government budget and of problems of Public Finance involves among other things the assumption that there are no goods and services (such as defence, justice, law and order) which our citizens must consume in common. All goods and services are assumed in this volume to be capable of private individual consumption.

(3) We shall assume at first that all production and consumption takes place in freely competitive markets. Any citizen is permitted to undertake on his own private enterprise the production of any product. There is no production by state enterprises. Any citizen is permitted to purchase for his own consumption any commodity or service available on the market.

(4) The only factors of production with which we shall be concerned in this volume fall into the two categories of land and labour. By land we mean all forms of original natural resource, but we assume in this volume that these natural resources are indestructible. In other words, we neglect problems connected with the use of wasting assets such as the mining of minerals or the depletion of forests. By labour we mean all forms of human work. We shall similarly assume in this volume that the quality of human effort is given; that is to say, we shall be neglecting problems connected with the investment of capital in the further education and improvement of human abilities. In our model there may be many different forms of labour (some men specially fitted for brain work, some for heavy physical work, some for delicate manipulation, and so on) and many different forms of land (some fertile, some infertile, some hilly, some flat, and so on). In other words there may be many more than two distinct factors of production; but all these factors are assumed to fall into

either of the two broad categories of land or labour. We assume that there are large, but given and unchanging, amounts of each type of land and of labour in our economy.

(5) In this volume we shall neglect entirely the factor 'capital'. We shall assume simply that the various forms of labour and land combine together to produce, instantaneously and without delay, certain outputs of goods and services ready for immediate final consumption by the citizens of our economy. There is no stock of real capital in the form of plant and machinery, or of stocks of raw materials, goods in process, or of finished products. Moreover, it is assumed that all citizens spend on consumption all of the incomes which they earn in the form of wages of labour or rent of land. No part of income is saved and no real capital is accumulated.

(6) In this volume we assume that there is no continuing technical progress. There is a certain state of technical knowledge available to all the citizens in the economy.

(7) There are no indivisibilities in the economy and there are in consequence constant returns to scale. This means that if given amounts of land and labour are being used, in the most efficient known way, to produce a given amount of a particular product, then an x per cent increase (or decrease) in the amounts of land and of labour available for the production would cause an x per cent increase (or decrease) in the level of the output of the product. The factors land and labour and the products themselves are all assumed to be infinitely divisible so that a change of x per cent (however large or small x may be) could not give rise to awkward absolute sizes for the productive activity. The absolute scale of production itself makes no difference to the amount of output per unit of input.

(8) There are no external economies or diseconomies in the community. This implies that the competitive markets work in such a way that, when a private citizen produces something, he in fact pays for all, but for not more than all, the real resources which he uses up in the production, and that he is in fact paid (or himself pays) for all, but for not more than all, the useful products (or the indirect disadvantages to others) to which his productive activity gives rise. It implies similarly that, when a private consumer consumes something, he in fact pays for all, but not for more than all, the real resources which his consumption uses up and that he is paid (or himself pays) for any accompanying benefits (or costs) which his act of private consumption may involve for other citizens.[1] One

[1] The communal goods which we assumed away in our assumption (2) (p. 26 above) when we stated that there was no Government expenditure on communal services like defence, police, etc., are merely an extreme example of the external economies assumed away in assumption (8). For if a private citizen were privately

example must suffice at this stage. If a producer causes a smoke nuisance which increases the laundry bills of those in his neighbourhood, but does not himself have to meet those bills, then his production is imposing an 'external diseconomy' on those whose linen is thus soiled. We assume away all such externalities.

(9) We assume in this volume that there is a large number of individual citizens and that each citizen has a given consistent and independent set of preferences. For example, if citizen A were given the choice between (*a*) working 2000 hours a year and having 300 loaves of bread and 5 shirts a year or (*b*) working 2200 hours a year and having 250 loaves of bread and 10 shirts a year, he would know whether he preferred (*a*) to (*b*) or (*b*) to (*a*) or was indifferent between them. Moreover, his set of choices is assumed to be consistent in the sense that if he prefers (*a*) to (*b*) and (*b*) to (*c*), then he prefers (*a*) to (*c*). His set of preferences is assumed to be independent in the sense that it is unaffected by what is going on around him (and in particular by what his neighbours are consuming) and it is given in the sense that it remains the same over time.

(10) Finally, in order to ease the exposition we shall make a very simple monetary assumption, namely that our citizens use a simple form of money—let us call it $1 notes—and that they spend on consumption goods each working day the whole of the money income which they earned from wages and rents on the previous working day. Since the amount earned on any working day in wages and rents must be equal to the amount received that day for the sale of that day's output of the products of labour and land, the money national income with our simple assumption will be constant. Suppose on day 1 $100 million has been earned. Then on day 2 $100 million will be spent, so that on day 2 $100 million will be earned. Then on day 3 $100 million will be spent . . . and so on. By this means we are able to consider what will determine the money prices of the various products that are produced, the money wage rates for various grades of labour, and the money rents for various sorts of land on the simple assumption that the total money income of the community is constant at $100 million a day.

It may help with the analysis of the rest of this volume to have in mind the simple schematic representation of our economy which is shown in Figure 1.

Every working morning in our competitive economy the workers and property owners (Mr A, Mr B, Mr C, Mr D) go off from their

to finance a police force, he would himself enjoy added security, but so would the other citizens. He would be paying the cost not only of his own, but also of his neighbours' security. His act of private consumption would confer an 'external economy' of increased security on others.

Homes to the Firms and Farms where they provide the services of Labour (*L*) and of the land or Natural resources (*N*) which they own. These resources produce an immediate output of goods and services for final consumption (*XYZ*) which find their way almost instantaneously to the Shops where they are bought on the same day by the housewives (Mrs A, Mrs B, Mrs C, Mrs D). This explains the day's circular clockwise flow of real goods and services shown by the unbroken line in Figure 1.

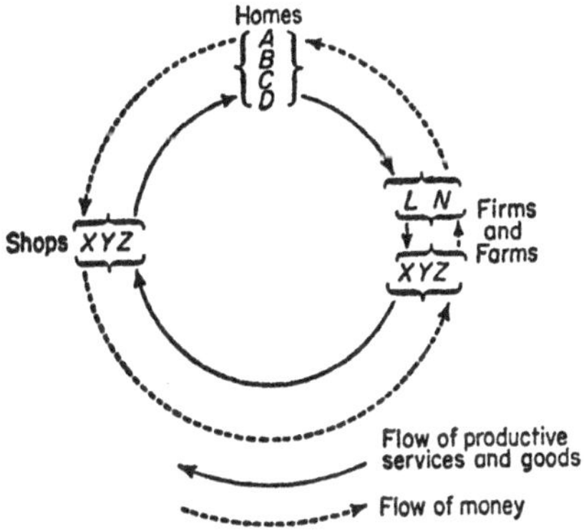

Figure 1

In the course of this same day the housewives have spent in the shops the whole of the $100 millions of money income which they received on the previous day. This money has been received in the firms and farms and paid, in wages of labour and rents of land, to the workers and property owners who, that same evening, take these receipts of income home to their housewives for expenditure in the shops on the following day. This explains the day's circular anticlockwise flow of money shown by the broken line in Figure 1.

There are thus in our present simplified economic system two markets: (i) the market for consumption goods as sold in the Shops to the final consumers; and (ii) the market for the productive factors, labour and land, as hired by the various Firms and Farms for the production of the goods supplied to the Shops. In this volume we shall be assuming that in both these markets conditions of perfect competition or of perfect potential competition prevail. Before we go further it is necessary to explain in some detail the meaning of these terms 'perfect competition' and 'perfect potential competition'.

Perfect competition for any product in the Shops (or for any factor of production in the Firms or Farms) implies:

(i) That there are a large number of individual competing sellers of each product (or factor);

(ii) that there are a large number of individual competing purchasers of each product (or hirers and employers of each factor);

(iii) that each product (or factor) is a standardized homogeneous entity so that there is no difference between one unit and another unit of the same product (or factor);

(iv) that there is perfect knowledge by each buyer and seller of the product (or factor) of the prices currently asked and offered by the other buyers and sellers in the same market; and

(v) that there are no transport or similar market costs which differentiate one buyer's position from that of another buyer or one seller's position from that of another seller.

As a first result of these conditions there could not be more than one price ruling in the market for any one product (or factor). For if there were a difference of price, the buyer who was being charged a higher price would attempt to obtain his requirements at a lower cost from the seller who was charging a lower price; and this seller in turn would be seeking a somewhat higher price from the buyer who was paying the higher price. As a result the high-priced seller would have to lower his price and the low-priced buyer would have to raise his price. Only when all bargains were at the same price would no buyer or seller seek to transfer his business.

There is a second and fundamental result of perfect competition. Each individual buyer or seller will take the market price of the product (or factor) at which he can buy or sell as given and on that basis will decide how much he wishes to buy or sell. No single buyer or seller alone by buying or selling more or less could hope to have any appreciable effect upon the ruling market price; for the amount which any individual buyer takes off the market or any individual seller puts on to the market is but a drop in the ocean of the total market. Of course, if all or a large proportion of the buyers (or of the sellers) decided simultaneously to buy (or sell) more or less of the product or factor, their combined decisions would affect the market price. This is known as the 'parametric' role of prices in a perfectly competitive market: the price of the product or factor is taken as a given constant by each individual decision-making unit (i.e. by each individual competing buyer or seller) but the level of each price is in fact the outcome of the sum of all the independently reached decisions of all the individual decision-making units.

What is important for our subsequent analysis are these two results of perfect competition, namely that only one price can rule in the market for a given product or factor and that each individual buyer or seller will take this ruling price as given in so far as his own individual action is concerned. But for these results to occur it is not in fact necessary that 'perfect competition', as we have just defined it, should prevail. It will be sufficient if conditions of what we may call 'perfect potential competition' prevail. The distinction is of great importance for our subsequent analysis of the productive process. We can explain it in the following way.

In what follows we shall assume that there are a large number of citizens and thus a large number of competing housewives purchasing the consumption goods in the Shops and a large number of competing workers and landlords selling the services of labour and of land to the producers in the Firms and Farms. But we shall not assume that there are necessarily a large number of competing Firms and Farms in any industry purchasing the services of labour and land and selling the consumption goods. With our two assumptions of freedom to compete (assumption 3) and of constant returns to scale (assumption 7) it is not necessary to assume that there are in fact a large number of small competing firms in any one industry in order to reach the conclusion that the individual firm cannot itself influence the prices of the factors which it buys or of the products which it sells.

The reason for this can be seen by starting from the extreme assumption that in any one industry (for example, the industry producing bread) there is one giant monopolistic firm. It would seem at first sight that this firm by restricting its output could create a scarcity of bread and thus drive the price of bread up above its cost of production and reap a monopoly profit. But if it did so, a small competitor would immediately come into the market and undercut the monopolist. For we are assuming that anyone is free to come in and compete (assumption 3) and that there is no disadvantage from the point of view of cost in producing on a very small scale (assumption 7). The monopolist producer would in fact be faced with 'perfect potential competition'. Although at the moment he is faced with no actual competition, he must in fact take the market price as being set at a level not higher than the cost of production of the myriads of small competitors that could at any moment come in and compete with him.

In fact the combination of assumptions 3 and 7 means that the size of the individual Firm or Farm is of trivial importance for our present analysis. We can conduct our analysis on the assumption that each industry is represented by only one single Firm or Farm (subject to perfect potential competition) or by a large number of small Firms or Farms (in actual perfect competition with each other) or by any intermediate number of Firms or Farms. In what follows it will often be most convenient to talk of an industry as if it were made up of only one single firm (subject to perfect potential competition); for then everything which we have to say about the firm can apply to the industry and *vice versa*. The size of the individual Firm or Farm becomes a matter of real importance only when we come on to consider economies of large-scale production which are excluded from this volume.

The grossly oversimplified economic system with which we are now dealing will, of course, tell us little about many of the basic economic objectives discussed in the Introduction (pp. 14–17). Since we assume a given state of technical knowledge, it will tell us nothing about the promotion of technical progress (p. 15). Since we assume no savings, it will tell us nothing about the optimum level of savings (p. 16). Since we assume a given population, it will tell us nothing about the economic problems of achieving an optimum population (p. 16). Since there is no change taking place in our stationary state, it will have little relevance to problems of economic security (p. 17).

Since our economy is a completely *laissez-faire* system, there will be complete freedom of choice of consumers among products and of workers among jobs, so that complete economic freedom will exist (p. 16). It will also be true that there will be full employment of the resources of land and labour (p. 14) if our economy does find an equilibrium state. For if any resource were unemployed, the owner of that resource would, in competition with the other competing owners of the same resource, be lowering the money price at which he would offer it in the market. So long as there was unemployed labour, the money wage rate would be falling in our perfectly competitive labour market. Or so long as there was unemployed land, the money rent per acre would be falling in our perfectly competitive real estate market. Conversely, so long as there was an excess of demand for, over the available supply of, labour (or land), the money wage rate (or the money rate of rent) would be being raised in our competitive factor markets. Prices of the factors of production would thus never be constant unless there were full employment. With a constant level of money expenditure on all factors taken together (assumption 10 on p. 28) a point could be reached at which the money wage rate and the money rate of rent were such as to give employment to all the available labour and land.[1] It should in passing be carefully noted that we are not arguing that the competitive factor markets will necessarily lead to a

[1] We rule out for the moment the possibility, which we will take up later, that there is so much of one factor that even when its price has fallen to zero and it is a free good there is still not a sufficient demand for its services to find useful employment for all of it.

stationary equilibrium position. There is in fact much to be said about the dynamic processes whereby market adjustments are made and whether these are stable or not; but these matters are not covered in this volume. All that we are asserting here is that if a stationary equilibrium is achieved there will be full employment of resources; for if there were not full employment of any factor, the price of that factor would not be constant and the economy would not, therefore, be in a stationary equilibrium.

There remain two of our economic objectives—namely those of an economically efficient allocation of resources (p. 15) and of an equitable distribution of income and property (p. 16)—about which quite a lot can be learnt even in the grossly over-simplified economy of this volume. A major function of our analysis in this volume will be to explain what economic efficiency means and to show how in the conditions now assumed an equilibrium based on the free operation of the price mechanism will achieve an economically efficient use of resources. But it will also be a major function of our analysis in this volume to point out that this 'efficient' equilibrium may also be a very 'inequitable' one. It will become apparent that a price situation which ensures an efficient use of resources may well involve an undesirable distribution of income. This volume will serve well to illustrate possible clashes between economic efficiency and distributional equity (cf. Chapter XII below).

CHAPTER II

CONSUMERS' CHOICE

In this chapter we shall consider the basic logic lying behind the choice of our consumers (Mrs A, Mrs B, Mrs C, Mrs D) as they select among the products available to them in the Shops.

Let us start with the simplest possible situation—Mrs A choosing between two products *X* and *Y*. In Figure 2 we measure along the horizontal axis the amount of *X* and up the vertical axis the amount of *Y* which Mrs A may be acquiring each week for consumption by herself and her family. Suppose that she is at the moment receiving *OI* of *X* and *OJ* of *Y* per week, a combination of consumption of

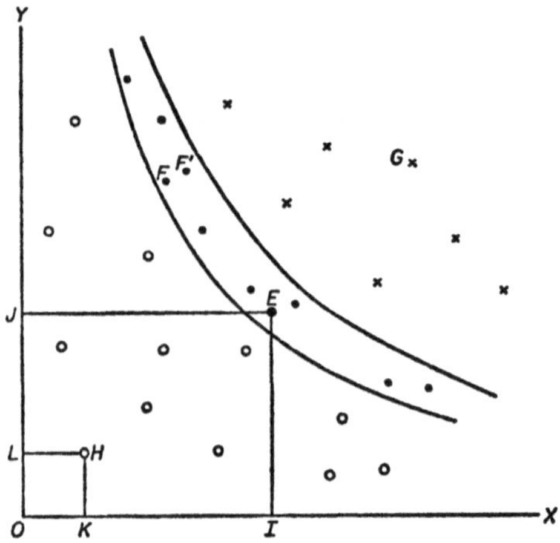

Figure 2

X and *Y* which can be represented by the point *E*. We now offer Mrs A alternative combinations of *X* and *Y* per week to consume, such as the combination at *H* which consists of *OK* of *X* and *OL* of *Y* per week. We ask Mrs A whether she prefers the new to the old combination and she can answer 'Yes', 'No', or 'Don't Know'. We mark in Figure 2 with a cross those new combinations which she prefers to the old, with a circle those new combinations which she likes less than the old, and with a dot those combinations between which and the old she is indifferent.

Her choice map will look something like that in Figure 2. Any new combination which leaves her neither better nor worse off than before will probably have to contain more *Y* if it contains less *X* (or more *X* if it contains less *Y*). The area of the dots will therefore lie North-West and South-East of *E*. The combinations like *G* which Mrs A prefers to the dots in the band of indifference must lie to the North and the East of this band; for they must contain either more *X* or more *Y* or more of both *X* and *Y* than some dot in the band

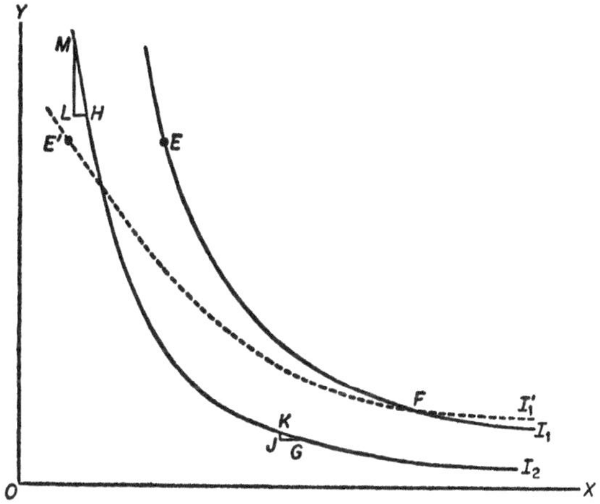

Figure 3

of indifference. Similarly the combinations like *H* to which Mrs A prefers her existing position will lie to the South and West of the band of indifference.

If Mrs A always prefers a combination which has more *X* and more *Y* to one which has less *X* and less *Y*, however small the difference may be, and if she is strictly consistent in her set of preferences, the band of indifference will shrink to a line separating the crosses from the circles. Consider the two points *F* and *F'* in the band of indifference. *F'* contains more *X* and more *Y* than *F*. Mrs A will, therefore, prefer *F'* to *F*. But if she is indifferent between *E* and *F*, she must, if she is consistent, prefer *F'* to *E*. *F'* should, therefore, be marked with a cross. If all points to the North-East of points like *F* are marked with a cross and all points to the South-West of points like *F* with a circle, then the band of indifference will be reduced to a line running North-West and South-East from *E*.

We can in this case represent Mrs A's preference map by a series of indifference lines as is done in Figure 3.

All combinations such as E and F which lie on the indifference curve I_1 are of the same importance as each other; and all points such as H and G on I_2 are of the same importance as each other.

There are three properties of these indifference curves which we must note.

(1) We have already explained why these lines must slope downwards from North-West to South-East.

(2) We can now see that they cannot cut—or indeed touch—each other. For, supposing that I_2 were cut by I_1'. E' is indifferent to F since both E' and F are on I_1'; H is preferred to E' since H contains more of both X and Y than does E'; and G is indifferent to H since both lie on I_2. It follows that G is preferred to F, since G is indifferent to H which is preferred to E' which is indifferent to F. But this is absurd since F contains more of both X and Y than does G. Indifference curves which cut would represent an inconsistent set of consumer's preferences. If choice is rational and consistent, the curve I_1 will lie always to the North and East of I_2 and any point on I_1 will be preferred to any point on I_2.

(3) The slope of any I-curve at any point measures how much more of the one product Mrs A would have to have to make up for the loss of a little of the other product. For example, Mrs A would be equally well off as at G if on the loss of JG of X she obtained JK more of Y. We may thus call the slope of the I-curve at any point the 'marginal rate of substitution' between X and Y. We shall assume that each I-curve is convex from below, i.e. has a slope which becomes gentler and gentler as one moves down it from North-West to South-East. This is a probable commonsensical assumption. At G Mrs A has a lot of X and little Y. If she has less of the plentiful X she would not feel the loss too much, but a little more of the scarce Y would be important to her. At G, therefore, a small increase in Y makes up for a given loss of X. But at H Mrs A has much Y and little X. The same loss of the now scarce X ($LH = JG$) must be offset by a much greater gain of the now already plentiful Y. The slope of I_2 is less steep at G than at H. We will call this phenomenon the 'diminishing marginal rate of substitution' between X and Y.

Figure 3 can be taken as a statement of Mrs A's needs and tastes. But her needs and tastes must be adjusted to the size of her purse and the state of the market to determine what she will buy. Figure 4 represents the size of her purse and the state of the market. Again we measure along the horizontal axis the amount of X per week and up the vertical axis the amount of Y per week available to Mrs A for her family's consumption. On this Figure we can draw the straight line AB sloping down from left to right, which we will call the budget-constraint line and which represents all the combinations of X and Y which Mrs A can purchase in the market.

The budget-constraint line is constructed in the following way. Suppose Mrs A has \$50 a week to spend; and suppose that the price of a unit of X is \$1 and of Y is \$2. Then if Mrs A spent all her income on X she could purchase 50 units of X a week. We measure

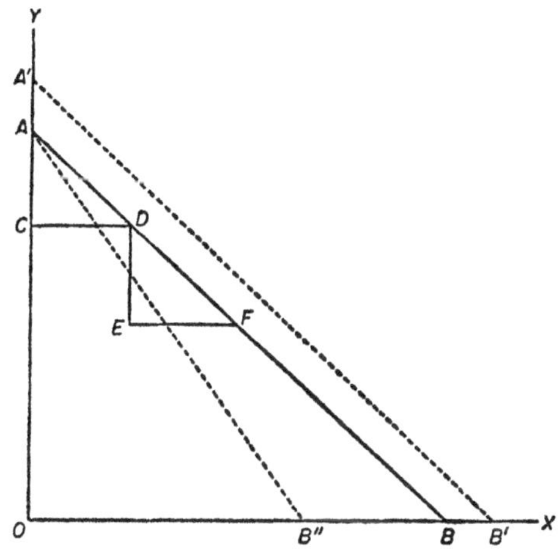

Figure 4

along OX a distance OB equal to 50. On the other hand if she spent all her income on Y she could purchase 25 units of Y, so that we measure up OY a distance OA equal to 25. Join the points AB with a straight line. Any point within the triangle OAB represents a combination of X and Y which is within Mrs A's purse. But since she would always like to have more of both products if it were possible, she will never be content with a combination like E but will always move as far North-East as possible, i.e. on to the line AB. At A she is spending all her money on Y. Suppose now she buys 5 units less of Y ($AC = 5$). She will then have \$10 free to spend on X. With this she can purchase 10 units of X ($CD = 10$). She will have moved from A to D. Suppose now she reduces her purchases of Y by another 5 units ($DE = 5$). Once more she has \$10 more to spend on X and can buy another 10 units of X ($EF = 10$). She has moved on the same straight line first from A to D and then from D to F. And so on, till she reaches B. By then she will have five times reduced her purchases of Y by 5 units in order to increase her purchases of X by five times 10 units. She will now be spending all her income on X.

Changes in Mrs A's income and changes in market prices can be represented by shifts in the budget constraint line *AB*. Suppose that Mrs A's weekly money income goes up by 20 per cent while the money prices of *X* and *Y* remain unchanged. Then Mrs A can purchase 20 per cent more *Y* if she buys only *Y* so that *OA′* is 20 per cent greater than *OA*. Similarly *OB′* is 20 per cent longer than *OB*. *A′B′* is parallel to *AB*, but is 20 per cent above (or to the right) of *AB*. The slope of *A′B′* is the same as the slope of *AB* which marks the fact that the price of *X* relatively to the price of *Y* is unchanged. By giving up 5 units of *Y* it is still possible to obtain 10 more units of *X*.

But the shift from *AB* to *A′B′* could represent not a rise in Mrs A's money income by 20 per cent with the money prices of *X* and *Y* unchanged, but a fall in the prices of both *X* and *Y* by $16\frac{2}{3}$ per cent the money income of Mrs A being unchanged. For if all prices fall by $16\frac{2}{3}$ per cent Mrs A's real purchasing power has gone up by 20 per cent.[1] The shift from *AB* to *A′B′* represents a 20 per cent increase in Mrs A's real income with the *relative* prices of *X* and *Y* unchanged; but it does not make any difference to Mrs A whether this occurs through a 20 per cent rise in her money income or through a uniform fall in the money price of every product by a corresponding percentage ($16\frac{2}{3}$ per cent).[2]

On the other hand a change in the money price of *X* relative to the money price of *Y* will cause a change in the slope of the budget-

[1] If the price of *X* is \$1 and Mrs A's income goes up by 20 per cent from \$50 to \$60, the number of units of *X* she can buy also goes up by 20 per cent from 50 to 60. If her income remains \$50 but the price of *X* falls by $16\frac{2}{3}$ per cent from \$1.000 to \$0.83, the number of units of *X* which she can purchase again goes up by 20 per cent from $\frac{\$50}{\$1} = 50$ to $\frac{\$50}{\$0.83} = 60$.

[2] This difference between the 20 per cent increase in money income and the corresponding $16\frac{2}{3}$ per cent decrease in prices raises an arithmetical point which threatens to haunt the reader throughout the following pages. Let us exorcise the spectre once and for all. Consider the movement of any index from 100 to 120. This can be represented as a rise of 20 per cent $\left(\frac{120 - 100}{100} = 20 \text{ per cent}\right)$. If the index now moves back from 120 to 100, this can be represented as a fall of $16\frac{2}{3}$ per cent $\left(\frac{120 - 100}{120} = 16\frac{2}{3} \text{ per cent}\right)$. This is the simple arithmetical reason for the difference between the 20 per cent *increase* in money incomes and the corresponding $16\frac{2}{3}$ per cent *decrease* in prices in the text. The rise in money incomes is measured as $\frac{120 - 100}{100}$ but the fall in prices as $\frac{100 - 86\frac{2}{3}}{100}$ which equals $\frac{120 - 100}{120}$. If the movement of an index is a small one (e.g. from 100 to 103) it makes very little difference whether one measures the percentage change

constraint line AB. Suppose that the money price of X were to rise by 20 per cent with Mrs A's money income and the price of Y unchanged. If she spent all her \$50 on Y she could purchase 25 units of Y as before (OA remains the same at 25 units). But if she spent all her \$50 on X at a price of \$1.20 instead of \$1.00 she could purchase only $41\frac{2}{3}$ units instead of 50. OB'' is $41\frac{2}{3}$ units in place of OB at 50 units. The line AB'' represents her new budget-constraint

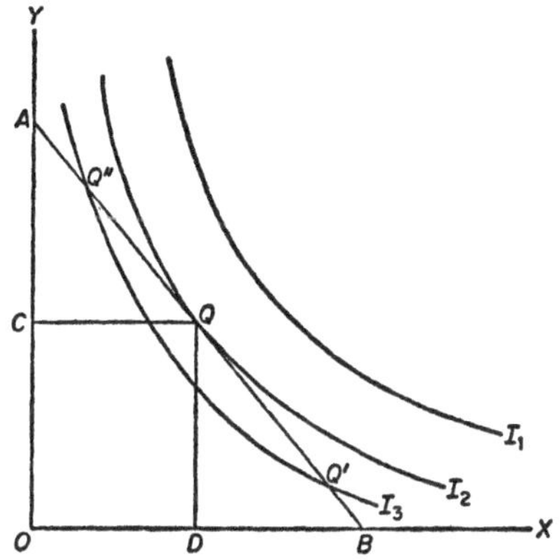

Figure 5

line. The steeper slope of AB'' represents the fact that for every 5 units of Y given up (i.e. for every \$10 released from expenditure on Y) she can now purchase only $\frac{\$10}{\$1.2} = 8\frac{1}{3}$ instead of 10 units of X.

By putting Figures 3 and 4 together we can confront Mrs A's needs and tastes with the size of her purse and the market situation. This is done in Figure 5. Mrs A has an income which, if all of it were spent on Y, would purchase OA units of Y. But by spending less on Y and more on X she can obtain a combination of products which

from the lower or the higher figure $\left(\frac{3}{100} = 3\text{ per cent and } \frac{3}{103} = 2{\cdot}91\text{ correct to two places of decimals}\right)$. In what follows we shall frequently speak as if these two measurements of a percentage change—i.e. a measurement from the lower and a measurement from the higher figure—were identical. That is to say, in terms of the problem discussed in the text, we shall frequently speak as if an x per cent rise in money incomes was equivalent in its effect on real income to an x per cent fall in money prices. This greatly eases the expression of the argument. However, it introduces minor arithmetical inaccuracies against which the reader is hereby once and for all forewarned.

she prefers. The highest indifference curve which she can reach is I_2, which she can just attain by purchasing the combination of *OC* units of *Y* and *OD* units of *X*. At this point the slope of the budget-constraint curve *AB* is equal to the slope of the indifference curve I_2. The relative market prices of *X* and *Y* are equal to the marginal rate of substitution between *X* and *Y* on her indifference-curve map. If she moves along her budget-constraint curve I_2 a little either to the North-West or the South-East of *Q*, she will be pulled away

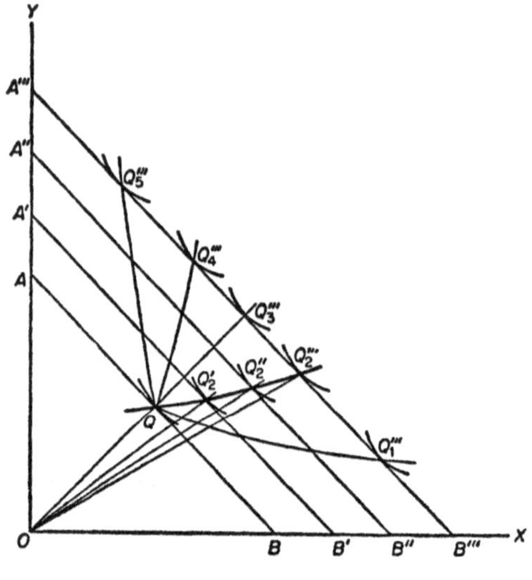

Figure 6

from the indifference curve I_2 towards a lower one such as I_3. On the other hand, there is no possible point on her budget-constraint curve which will bring her into contact with a higher indifference curve such as I_1. We can put the same point the other way round. Suppose Mrs A is purchasing a combination of *X* and *Y* such that the relative prices of *X* and *Y* differ from the marginal rate of substitution between *X* and *Y* on her indifference map (as at *Q′* or *Q″*). It is clear from Figure 5 that in such a case she can always move along her budget-constraint line in such a way as to reach a higher indifference curve.

We can now see how a change in her money income and a change in market prices would affect Mrs A's purchases. Let us start with a change in her money income which is represented in Figure 6. Mrs A starts with a money income and a set of market prices which put her on the budget constraint line AB, on which she chooses the point Q which is tangential to her highest attainable indifference curve. She then enjoys successive increases in her money income, market prices remaining unchanged, so that her budget constraint line rises to $A'B'$, to $A''B''$, and finally to $A'''B'''$. As her income increases in this way she moves along a path $Q' - Q'' - Q'''$, at each stage choosing that combination of X and Y at which her new budget constraint line is tangential to her highest attainable indifference curve. The path $Q - Q' - Q'' - Q'''$ we may call her 'income-consumption curve'.

The position of the path $Q - Q' - Q'' - Q'''$ depends upon the nature of her needs and tastes, i.e. upon the shape of her indifference curves. One possible set of indifference curves might bring her along the path $Q - Q_2' - Q_2'' - Q_2'''$. Figure 6 shows a set of indifference curves which would bring this result. In this case as her income increases she buys a lot more X and a little more Y. But if Y instead of X were the commodity which she most wanted when her income went up, then her indifference curves would be differently shaped and she would move along a path like $Q - Q_4'''$. Figure 6 shows five different possible paths all relating to the same relative prices of X and Y, but each relating to a different set of tastes and needs for the two products X and Y.

We can now give certain definitions which will help to describe these different reactions. We define 'the income elasticity of demand for X' as the percentage change in the amount of X bought as a result of a one per cent increase in spendable income, the prices of X and Y being constant. Suppose Mrs A's income-consumption curve was on the straight line passing through O and Q, i.e. the line $Q - Q_3'''$. In this case the ratio of Y to X in Mrs A's purchases would remain unchanged as her income rose. Y and X would increase in the same percentage as each other and, therefore, in the same percentage as total spendable income. In this case her income elasticity of demand for X and her income elasticity of demand for Y would both be one; for a one per cent increase in spendable income would cause her to purchase one per cent more X and one per cent more Y.

On the path $Q - Q_2'''$, as Mrs A's income goes up, so the ratio of the amount of Y bought to the amount of X bought falls. The slope of the lines joining O and Q, O and Q_2', O and Q_2'', and O and Q_2''' measure at each point the ratio of the amount of Y to the amount of X bought and these slopes become gentler and gentler as Mrs A's income increases. In this case when her income goes up by one per cent her expenditure on X goes up by more than one per cent and her expenditure on Y by less than one per cent, so that on the line

$Q - Q_2'''$ the income elasticity of demand for X is greater than one and for Y is less than one.

The path $Q - Q_1'''$ represents an exaggerated form of a high income elasticity of demand for X and a low income elasticity of demand for Y. In this case when Mrs A's income goes up she purchases a great deal more X and *actually less* Y than before. This might happen if X was a rich person's good and Y a poor person's good. When the standard of living goes up, people may consume more meat and less bread. In this case Y is said to be an 'inferior good'. The income elasticity of demand for X is a high positive figure but the income elasticity of demand for Y is a negative figure because when Mrs A's income goes *up* by one per cent the amount of Y which she buys goes *down* by a certain percentage.

By a similar process of reasoning it can be seen that on the path $Q - Q_4'''$ the income elasticities of demand for X and Y are both positive, but that for X it is less than one and for Y it is greater than one. And along the path $Q - Q_5'''$ the amount of X bought actually goes down. X is now an inferior good; and the income elasticity of demand for X is a negative figure while that for Y is a large positive figure.

So much for the description of the different ways in which Mrs A may react to a change in her income. Let us now give a similar description of the way in which she may react to a change in the price of one of the products, her income and the price of the other product remaining unchanged. In Figure 7 we suppose that Mrs A's income and the price of Y both remain constant, so that the amount of Y which she could purchase with all her income remains fixed at OA. But the price of X falls. It starts at a high level so that OB measures the amount of X which she could buy with all her income; but as the price of X falls she could purchase larger amounts of X (OB', OB'', and finally OB''') with the whole of her income. Her budget constraint line swings round from AB to AB' to AB'' to AB''' as the price of X falls. The ever-diminishing downward slope of this line represents the fact that as the price of X falls, Mrs A can obtain larger and larger increments of X for every unit of Y which she gives up. Mrs A's combination of purchases of X and Y will move along a path $Q - Q' - Q'' - Q'''$, each combination being that at which the ruling budget constraint line is tangential to her highest indifference curve. We will call the line $Q - Q' - Q'' - Q'''$ Mrs A's 'price-consumption curve'.

Once again, according to her tastes and needs, i.e. according to the configuration of her indifference curves, there are different courses which this price-consumption curve may take. Just as in the former case we needed the idea of an income elasticity of demand for X to describe Mrs A's reaction to a change in income, so we now need the idea of a 'price elasticity of demand for X' to describe Mrs. A's reaction to a change in the price of X. We define Mrs A's price elasticity of demand for X as the percentage change in the

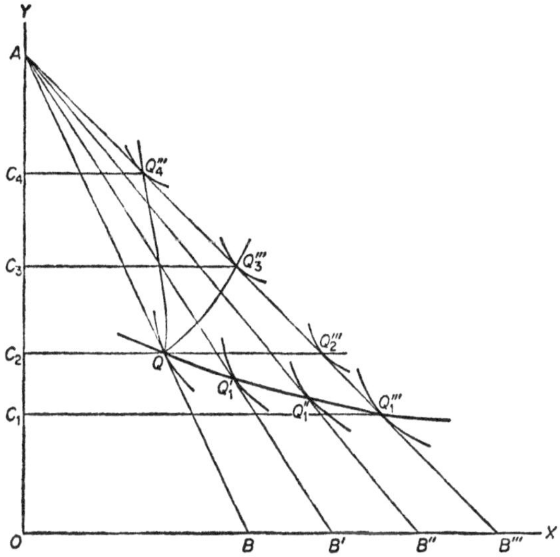

Figure 7

amount of X which Mrs A would buy as a result of a one per cent increase in the price of X, her income and other prices remaining unchanged. Table II gives numerical examples of price elasticities

Price of X	Quantity of X Bought				Total Expenditure on X (Price × Quantity)			
$	(a)	(b)	(c)	(d)	(a)	(b)	(c)	(d)
1·01	100				$101			
1·00	105	101	100·5	99	105	101	100·5	99
	Price Elasticity of Demand for X							
	−5	−1	$-\frac{1}{2}$	+1				

Table II

of demand for *X*. We suppose that the price of *X* is initially $1.01 and that at this price Mrs A purchases 100 units a week. The price then falls by 1 per cent to $1.00. We then trace four different reactions by Mrs A. In case (*a*) her purchases rise by 5 per cent from 100 to 105. This represents a price elasticity of demand of -5. For the percentage change in the price is -1 and the percentage change in the amount bought is $+5$. A change of $+1$ per cent in the price would, therefore, presumably cause a change of -5 per cent in the amount bought. In case (*b*) the -1 per cent change in price causes a $+1$ per cent change in the amount bought and the price elasticity of demand is -1. In case (*c*) the -1 per cent change in price causes a $+\frac{1}{2}$ per cent change in the amount bought and the price elasticity is $-\frac{1}{2}$. In case (*d*) the -1 per cent change in price has caused a -1 per cent change in amount bought and (we will consider later whether this is a possible case) the price elasticity of demand is $+1$.

In the four columns on the right of Table II we show the total amounts of money which Mrs A will be spending on *X* on these various assumptions. Initially she is buying 100 units at $1.01 a unit, i.e. spending $101 on her purchases of *X*. In case (*a*) this goes up to $105; in case (*b*) it stays unchanged at $101; in case (*c*) it goes down to $100.5; and in case (*d*) to $99. Case (*b*) marks a clear dividing line. In this case of a price elasticity equal to -1, the 1 per cent fall in price is just counterbalanced by the 1 per cent rise in the amount purchased so that the amount spent remains unchanged. In case (*a*) the increase in amount bought outbalances the fall in price and total expenditure goes up. In case (*c*) the increase in the amount bought is outweighed by the fall in price and total expenditure falls. *A fortiori* total expenditure falls in case (*d*) where both price and quantity fall. Where the price elasticity of demand is -1, total expenditure on *X* remains unaffected by a change in the price of *X*. Where the price elasticity of demand for *X* is a larger negative figure (e.g. -5), a fall in price and expenditure move in opposite directions. Where the price elasticity of demand for *X* is a smaller negative figure or actually a positive figure (e.g. $-\frac{1}{2}$ or $+1$), price and expenditure move in the same direction.

These relationships are illustrated in Figure 7. The price of *Y* is constant. Let us choose units of *Y* such that 1 unit of *Y* has a price of $1. Then *OA* measures Mrs A's total money income, because it is the number of dollar's worth of *Y* which she could purchase with the whole of her income. In fact in the initial position at *Q* she is purchasing only OC_2 units of *Y*, i.e. she is spending OC_2 dollars on *Y* and is using the remainder of her income—namely AC_2 dollars—to purchase C_2Q units of *X*. At the final low price of *X* represented by the budget-constraint line AB''' she is spending OC_1 on *Y* and

AC_1 on X. Her expenditure on X has risen when the price of X has fallen. Her price elasticity of demand for X is (numerically) larger than one.[1] The downward falling curve $Q - Q_1'''$ represents an example of case (*a*) of Table II where the expenditure on X and the price of X move in different directions.

The path $Q - Q_2'''$ on the horizontal line C_2Q illustrates case (*b*) of Table II where the total expenditure on Y (namely AC_2) remains unchanged as the price of X falls from AB to AB'''. The price elasticity of demand for X is -1.

The path $Q - Q_3'''$ represents case (*c*) of Table II. The fall in the price of X leads to a larger purchase of X (Q_3''' is to the East of Q) but to a smaller expenditure on X (Q_3''' is to the North of Q).

The path $Q - Q_4'''$ represents case (*d*) of Table II. The fall in price has caused the quantity of X to fall (Q_4''' is to the West of Q) and *a fortiori* expenditure on X to fall (Q_4''' is to the North of Q). Is this in fact a possible case? Figure 7 shows that there is nothing in the three asumptions about the nature of indifference curves given on page 36 which would prevent the line AB being tangential to one indifference curve at Q and the line AB''' being tangential to a higher indifference curve at Q_4'''. But what does this mean in terms of Mrs A's needs and tastes? Suppose X were bread and Y were meat. The price of bread falls. Bread is an important item in Mrs A's cost of living. The fall in its price, therefore, appreciably raises her standard of living. But bread is a very inferior good so that, being better off, she buys meat rather than bread. The rise in her standard of living causes her to shift from bread to meat more than the improvement in the price of bread relatively to meat causes her to shift from expensive meat to cheaper bread. She actually buys less bread as a result of the fall in its price.

This last point brings out the fact that a fall in the price of X will have a double effect so far as the purchases of X by Mrs A is concerned. (1) In the first place, a fall in the price of X, with her income and the price of Y unchanged, will reduce Mrs A's cost of living. Her standard of living is raised. It is equivalent to some rise in her income at constant prices of X and Y, and this in itself would cause her purchase of X to change. This we may call the 'income effect' of the change in the price of X. (2) In the second place, X will now be cheaper relatively to Y and—if we abstract from the fact that the fall in the cost of living due to the fall in the price of X has made her better off—this alone would cause her to switch her purchases

[1] In the case of negative elasticities such as those shown in cases (*a*), (*b*), and (*c*) of Table II, we shall talk of them being (numerically) large, when we mean that they are a large negative figure. Thus -5 is a '(numerically) large' and $-\frac{1}{2}$ is a '(numerically) small' price elasticity of demand.

from the now relatively expensive Y to the now relatively cheap X. This we may call the 'substitution effect' of the change in the price of X. Figure 8 enables us to distinguish these two effects.

Suppose that with a constant price of Y of \$1 and with an income of OA, the price of X falls so that Mrs A's budget constraint line moves from AB to AB'. Suppose that as a result of this her pur-

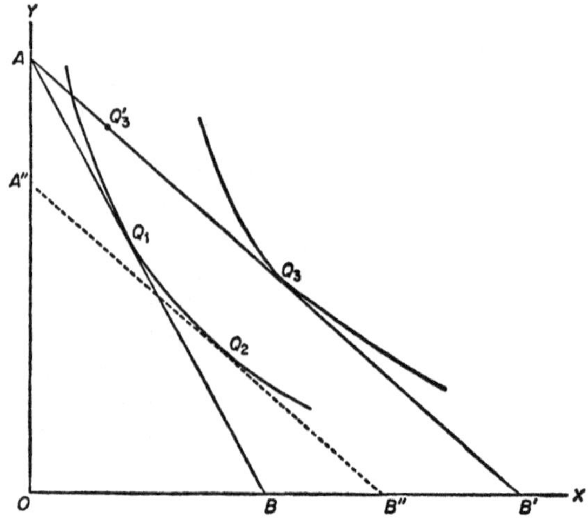

Figure 8

chases move from the combination Q_1 to the combination Q_3. She is better off. Q_3 is on a higher indifference curve than Q_1. Suppose now that her income were simultaneously reduced by an amount (AA'') which, at the new and lower price of X, makes her just as well off as before the change, the fall in the price of X being just offset by the fall in her income. She will now have a budget constraint line $A''B''$ which is parallel to AB' but which is tangential at Q_2 to her first indifference curve. At Q_2 she is neither better nor worse off than at Q_1 her initial position.

We may call the movement from Q_1 to Q_2 the 'substitution effect' of the fall in the price of X. It shows the extent to which she will buy more X and less Y simply because the price of X has fallen relatively to the price of Y, quite apart from the effect on her purchases of the fact that the fall in the cost of living has made her better off. The movement from Q_2 to Q_3 shows the 'income effect' of the fall in the price of X because a movement from Q_2 to Q_3 could be brought about only by a rise in her income from OA'' to

OA at the new relative prices of X and Y. The complete move from Q_1 to Q_3 can therefore be regarded as the sum of (i) a movement from Q_1 to Q_2 due to a change in relative prices at a constant *real* income and (ii) a movement from Q_2 to Q_3 caused by the rise in *real* income which the fall in the price of X represents.[1]

The substitution effect illustrated by the movement from Q_1 to Q_2 in Figure 8 enables us to define the 'elasticity of substitution' between X and Y in Mrs A's consumption, which is a measure of the ease with which the one product can replace the other product in Mrs A's needs and tastes. Suppose, as is shown in Figure 9, that as a result of a change in relative prices represented by the change in the slope of the budget constraint line from AB to $A''B''$ Mrs A's purchases shift from Q_1 to Q_2 on the same indifference curve I. This 'substitution effect' is much greater if Mrs A's indifference curve, as in the case of I in Figure 9, has a very gentle curvature than it is if, as in the case of I', her indifference curve has a much sharper curvature. In the latter case the substitution effect is only from Q_1' to Q_2'.

We can define the elasticity of substitution between X and Y as the percentage change in the ratio of the quantity of Y purchased to the quantity of X purchased that would be brought about by a one per cent rise in the ratio of the price of Y to the price of X. In other words suppose that the $\frac{\text{Price of } Y}{\text{Price of X}}$ rose by 1 per cent and that in consequence the $\frac{\text{Amount of } Y \text{ purchased}}{\text{Amount of } X \text{ purchased}}$ fell by 2 per cent, the elasticity of substitution between X and Y would be -2. Now the $\frac{\text{Price of } Y}{\text{Price of X}}$ is equal to $\frac{OB}{OA}$[2] which is the slope of the budget constraint line AB; and the $\frac{\text{Amount of } Y \text{ purchased}}{\text{Amount of } X \text{ purchased}}$ is equal to $\frac{OC}{CQ_1}$ which is

[1] We have already considered on the path $Q - Q_4''$ in Figure 7 the possibility that Mrs A might buy less X as a result of the fall in its price. For this to happen X would have to be a very 'inferior' good. Figure 8 helps us to appreciate better this point. If Q_3 lay to the West of Q_2, X would be an 'inferior' good. The rise in income from OA'' to OA would have reduced the demand for X. But for Q_3 to lie to the west of Q_1, as in the case of Q_3' in Figure 8, the 'inferiority' of X must be so great as to shift Q_3 to the West of Q_2 by more than the 'substitution' effect, i.e. by more than the amount that the change in relative prices had shifted Q_2 to the East of Q_1.

[2] If the price of Y is half the price of X, then with any given amount of money one can purchase twice as many units of Y as of X.

the slope of the line OQ_1. Thus the elasticity of substitution can be measured by the percentage change in the slope of the line OQ which is caused by a one per cent change in the slope of the line AB. Clearly the change in slope from OQ_1 to OQ_2 on an indifference curve like I is much greater than the change in slope from OQ'_1 to OQ'_2 on an indifference curve like I'; but both are brought about by the same change in the slope of the budget-constraint line from AB to $A''B''$.[1]

Once again an elasticity of -1 marks an important dividing line.

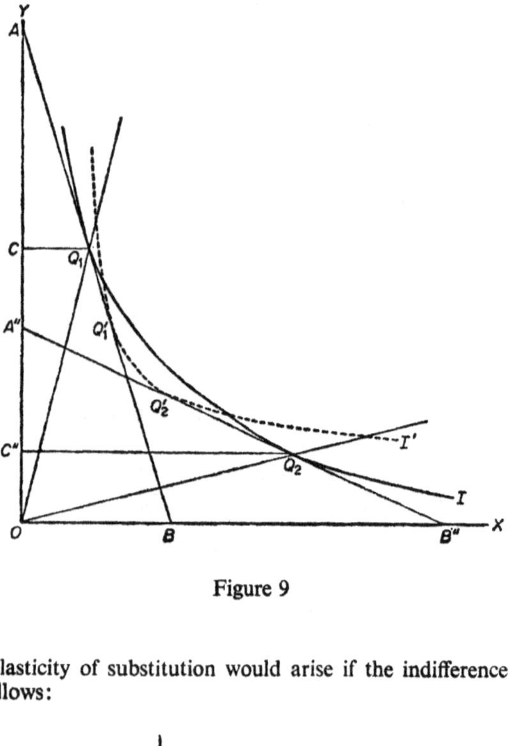

Figure 9

[1] A zero elasticity of substitution would arise if the indifference curve were shaped as follows:

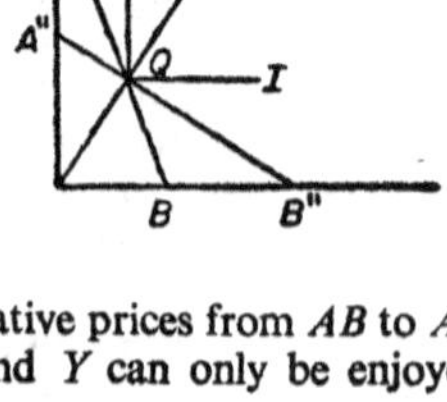

In this case a change in relative prices from AB to $A''B''$ would cause no change in relative quantities. X and Y can only be enjoyed in a fixed proportion. A

We have already seen that $\frac{OC}{AC}$ measures the ratio of expenditure on Y to expenditure on X at the point Q_1. Mrs A is spending OC of her income in purchasing Y and AC of her income in purchasing CQ_1 of X. Now if the elasticity of substitution between X and Y is equal to -1, she will spend the same proportions of her income on X and on Y after the change as before the change. For if X and Y are the amounts of X and Y bought, P_y and P_x are the prices of Y and of X, and E_y and E_x are the amounts of money spent on Y and on X, we have $\frac{E_y}{E_x} = \frac{YP_y}{XP_x} = \frac{Y}{X} \times \frac{P_y}{P_x}$. If the ratio $\frac{P_y}{P_x}$ went up by 1 per cent without any change in $\frac{Y}{X}$, the ratio $\frac{E_y}{E_x}$ would go up 1 per cent. If on the other hand the ratio $\frac{Y}{X}$ went down by 1 per cent without any change in $\frac{P_y}{P_x}$, the ratio $\frac{E_y}{E_x}$ would go down by 1 per cent. But if the elasticity of substitution is -1, the ratio $\frac{Y}{X}$ will go down by 1 per cent when the ratio $\frac{P_y}{P_x}$ goes up by 1 per cent. The change in the price ratio would exactly offset the change in the quantity ratio, so that the expenditure ratio would remain unchanged. If the elasticity of substitution were a (numerically) larger figure (-2, for example) then the quantity ratio would go down by more than the price ratio went up; and the rise in the price of Y relatively to the price of X would cause the ratio of expenditure on Y to expenditure on X to fall. Conversely if the elasticity of substitution were (numerically) only a small figure ($-\frac{1}{2}$, for example), the ratio of the

(numerically) infinitely large elasticity of substitution would arise if the indifference curve were a straight line:

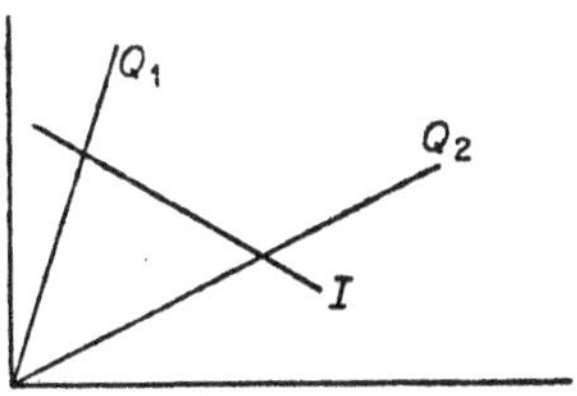

In this case a zero percentage change in relative prices would be sufficient to bring about any given percentage change in relative quantities.

quantities would move less than the ratio of the prices and the ratio of expenditure on Y to expenditure on X would rise when the price of Y rose relatively to the price of X.

In Figure 9 the indifference curve I represents a case in which the elasticity of substitution is (numerically) larger than one. For $\frac{OC}{CA}$ is clearly greater than $\frac{OC''}{C''A''}$; the relative rise in the price of Y has caused the proportion of income spent on Y to fall. Conversely, the indifference curve I' represents a case in which the elasticity of substitution is (numerically) smaller than one. If C were brought down to a level with Q_1' and C'' were brought up to level with Q_2', clearly $\frac{OC}{CA}$ would be less than $\frac{OC''}{C''A''}$. The rise in the relative price of Y would have caused the proportion of income spent on Y to rise.

We have now in the present chapter defined and described the possible reactions of a single consumer (Mrs A) to a change in prices or a change in her spendable income when she has to choose between only two products X and Y. We must now generalize these definitions to cover the case in which there are more than two products.[1]

Suppose then that the prices of X, Y, and Z all remain constant and that Mrs A's income goes up. We may still define the income elasticity of demand for any one of these products (say X) as the percentage change in the amount of X which Mrs A would purchase if her income went up by one per cent, all prices remaining unchanged. The income elasticity of demand for all the products could be 1; that is to say, it would be possible, when her income went up by 1 per cent, for Mrs A to increase her purchases of each and every individual product by 1 per cent. But the income elasticity of demand for one (or more of the products) could be greater than 1 provided that at the same time it was less than 1 for at least one of the products; that is to say, if Mrs A increases the proportion of her income which she spends on one (or more products) there must be at least one product on which she spends a smaller proportion of her income. Finally, one (or more) of the products might be an 'inferior' good and have a negative income elasticity of demand provided that there were at least one product which was not an inferior good and for which the income elasticity of demand was greater than one; that is to say, Mrs A when she becomes richer

[1] The case of three products, X, Y and Z, will for most purposes give us all the clues that are necessary to extend the definitions to cover any number of products.

may actually buy less of some goods, but in that case she must increase the proportion of her income which is spent on at least one good.

The generalization to many products of the effects of a change in income is thus in principle simple. But the generalization to many products of the effects of a change in the price of a single product introduces some new considerations.

Let us suppose that there are a large number of products; that the prices of all these products are constant except that of X which is

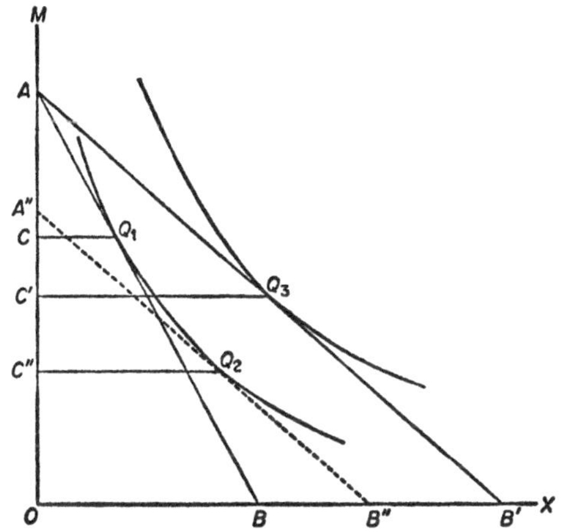

Figure 10

reduced; and that Mrs A's money income is constant. We can now re-interpret our diagrams, measuring Mrs A's money income (M) up the vertical axis and the amount of X along the horizontal axis. This is done in Figure 10.

Since the prices of Y and Z and of all other commodities except X are constant, we can measure up the vertical axis a composite commodity of '\$1-worth-of-all-commodities-except-X'. The fact that their prices are all constant gives them all a common measure, namely \$1-worth. We assume that Mrs A divides her expenditure on these 'commodities-except-X' among the various commodities other than X in the way which gives her the greatest satisfaction. OA measures Mrs A's money income, while OC measures the amount she spends on all commodities other than X and AC the amount she spends on X when the price of X is represented by the budget-constraint line AB. When the price of X falls, so that Mrs A's budget constraint line swings round to AB', she purchases $C'Q_3$ instead of CQ_1 units of X; and the change in her purchases can as before be split into the 'substitution effect' (Q_1 to Q_2) and the 'income effect' (Q_2 to Q_3).

The substitution effect now measures the ease with which X can be substituted for all other products in general, and we can apply to it exactly the same measure of the elasticity of substitution as we did in the two-commodity case. The elasticity of substitution between X and all other products is the percentage change in the ratio $\frac{\text{\$-worth of other products bought}}{\text{amount of } X \text{ bought}}$ which is caused by a one per cent rise in the ratio $\frac{\text{price level of all other goods}}{\text{price of } X}$, when all individual prices except that of X remain unchanged and when Mrs A's money income is so reduced (i.e. from OA to OA'') as to leave her exactly as well off as she was before the fall in the price of X.

Both in the two-commodity case (Figure 8) and the many-commodity case (Figure 10) Q_2 lies to the South-East of Q_1. In other words, because the indifference curves slope down from North-West to South-East and are convex from below (see page 36), the substitution effect is always in the same direction. When the price of X falls relatively to that of other things then—apart from any income effects—purchases of the relatively cheaper product X go up and purchases of the other relatively more expensive products go down. The cheaper product is substituted for the more expensive products.

This is true whether the 'more expensive products' are a single product Y (as in the two-commodity case of Figure 8) or a whole range of other products (as in the many-commodity case of Figure 10). In the former case it means, of course, simply that less Y is bought. In the latter case it means that less of other goods in general are bought; but it does not necessarily mean that less is bought of every individual good other than X.

Here we have the possibility of a new relationship, namely that of 'complementarity'. Consider the three products Pens, Ink, and Pencils. Suppose the price of Pens to fall (Pens are product X in Figure 10). Apart from any income effects more Pens will be bought and less of other products must be bought to finance the increased purchase of Pens. People will shift from writing with the now relatively expensive Pencils to writing with the now relatively cheap Pens. But Pens are no use without Ink, so that, while the purchase of Pens will go up and the purchase of all other products in general will go down, nevertheless the purchase of one of these other products—Ink—will go up. In Figure 10 the purchase of other goods in general will have gone down from OC to OC''; but this net fall may be made up of a very large fall in the purchase of some products (e.g. Pencils) combined with some partially offsetting rise in the purchases of one or a few products (e.g. Ink). In such a case Ink and Pens are said to be 'complementary' in Mrs A's demand. Complementarity is thus a relationship which can occur only when there are three or more products. The price of one product (Pens) falls; income effects apart, more of this product and therefore less of other products in general will be purchased; but while purchases of all these other products combined will have gone down, there may be among them some one product (Ink) which has gone up. Pens and Ink are then 'complements' in Mrs A's needs and tastes.

CHAPTER III

THE MARKET FOR CONSUMPTION GOODS

In the last chapter we gave an account of the way in which a single consumer, Mrs A, may react to a change in her income or in the market conditions in which she has to make her purchases. In this chapter we intend to apply the analysis of the last chapter to the total market for consumption goods constituted by the whole body of competing consumers.

Let us consider the schematic representation of our simple economic system on page 29. It contains two markets: the Shops on the left in which consumption goods are sold and bought and the Firms and Farms on the right where the factors of production are hired and the goods are produced. At the moment we are concerned only with the Shops. That is to say, in this chapter we shall assume (i) that each of a large number of consumers—Mrs A, Mrs B, Mrs C, Mrs D—has a fixed money income with which she comes to the Shops and (ii) that there is a fixed flow into the shops each day of each of the various products—X, Y, and Z. Our purpose is to see what determines the market prices of X, Y, and Z when the fixed money incomes of Mrs A, B, C, and D meet the fixed supplies of the products.

This is a very partial analysis because the market prices of X, Y, and Z will in fact affect what goes on in the Firms and Farms in two ways: first, by affecting the relative amounts of X, Y, and Z which are produced and put into the shops and, second, by affecting the demand for various factors of production—such as labour and land—and thus affecting the distribution of our fixed money national income among the owners of the factors of production, Mr A, B, C, and D. In other words, in this chapter we ask at what levels the prices of the various consumption goods would stand, if the distribution of money incomes and the supplies of these consumption goods were given. We shall have to enquire in later chapters how in the Firms and Farms the prices of the consumption goods affect the distribution of money incomes and the supply of goods.

We will start our enquiry into the formation of prices in the Shops with two very special assumptions: (i) that there are only two products, X and Y, on sale in the Shops and (ii) that each consumer has the same money income and the same tastes and needs as every other consumer.

So long as we make this second assumption (ii), there is no difficulty in applying the indifference-curve analysis of the previous chapter to the whole community of consumers. Suppose that any one consumer's, say Mrs A's, indifference map between X and Y was as shown in Figure 11 (i). Mrs A is indifferent between $O'D_1'$ of X with

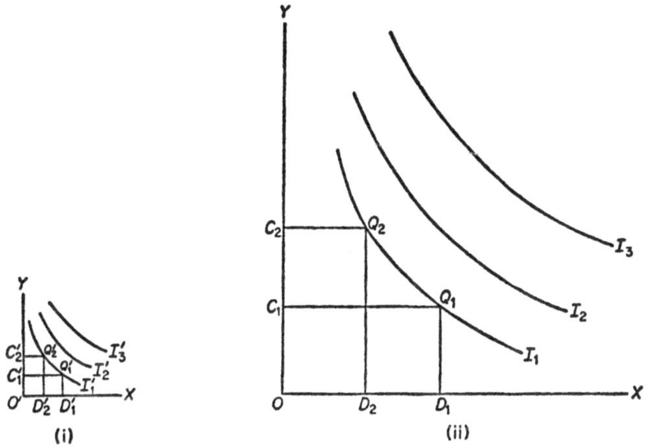

Figure 11

$O'C_1'$ of Y and $O'D_2'$ of X with $O'C_2'$ of Y. Both combinations lie on her indifference curve, I_1'. But if there are 1000 consumers with the same incomes and the same tastes[1] and confronted with the same prices in the Shops, Mrs A will be purchasing $O'D_1'$ of X and $O'C_1'$ of Y only if her 999 neighbours are also each purchasing $O'D_1'$ of X and $O'C_1'$ of Y and are also each on their own indifference curve, I_1'. We can, therefore, draw a set of community indifference curves in Figure 11 (ii) which are exactly similar to those in Figure 11 (i) except that in (ii) every dimension is 1000 larger than in (i). OD_1 is 1000 times $O'D_1'$ and represents the fact that there is a total supply of OD_1 on the market of which $O'D_1'$ is being purchased by each of 1000 identical consumers. Thus the combination of OD_1 with OC_1 on the market must mean that there are 1000 consumers each

[1] By saying that Mrs A and Mrs B have the same needs and tastes we do not imply that any given combination of goods (say Q_1' in Figure 11) will make Mrs A and Mrs B equally 'happy' or 'satisfied' in any absolute sense. We imply only that their indifference maps are similar, i.e. that if Mrs A is indifferent between Q_1' and Q_2' then Mrs B is also indifferent between Q_1' and Q_2'.

consuming $O'D_1' + O'C_1'$ and each on her indifference curve, I_1'. If total market supplies changed to $OD_2 + OC_2$, then each individual consumer's consumption would change to $O'D_2' + O'C_2'$; and as can be seen from (i), each consumer is on the same indifference curve. This is represented on (ii) by making the community indifference curve I_1 pass through Q_2 as well as Q_1. These are both total supplies which, when equally divided among all consumers, will put each consumer on her same indifference curve, I_1'.

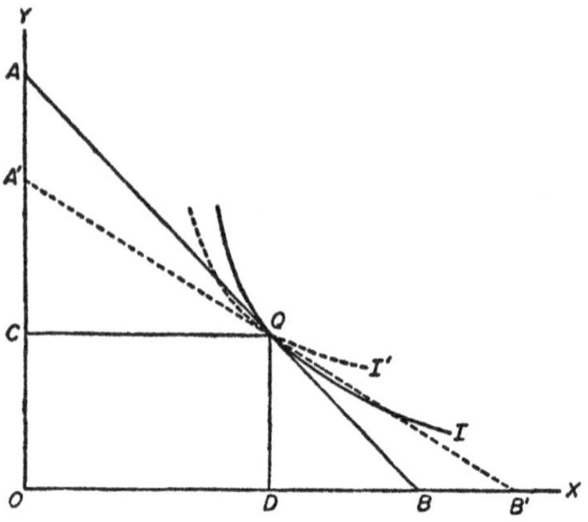

Figure 12

The slope of the community indifference curve at Q_1 is the same as that of the individual indifference curve at Q_1', the slope of I_1 at Q_2 is the same as the slope of I_1' at Q_2'; and so on. This can be seen in the following way. Suppose that the slope of I_1' at Q_1' were 1 in 2 or, in other words, Mrs A must at this point have 2 more units of *X* to make up for the loss of a 1 unit of *Y*. Then as far as market supplies are concerned, in order that every consumer should remain equally well off, there must be 2000 more units of *X* supplied in order to make up for the loss of 1000 units of *Y*. In other words the slope of I_1 at Q_1 is 1000 in 2000 or 1 in 2, which is the same as the slope of I_1' at Q_1'.

We can use this set of community indifference curves very simply to show the way in which the prices of *X* and *Y* will be determined in the Shops. This is done in Figure 12. We suppose that *OD* of *X* and *OC* of *Y* are being put on the market each week. Then there is a point *Q* which represents this combination of *X* and *Y* which consumers must purchase. There is an indifference curve *I* which passes through this point *Q*. Draw the line *AB* tangential to *I* at the point Q. The line AB will describe the resulting market prices of X and Y. This can be understood in the following way.

Let Figure 12 shrink until it is only 1/1000 of its present size, so that it represents the indifference map of one of our 1000 identical consumers, Mrs A. Mrs A must be induced to purchase OD of X and OC of Y, i.e. 1/1000 of the total supplies of each product; for this is the only way in which the market can be cleared. But Mrs A can be induced to do this only if she has a budget constraint line AB. In other words the money price of Y must be such that her money income (1/1000 of the total national income) must be able to purchase OA units of Y; and the money price of X must be such that her money income could purchase OB of X. The slope of the line AB then represents the price of X relatively to the price of Y. Mrs A could purchase any combination of X and Y on her budget constraint line AB; and she chooses the combination Q which is on her highest indifference curve.

Inflate Figure 12 by 1000 times back into a picture of the whole community. The price of Y must be such that the whole national income could purchase OA units of Y at the current market price of Y. In other words, the money price of Y equals $\frac{\text{National Money Income}}{OA}$ and the money price of X equals $\frac{\text{National Money Income}}{OB}$. The line AB represents the relationship between the market prices of X and Y. The community has a money national income with which, at current prices, it could purchase OA units of Y. But it spends only a fraction $\frac{OC}{OA}$ of its national income on Y. The other fraction $\frac{AC}{OA}$ it devotes to the purchase of X and it is able at the current price of X to purchase QC of X by refraining from purchasing AC of Y. Its purchases of OC of Y and OD of X just clears the market at Q.

Suppose that tastes had been different and that at the combination of a 1/1000 part of OD and of OC, each consumer had a higher marginal valuation of Y relatively to X. Mrs A would need to receive more X to make up for the loss of a unit of Y. The slope of the indifference curve at Q would be less steep (as in the case of I'). In this case the market price line would be $A'B'$. The money price of Y would be higher (the same money national income would purchase only OA' instead of OA units of Y) and the money price of X would be lower.

If we now suppose that the supply of one of the products is changed, the effect on the prices of the products is less easy to determine. Suppose, for example, that money incomes remain unchanged, that the weekly supply of *Y* is unchanged, but that the weekly supply of *X* in the Shops is increased. What will be the effect on the money prices of *X* and *Y*? There is one thing which we can say for certain, namely that the money price of *X* or the money price of *Y* or both money prices must fall. The same supply of *Y* and a larger supply of *X* has got to be purchased with the same

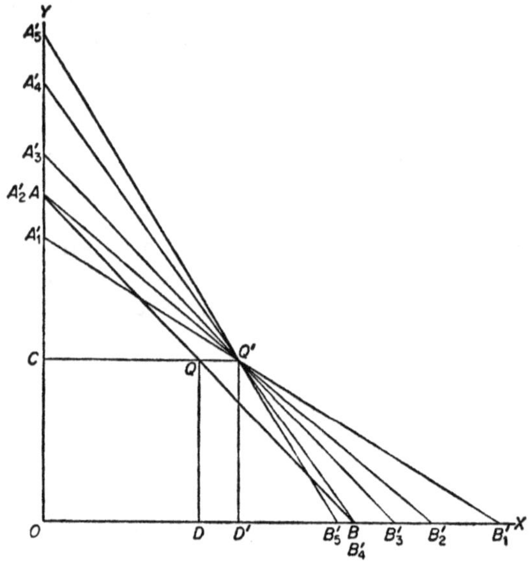

Figure 13

total money income and the price of something must fall. But it turns out that this is practically everything that one can say for certain. Whether the price of *Y* or even the price of *X* will fall depends upon the nature of the consumers' tastes and needs.

This is illustrated in Figure 13. We start with supplies of *OC* of *Y* and *OD* of *X* on the market. The supply of *Y* remains unchanged and the supply of *X* rises to *OD'*. At the point *Q* the slope of the indifference curve gave a market price line *AB*. According to the slope of the indifference curve which passes through the new combination *Q'* we may have a new market price line of any kind ranging from $A_1'B_1'$ to $A_5'B_5'$. Let us consider what these various possibilities mean.

Consider first the possibility $A_2'B_2'$ where *A'* coincides with *A*. This means that consumers' needs and tastes are such that when the supply of X on the market is increased the money price of X falls but the money price of Y remains unchanged. The fall in the money price of X is represented by the fact that OB_2' is greater than OB, so that with their given money incomes consumers could purchase more X than before; and the constancy in the money price of Y is represented by the fact that OA_2' equals OA. This case is in fact the case in which the price elasticity of demand for X is -1. In this case consumers can be induced to purchase more X by a fall in the price of X with their incomes and the price of Y constant. They spend the same amount of money on Y as before and have left over the same amount as before for expenditure on X. The situation is the same as that in Figure 7 on the path $Q-Q_2'''$ which shows a price elasticity of demand of -1.

In Figure 13 the line $A_1'B_1'$ shows a situation in which the price elasticity of demand for X is (numerically) less than one (e.g. $-\frac{1}{2}$). In this case the price of X falls when more X is put on the market ($OB_1' > OB$). But in consequence consumers spend less of their income on the cheaper product X and have more left over to spend on Y so that the money price of Y rises ($OA_1' < OA$). The line $A_3'B_3'$ on the other hand shows the case where the price elasticity demand for X is (numerically) greater than one (e.g. -2). In this case when the price of X falls consumers spend more of their income on the greater supply of X and, in consequence, spend less than before on the fixed quantity of Y. The prices of Y and of X both fall ($OA_3' > OA$ and $OB_3' > OB$).

Suppose that $A_3'B_3'$ were parallel to AB which would mean that the money prices of X and of Y had both fallen by exactly the same percentage so that their relative prices (i.e. the slope of AB) were unchanged. Then the income elasticity of demand for Y would be zero and Y would be just on the border line of being an inferior good (cf. a horizontal path for $Q - Q'''$ on Figure 6). The equal proportionate fall in the prices of both X and Y would be equivalent to a rise in spendable incomes with constant prices; and the consumers' needs and tastes would have to be such in this case that they would spend the whole of this increase in income on X and none on Y. If $A_3'B_3'$ were more gently sloped than AB, then the income elasticity of demand for Y would be greater than zero and Y would not be an inferior good; for if both prices had fallen by the same percentage consumers would be trying to purchase more Y and this would drive the price of Y up relatively to the price of X. On the other hand if $A_3'B_3'$ were more steeply sloped than AB, then Y is an inferior good; for in this case if both prices had fallen by the same percentage consumers would be trying to purchase a smaller absolute amount of Y and this would be lowering the price of Y still further.

The line $A'_4B'_4$ where B'_4 coincides with B represents a case in which Y is so inferior a good that the price elasticity of demand for Y is zero. This is a case in which there has been no change in the price of X ($OB'_4 = OB$) but a heavy fall in the price of Y ($OA'_4 > OA$). Consumers, having the same income and faced with the same price of X, purchase no more Y when the price of Y falls but purchase only more X. The extreme case of inferiority for Y is represented by the line $A'_5B'_5$ where the increase in the supply of X causes the price of X to *rise* and the price of Y to fall very heavily. This is the case where the price elasticity of demand for Y has become a positive figure so that a *fall* in the price of Y would actually cause a *reduction* in the amount of Y purchased, if money incomes and the price of X remained unchanged. Suppose we were at Q' on the line $A'_4B'_4$ and consumers wanted then to purchase less Y and more X; the price of Y would fall still further and the price of X would actually rise above its initial level.

This is a very paradoxical, but nevertheless a possible, result where an increase in the supply of X causes a *rise* in the money price of X and a heavy fall in the money price of Y. We can perhaps understand the final outcome by imagining the following sequence of events. The immediate effect of the increase in the supply of X is to cause the price of X to fall. This makes people better off. X is the commodity they want when they are better off. They therefore attempt to purchase less Y and still more X. But this causes the price of Y to fall and of X to rise. Consumers now enjoy a larger total real purchasing power not so much because X is cheaper but because Y is cheaper than before. Y is so markedly 'inferior' that this attempted shift from Y to X goes on until the money price of X has made up more than the whole of its initial fall and is actually higher than it was initially.

We are now ready to modify the first of the two special assumptions which we made on page 54, namely that there were only two products X and Y. Our analysis does not need any very great modification to allow for the existence in the Shops of a large number of different products. If there are 1000 identical consumers, then the prices in the Shops must be such as to cause Mrs A, with her 1/1000 part of the national money income, to wish to take 1/1000 part of the supply of each product. The money price will rise for any product of which she is trying to take more than 1/1000 part of the total supply; and it will fall in the case of any product of which Mrs A is taking less than 1/1000 part of the total supply off the market.

If the market were in equilibrium and all the consumers' tastes changed simultaneously so that, at the initial equilibrium prices, they wished to purchase more Y and less X, then the immediate effect would be that the price of X would be driven down and the price of Y would be raised. There might now well be further repercussions on the prices of Z and many other products. When the price of X fell this might cause consumers to shift from purchasing Z to purchasing X, if for some purpose the now cheaper X was a good substitute for the still expensive Z. Or, if in some uses X and Z were complements, the fall in the price of X might encourage the use of X for a purpose which required also an increased use of Z. Thus the fall in the price of X might well lead to a sympathetic fall in the prices of products which were good substitutes for X in some uses and a sympathetic rise in the prices of products which were complementary to X in some uses. Similarly, sympathetic rises might take place in the case of products which were good substitutes for Y and sympathetic falls in the case of goods complementary to Y. And there might then be some further price changes which were sympathetic to these sympathetic price changes; and so on in an endless intertwining of repercussions. But finally we must imagine the market settling down to a new pattern of prices, in which some—including that of Y—have gone up and some[1]—including that of X—down, and in which the consumers with their new tastes are now prepared to clear the supplies in the Shops.

Rather similar repercussions must be imagined if there is an increase in the supply of any one product, X, coming on to the market. If we rule out as too improbable the possibility that all other products together make up an 'inferior' group of products, we can assume that this causes the money price of X not only to fall absolutely but also relatively to the prices of the generality of other products. But there may then be important sympathetic falls in the prices of particular products which are good substitutes for X and rises in the prices of any particular products which are complementary to X. And there may be further price changes sympathetic to these first sympathetic price changes; and so on. But once again we can imagine the market settling down to a new equilibrium in which with unchanged money incomes and unchanged needs and tastes the consumers are taking the same amounts as before of products Y, Z, etc., but larger amounts of X.

Let us next modify the second assumption made on page 54, namely that each consumer had the same money incomes and the needs and tastes. In order to analyse this situation let us revert to the assumption that there are only two products, X and Y. We now imagine a series of consumers—Mrs A, B, C, and D, etc.—perhaps

[1] Since total money incomes are constant and the total supply on the market of each product is unchanged, if some prices have gone up others must have gone down. The total value of the turnover in the Shops must be unchanged.

with different tastes and needs and with different money incomes to spend—M_a, M_b, M_c, M_d, etc. The total of these private incomes $M_a + M_b + M_c + M_d +$, etc., adds up to the total national income, M. Our problem is to determine how the prices of the two consumption goods (P_x and P_y) are determined when given supplies

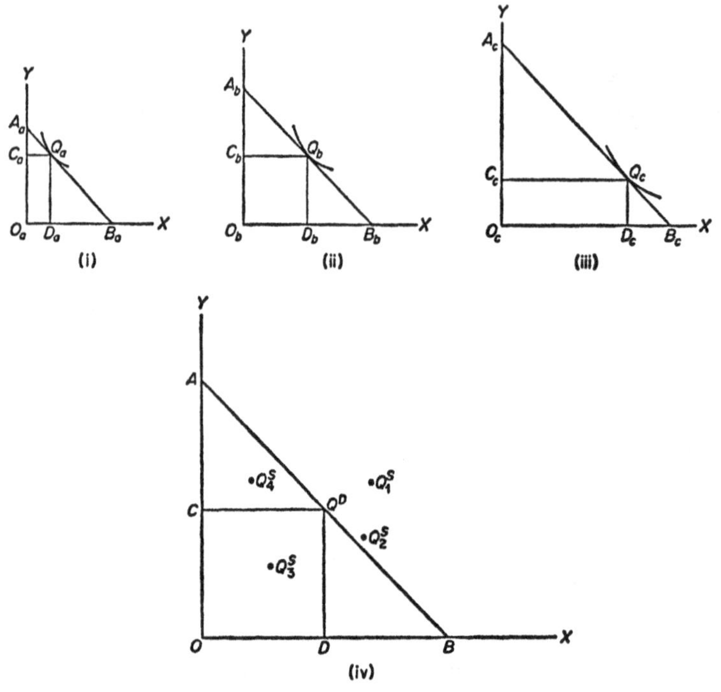

Figure 14

of X and Y are coming on to the market, when the total money income to be spent on X and Y is M, when this total income is distributed in a fixed manner between the various consumers, M_a going to Mrs A, M_b to Mrs B, and so on ($M_a + M_b + M_c + \ldots = M$) and when the different consumers may have different indifference maps.

We can tackle this problem by means of Figure 14. Let us arbitrarily choose two prices P_x and P_y and see whether they give an equilibrium solution or not and, if not, what will happen to these prices. With prices P_x and P_y and with an income of M_a, Mrs A could purchase $\frac{M_a}{P_x}$ units of X if she spent all her income on X or

$\frac{M_a}{P_y}$ units of Y if she spent all her income on Y. In Figure 14 (i) we draw O_aA_a equal to $\frac{M_a}{P_y}$ and O_aB_a equal to $\frac{M_a}{P_x}$, so that A_aB_a is Mrs A's budget constraint line. She will move along this line to her highest indifference curve at Q_a and will purchase O_aC_a units of Y and O_aD_a units of X. Figure 14 (ii) and (iii) give similar constructions for Mrs B and C. Since the market prices (P_x and P_y) are the same for all consumers the slope of the individual budget constraint line is the same for each consumer. But Mrs B is richer than Mrs A and her budget constraint lies further to the right than does Mrs A's. Similarly, Mrs C is richer than Mrs B.

The combinations of X and Y demanded by Mrs A, B, and C are shown by the points Q_a, Q_b, Q_c. These show a higher proportion of X to Y in Mrs B's purchases than in Mrs A's and in Mrs C's than in Mrs B's. This might be due to the fact that X was a rich person's product and Y a poor person's product; or it might be due to quite other differences of individual need and taste. For our present purpose the reason is irrelevant. For whatever reason the total market demand for X is $O_aD_a + O_bD_b + O_cD_c + \ldots$ We show this as OD in Figure 14 (iv). Similarly we show the total of the individual demands for $Y(O_aC_a + O_bC_b + O_cC_c + \ldots)$ as OC in Figure 14 (iv). Q^D shows the total market demand for X and Y at the arbitrary prices P_x and P_y; and OA $(=O_aA_a + O_bA_b + O_cA_c + \ldots)$ shows the value of the total money income in terms of Y and OB its value in terms of X.

If by accident Q^D also represents the supplies of X (CQ) and of Y (DQ) which are being supplied on the market, then the prices P_x and P_y are the equilibrium prices which clear the market. But suppose that while the demands for X and Y are at Q^D, the supplies of X and Y are at a different point, namely Q^S. In Figure 14 (iv) we show four possible supply points: at Q^S_1 there is an excess supply over demand for both X and Y and P_x and P_y will both fall; at Q^S_3 both X and Y are in excess demand and P_x and P_y will both rise; at Q^S_2 Y is in excess demand and X in excess supply so that P_y will rise and P_x fall; and at Q^S_4 Y is in excess supply and X in excess demand so that P_y will fall and P_x rise. Let us consider this last case in more detail. The lengths O_aA_a, O_bA_b, O_cA_c, etc., will all lengthen as a result of the fall in P_y while all the OB's will be shortened because of the rise in P_x. The points Q_a, Q_b, Q_c, etc., will thus all tend to move in a North-Westerly direction. For the community as a whole the market demand point Q^D will move North-West towards the market supply point Q^S_4. If Q^D then passed, for example, somewhat to the right of Q_4^S, both X and Y would be in excess demand; P_y as well as P_x would tend to rise; the OA's as well as the OB's would be shortened; and Q^D would be brought South-West towards Q_4^S. We are not at present concerned with this dynamic process of adjustment. It is clear, however, that there will be a set of prices P_x and P_y which will make Q^D coincide with Q^S. For our present purpose we simply assume that the market mechanism will on the general lines indicated successfully find this point of equilibrium.

In Figure 15 we reproduce the market equilibrium for the whole economy. Total supplies on the market are OD of X and OC of Y.

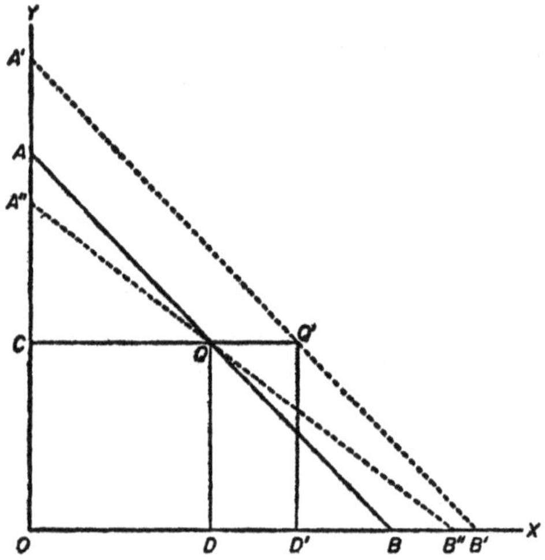

Figure 15

The prices of X and Y have been set in the way already described so that the national money income would purchase OA of Y or OB of X at current prices. Consumers as a whole have incomes which, at current prices, would enable them to purchase any combination on the market price line AB. In fact prices are such that they choose the combination Q which corresponds to the supplies actually available.

Suppose now that an important group of consumers changed their tastes and at current prices wished to purchase more Y and less X. This would drive up the price of Y and lower the price of X. The market price line in Figure 15 would swing round on the point Q to a position such as $A''B''$. The new market price line would have to pass through the point Q because total supplies on the market have not changed and the market price line, which represents the new combinations which consumers as a whole could purchase at the new prices, must pass through the combination Q which they do in fact continue to purchase in the new conditions.

Let us now consider the effect of this change on some individual consumer—say Mrs A—whose tastes have not changed. Suppose Mrs A enjoys 1/1000 of the national income. Then she has a budget constraint line which, on a scale of 1 in 1000, is an exact replica of the market price line AB of Figure 15 before, and of $A''B''$ of Figure 15 after, the change of taste of her neighbours. This is shown in Figure 16. It is clear that she will gain as a result of the change if as at Q_a^1 her tastes are such that she consumes an exceptionally large

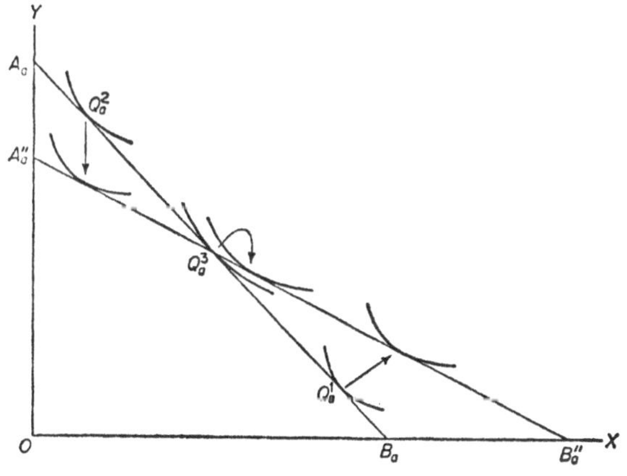

Figure 16

proportion of X, the product which has fallen in price because her neighbours do not want it. She will lose if she consumes, as at Q_a^2, an exceptionally large proportion of the product which is now more highly priced because her neighbours are competing more heavily for it.[1]

Figure 15 will also enable us to analyse the effect on individual consumers of an increase in the total market supply of X. There will now be a new market price line such as $A'B'$ which must pass through Q', the new market supply combination of X and Y. In Figure 15 we have drawn $A'B'$ so that the increase in X has caused the prices of both X and Y to fall ($OA' > OA$ and $OB' > OB$). In this case no

[1] It is interesting to observe that in this case she will gain moderately if, as at Q_a^3, she consumes the national average of X and Y. She could now go on purchasing the same combination as before. Q_a^3 is on $A''B''$ as well as on AB. But the change in the relative prices of X and Y will induce her to improve her position by buying a little more of the cheaper X and less of the more expensive Y.

individual consumer could fail to gain from the increased supply of X. Any one with a fixed money income must gain when the price of every product falls.

But if in the market as a whole the price elasticity of demand for X were (numerically) smaller than one (e.g. $-\frac{1}{2}$), then the price of Y might rise as in the case of $A_1'B_1'$ in Figure 13. Or, at the other extreme, if Y were such an inferior product that a fall in the price of Y would cause the amount of Y demanded to fall, the price of X would rise as in the case of $A_5'B_5'$ in Figure 13. (cf. p. 60 above). In either of these two cases an individual consumer such as

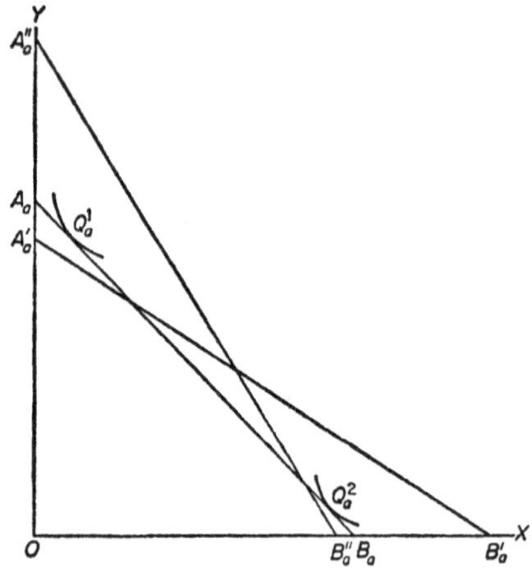

Figure 17

Mrs A might conceivably be hurt by the increased market supply of X as is shown in Figure 17.

Mrs A's budget constraint line in the initial position of equilibrium is A_aB_a. The supply of X increases in the market.

In the case of the new budget constraint line $A_a'B_a'$ the market price elasticity of demand for X is (numerically) less than one (e.g. $-\frac{1}{2}$) so that the price of X falls very much; and the price of Y rises because on the average consumers spend more on Y than before. If Mrs A spent a very large proportion of her income on Y (as at Q_a^1) she might be hit by the increased plenty of X on the market.

The case of the budget constraint line $A_a''B_a''$ represents a much more paradoxical position. Because Y is such an inferior good on the average of consumers in the market, the increased supply of X and the consequential rise in standards of living causes such a shift of expenditure away from Y onto X that the money price of X

actually rises. If Mrs A now consumes an exceptionally large proportion of the product *X* which has increased in supply (as at Q_a^2), it is conceivable that she is hurt by the increased supply of *X* on the market. The heavy consumers of *Y* are now so advantaged by the fall in the price of *Y* that they drive up the price of the more plentiful *X* against the already heavy consumers of *X*. If the rich man's good is increased in supply, making the general public better off, the higher standards of the poor may cause them so to compete for the rich man's good that the rich man is worse off. This possible event is a most unlikely curiosity. Normally, of course, an increased supply of *X* will be particularly favourable to the heavy consumers of *X* because the price of *X* will fall more than that of other products.

We can apply these principles to the general case in which there are many products and many consumers with differing incomes and needs and tastes. A market change, due either to a change in consumers' tastes or to a change in market supplies, will cause a series of price changes of the kind which we have examined. Consumers with fixed money incomes will gain from price falls and lose from price rises. A consumer who consumes an exceptionally high proportion of a particular product will suffer an exceptionally heavy gain (or loss) if there has been an above-average fall (or rise) in the price of that product.

This is the first set of principles to bear in mind in considering the effect of market changes on the distribution of real income between the individual citizens of the community. But there is a much more important set of factors affecting the distribution of incomes among persons, namely the effect of market changes upon the distribution of money incomes among persons. We shall turn to this problem in the next and following chapters.

CHAPTER IV

THE TERMS OF TRADE

We have now considered what goes on in the Shops when given streams of money incomes meet given flows of various products on to the market. We explained at the beginning of the last chapter (p. 54) that we were neglecting the effect of price changes in the Shops upon what went on in the Firms and Farms; and we explained that in fact there were two sets of influences in the Firms and Farms which might have repercussions in turn upon the market for finished products in the Shops. For, first, a change in product prices might affect the supplies of *X*, *Y*, and *Z* produced in the Firms and Farms for the Shops; and, second, this might cause a change in the demand for various factors of production and thus in the relative earnings of various citizens and so in the personal distribution of the fixed national money income between the individual consumers. In this chapter we shall construct and discuss a set of assumptions about what goes on in the Firms and Farms which will enable us to continue with our assumption that the supplies of the products *X*, *Y*, and *Z* are unaffected by changes in the prices of *X*, *Y*, and *Z* but to drop the assumption that such price changes have no effect upon the distribution of incomes.

This result would occur if the factors of production (i) were fixed in amount, (ii) were very specialized in the production of different commodities, and (iii) were very unequally owned. Let us start with a very extreme example. Suppose

(i) that there are two factors of production, land (*N*) and labour (*L*), each fixed in amount;

(ii) that there are two products, food (*X*) and clothing (*Y*), food being produced by land without the co-operation of any labour and clothing being produced by labour without the co-operation of any land; and

(iii) that there are two classes of citizens, landlords (*A*) who own all the land and do no work and workers (*B*) who do all the work and own no land.

The outputs of *X* and *Y* would now be fixed, the output of *X* being the given output of the available supply of *N* and the output of *Y* being the given output of the available supply of *L*. But variations in the price of *X* and *Y* would cause variations in the rents of land and the wages of labour and thus in the distribution of the national income between the classes *A* and *B*.

In order to continue with the simple model of the economy which we explained in Chapter I we will assume that the *X* produced by the landlords on their Farms is all sold at the current market money price in the Shops; the landlords' wives receive this money income; and next day they spend it in the Shops partly on buying some *Y* produced by the workers in the Firms but partly on buying back, as it were, some of the *X* which has been produced on the landlords' Farms the previous day. Similarly, we suppose that the workers sell

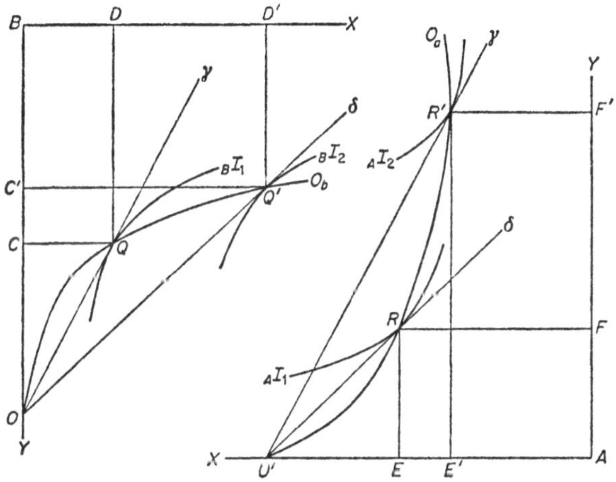

Figure 18

in the Shops at the ruling price all the *Y* produced by them in the Firms, their wives receiving the wages thus earned and spending them on purchasing *X* and *Y* from the Shops.

If we assume that each landlord's family is exactly similar to every other landlord's family in the sense that (i) each owns the same amount of land and thus receives the same money income from rents and (ii) each has the same set of tastes and needs, and if we make a similar assumption about the workers and their families, we can treat the present case very simply. We can for each of the two groups of families in the community construct a group indifference map out of the indifference map of a representative family in that group on the principles which have already been explained at length (pp. 55–56).

At the top left half of Figure 18 we draw a group indifference map for the whole of the workers' families. We measure horizontally to the right from *B* the amount of *X*, and downwards vertically from *B* the amount of *Y*, consumed by the working class. Thus the point *Q* represents a working-class consumption of *BD* of *X* and *BC* of *Y*. Since all are alike in incomes and needs and tastes, each workers' family will be consuming 1/1000 of *BD* plus 1/1000 of *BC*, if there are 1000 workers. Each individual working-class family will be on an indifference curve which we may call ${}_BI'_1$. On the group indifference curve marked ${}_BI_1$ we have represented all those combinations of total consumption of *X* and of *Y* by the workers as a whole which, when spread evenly over all the workers, would put each individual working-class family on this same individual indifference curve, ${}_BI'_1$.

At the bottom right half of Figure 18 we do the same for the landlords as a class. We measure the amount of *X* consumed by the landowning class to the left along the horizontal axis from the origin *A* and the amount of *Y* consumed by the land-owning class up the vertical axis from the origin *A*. Thus the point *R* represents the consumption of *AE* of *X* and of *AF* of *Y* by the landowning class. If there are 100 landlords, each landlord's family will be consuming 1/100 part of each of these quantities. All points on the *A*-group indifference curve marked ${}_AI_1$ represent combinations of *X* and *Y* which, when they are divided into 100 equal parts, would suffice to keep each individual landlord's family on the same individual indifference curve, say ${}_AI'_1$.

Suppose now that the 1000 workers between them can produce an amount of *Y* equal to *OB* (each individual worker producing 1/1000 of *OB*). This amount of *Y* is sold in the Shops. Whatever the money price of *Y* ruling in the Shops the market price line for the workers must pass through the point *O*. If the price of *Y* is high, the money incomes of the workers will be high; but, the price of *Y* being high, this money income would purchase only *BO* of *Y* if it were all spent on *Y*. If the price of *Y* were low, the money incomes of the workers would be low; but, the price of *Y* being low, this money income would purchase as much as *BO* of *Y* if it were all spent on *Y*. The workers in fact will in all circumstances receive a money income which, if all spent on *Y*, would purchase that amount of *Y* (namely *BO*) which they have in the first instance sold in the Shops. According to the money price of *X* relatively to the money price of *Y*, the market price line for the workers, starting from *O*, will have a steep slope such as that of the line γ or a gentle slope such as that of the line δ. In the case of γ the workers' wives by refraining from repurchasing *OC* of the *Y* sold by their husbands to the Shops can purchase *CQ* of *X*. In the case of δ by refraining from purchasing *OC′* of *Y* they can obtain *C′Q′* of *X*. Since the slope of

δ is less steep than that of γ, more X can be obtained for each unit of Y given up on δ than on γ. On δ the price of X is lower relatively to the price of Y than it is on γ. When the relative prices or, as they may be called, the terms of trade between X and Y are represented by the price line γ, the workers will in fact choose the combination Q. For this is the point at which their market price line γ is tangential to their highest attainable indifference curve $_BI_1$. When the price improves for them to the line δ, they will purchase the combination Q', bringing them on to a higher indifference curve $_BI_2$. The curve $O - O_b$ which is often called group B's 'offer curve' maps out all the points Q at which the market price lines through O are tangential to group B's indifference curves. It is in fact analytically the same construction as the price-consumption curve shown in Figure 7 for all consumers in the conditions discussed in Chapter II. Since OC represents the total amount of purchasing power in terms of Y which group B will spend on X, group B's price elasticity of demand for X is (numerically) greater than one when the curve $O - O_b$ is sloping up from O in a North-Easterly direction, is (numerically) equal to one when $O - O_b$ is horizontal and moving due East, and is (numerically) less than one when it is sloping down to the South-East, as the price of X falls in terms of Y.

Similarly in the bottom right half of Figure 18 we suppose that the landlords with the land available to them can produce AO' of X of which each landlord receives 1/100 part. This they can sell in the Shops in competition with each other, receiving an income which, whatever the price of X may be, will give their wives a purchasing power over AO' units of X. If the money price of X relatively to that of Y gives a 'terms of trade' of δ, then their wives by refraining from the repurchase of $O'E$ of X can obtain AF of Y. In fact, this brings them to a consumption combination R which is on their highest attainable indifference curve $_AI_1$. The terms of trade γ represents a rise in the price of X relatively to that of Y. The landlords' families will be better off and will now move to the consumption combination R' by refraining from the repurchase of $O'E'$ of their output of X in order to purchase $R'E'$ of Y in the Shops. The curve $O - O_a$ is group A's 'offer curve'. It corresponds to the price-consumption curve of A for Y. Since $O'E$ represents the amount of purchasing power in terms of X which group A spends on purchasing Y, group A's price-consumption curve has an elasticity (numerically) greater than one so long as it slopes up North-East from O', an elasticity equal to one if it rises due North, and an elasticity (numerically) less than one if it moves in a North-Westerly direction as the price of Y in terms of X falls.

By bringing the points O and O' together we can from Figure 18 construct the box diagram given in Figure 19. Group B is producing *BO* of *Y* and group A is producing *AO* of *X*. Suppose the terms of trade were as shown by the line δ. Then group A would be trying to consume the combination shown at *R* because, as is indicated by the offer curve $O - O_a$ by giving up *OE* of *X* in return for *ER* of *Y* group A can now attain the highest achievable indifference curve. Group B on the other hand would wish to give up *OC* of its output of *Y* to purchase *CQ* of group A's output of *X* in order to achieve the consumption combination at *Q* which, as group B's offer curve shows, brings group B to the highest attainable indifference curve.

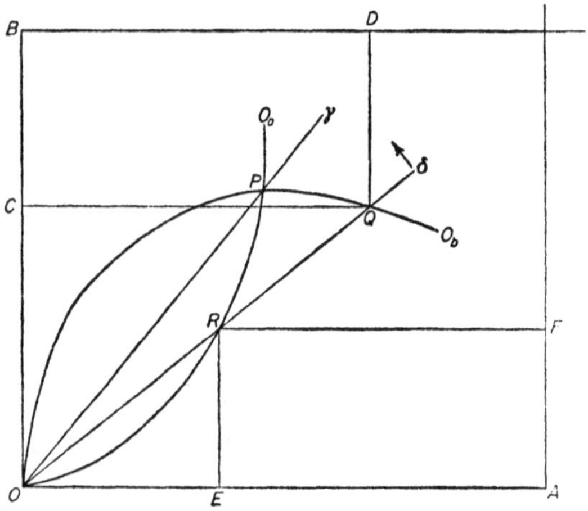

Figure 19

In this situation the demand for *X* would exceed the supply since group A's consumption (*AE*) plus group B's consumption (*BD*) is greater than the total output (*AO*). Conversely, the supply of *Y* (*BO*) would exceed the demands of group A (*AF*) and of group B (*BC*). The money price of *X* would rise and of *Y* would fall. The terms of trade would move in favour of *X* and against *Y*. The price line δ would swing round in the direction of the arrow. Equilibrium would be possible only at the terms of trade represented by γ, the price line which passes through the point *P*, where the two offer curves intersect. It can be seen from the Figure that at this point *R* and *Q* would coincide and for both products total demand would be equal to total supply.

It is perhaps worth noting that in the case of offer curves with price elasticities (numerically) less than one there may be more than one possible equilibrium level of the terms of trade. This is illustrated in Figure 20 where the two offer curves intersect at Q_1, Q_2, and Q_3. At all the three terms of trade represented by straight lines passing from O through Q_1, Q_2, or Q_3, total demand and supply would be equal. The point Q_2 would, however, represent a very unstable point. For supposing that the terms-of-trade line happened to pass slightly above the point Q_2, as in the case of the line γ shown in Figure 20, then, as can be seen in the Figure, the demand for X would exceed the supply ($RF + CQ > AO$), while the supply of Y would exceed the demand ($BO > DQ + RE$), so that the price line would be pulled in the direction shown by the arrow, away from Q_2 towards

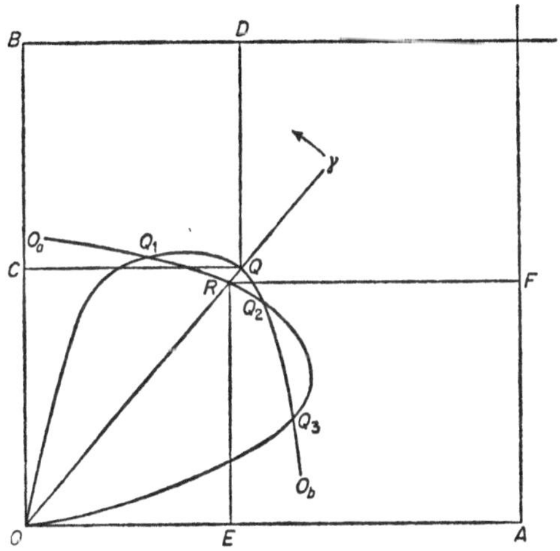

Figure 20

Q_1. Similarly, it can be seen that if the price line passed between Q_2 and Q_3 it would be pulled away from Q_2 towards Q_3.

But Q_1 and Q_3 are both equilibrium points. The existence of more than one equilibrium point is probable only if X and Y are bad substitutes for each other and are demanded in rather fixed proportions by both groups, A and B. The commonsense of this possibility can then be seen in the following way. Suppose the terms of trade are very unfavourable to group B. Group B has to give up a lot of Y to get a little X. This little X goes with the little Y left over to group B to make up a low level of balanced consumptions of X and Y. At the same time group A has received a lot of Y and is giving up little X and, therefore, has much of both X and Y to consume—a high-level balanced consumption. Both groups A and B might be in equilibrium. At vastly different terms of trade greatly in favour of group B the roles are simply reversed. Group B gives up little Y for much X and has a high-level balanced consumption, while group A gives up much X for little Y and has a low-level balanced consumption. Again both groups A and B might be in equilibrium.

We can now use this box diagram to observe the effects of a change of tastes on the part of one group. Suppose that group A's demand for Y increases and for X decreases in the sense that at any given terms of trade group A would sell more X in order to buy more Y. This is shown in Figure 21.

Before the change group A's offer curve was shown by $O - O_a$. After the change group A's offer curve has shifted to $O - O_a'$. At the

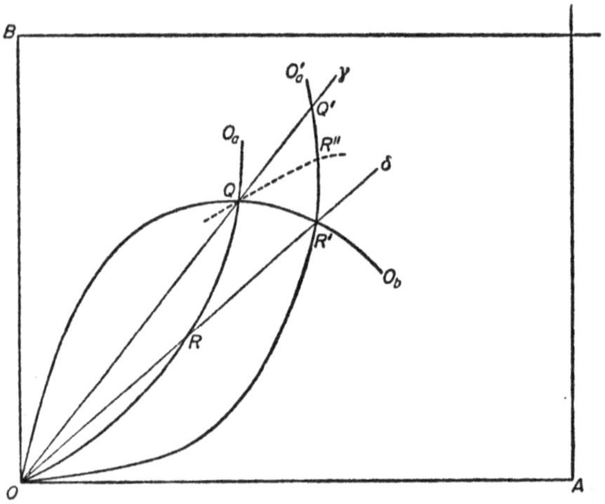

Figure 21

terms of trade γ group A consumed the combination Q, but after the change consumes at Q' a larger amount of Y and a smaller amount of X. Similarly, at the terms of trade δ group A formerly consumed at R and after the change at R'. The initial equilibrium terms of trade would have been γ, since the line γ passes through the point Q where $O - O_b$ and $O - O_a$ intersect. After the change of group A's tastes the terms of trade will have moved to δ since the line δ passes through R where $O - O_b$ and $O - O_a'$ intersect. The increased demand for Y and the decreased demand for X by group *A* will have raised the money price of Y and lowered that of X and group *B* will be better off.

How much the terms of trade will have moved in favour of group B and against group A will clearly depend, not only upon the shift in group A's offer curve, but also upon the shape of group B's offer curve. Between Q and R' group B's offer curve is inelastic. Suppose that the curve had been elastic as on the broken line between Q and R''. The terms of trade would have moved much less against group A as a result of the increase in group A's demand for X. The reason is clear. Group A's increased demand for Y and decreased demand for X causes the price of Y to rise and of X to fall. If a small fall in the price of X relatively to that of Y causes group B to purchase much more X and to spend more Y on the purchase of X then A's increased demand for Y can be met without very extensive price changes.

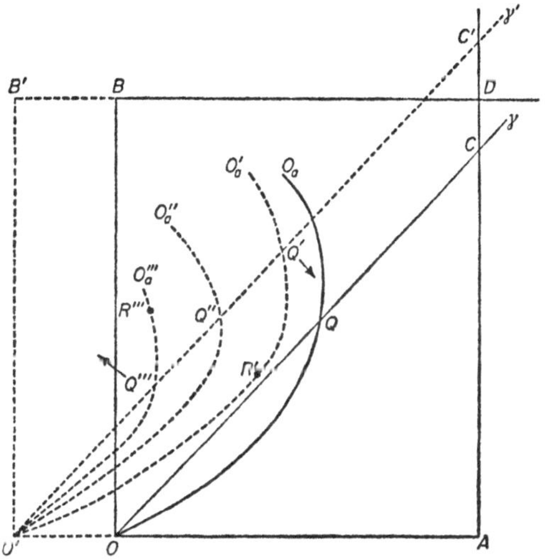

Figure 22

Suppose next that there were some change in the productivity of the soil and that more X per acre is produced, so that the total output and the output per landlord of X is increased. The result of this on the terms of trade is illustrated in Figure 22. We start with a production of X of AO and of Y of BO. The line γ represents the equilibrium terms of trade and the point Q represents the initial equilibrium trading point. It is on group A's offer curve $O—O_a$ which cuts the line γ at the point Q. To avoid confusion in the diagram we have not shown group B's offer curve; but since Q is the equilibrium trading point we know that group B's offer curve must pass through Q.

The increased output of X is represented by the fact that group A can now produce AO' instead of AO of X. As far as group B is concerned this means simply that group B's origin is shifted to the left from B to B' and all group B's indifference curves and so B's offer curve is simply shifted by an amount of $B'B$ or $O'O$ to the left.

If we take the same price line as before (γ' is parallel to γ) group B's offer curve will cut the price line at the same point. In other words group B's offer curve, having been shifted by an amount $O'O$ to the left, passes through Q'' where Q'' is a point directly to the left of Q by the same distance. If the new equilibrium point were at Q'', group B's position would be completely unchanged by the increased output of X.

The outcome clearly depends upon what has happened to group A's offer curve which we must redraw because group A's initial real income in terms of X has gone up by an amount OO'. In other words, still taking the point A as the origin of group A's consumption map, we have to draw group A's offer curve starting with an income for group A in terms of X of AO' instead of AO. What the new offer curve of group A looks like depends upon the nature of group A's indifference map. $O' - O_a'$, $O' - O_a''$, and $O' - O_a'''$ represent three possible positions of group A's new offer curve.

The curve $O' - O_a''$ passes through Q''. In this case there is no change in the terms of trade. Group B's position is unchanged. Starting with the same real income in terms of Y ($B'O' = BO$) and faced with the same terms of trade (γ' is parallel to γ), group B is in exactly the same market position as before. Group A is, of course, better off, starting with a larger real income in terms of X ($AO' > AO$) and faced with the same terms of trade as before. This case will occur if and only if group A's income elasticity of demand for Y is zero. Group A's income goes up by $O'O$ in terms of X and at unchanged terms of trade, group A adds the whole of this amount of X to its own consumption of X leaving its consumption of Y unchanged.

The curve O'–O_a''' passes South-West of Q'' and cuts γ' at Q'''. This is an example of what would happen if Y were an inferior good in group A's consumption, so that when group A's income went up and prices remained unchanged group A would purchase less Y than before in order to spend more than the whole of the increase in income on X. Q''' is South-West of Q. In this case unless the terms of trade changed group B's consumption would be at Q'' and group A's at Q'''. There would be an excess demand for X and an excess supply of Y. The terms of trade would move against group B in the direction of the arrow pointing from Q'''. If B's offer curve ran from Q'' through R''', then R''' would be the new equilibrium point. Group B would be worse off than before because of the increased supply of X. Group A has become rich by producing more of the 'rich man's product' and therefore buys less of the poor man's product; and this has hurt group B which produces the poor man's product.

$O'-O_a'$ shows the more normal case in which group A's income elasticity of demand for Y is positive. When group A's income increases, prices remaining the same, group A in this case buys more X and more Y. Q' is North-West of Q. Now unless there is a change in the terms of trade there will be an excess demand for Y and an excess supply of X, since group B's consumption point is at Q'' and group A's at Q'. The terms of trade will move in the direction of the arrow from Q' in favour of group B and against group A. Group B will be better off than before, having the same real income in terms of Y but being able to trade it on better terms. Other things being equal, it is good to trade with rich people because they are likely to have a high demand for your product.

Group A starts with a larger income in terms of X but in the present case can trade on worse terms. If group B's price elasticity of demand for X is (numerically) less than one, it is possible that the net outcome of the two changes will be to make group A worse off than before. Suppose in the case of Figure 22 that group B's offer curve (which is not drawn on the Figure) ran from Q'' South Eastwards through R'. Then R' would represent the new equilibrium position. The slope of group A's indifference curve at R' is that of the line $O'R'$ and the slope of group A's indifference curve at Q is that of the line γ. If the line $O'R'$ extended passed below Q, then R' might be on a lower indifference curve for group A than is Q.

If the farmers (group A) produce more wheat (X) and if they do not want to consume more wheat themselves but want to sell it to get more manufactured goods (Y), and if the manufacturers (group B) do not want to eat more wheat unless the price of wheat is very greatly reduced, then the farmers may in competition among themselves so spoil the market for wheat that they are worse off as a result of a good harvest. This is the well-known problem of the producers of primary products.

It is of some interest to consider in the three cases of $O' - O_a'$, $O' - O_a''$, and $O' - O_a'''$ of Figure 22 what will have happened to the absolute level of the money prices of X and Y. Since the output of Y is constant but the output of X has increased, and since we are assuming total money expenditure on both goods to be constant, the prices of X or of Y or of both X and Y must have fallen. If the money price of Y is constant, then the money income of group B is constant; therefore, the money income of group A must also be constant; and therefore the distribution of money income between the two groups is unchanged. If the money price of Y has risen, the money income of group B will be up and that of group A must, therefore, have fallen; and the distribution of the money income will have changed in favour of group B. Conversely, if the money price of Y has fallen, the distribution of the national income will have moved in favour of group A.

Now in the case of the new offer curve O'–O_a'' in Figure 22 the money prices of both X and Y will have fallen. Since the terms of trade are unchanged (γ' parallel to γ) both money prices must have moved together and both must, therefore, have fallen. The distribution of the national income has moved in favour of group A which has a larger income in terms of X and thus against group B which has no change in its real income.[1]

In the case of $O' - O_a'''$ in Figure 22 the terms of trade have moved against Y. The absolute money price of Y will, therefore, have fallen still more than in the case just examined, since the money price of Y must now have fallen by a larger proportion than the price of X. If Y is sufficiently inferior in group A's consumption it is possible that the terms of trade will have moved so heavily against Y that, with a constant money expenditure on X and Y together, the price of Y will have fallen so much that the price of X does not fall at all or even rises.[2] In this case there will have been a very marked shift in the distribution of income against group B.

In the case of $O' - O_a'$ in Figure 22 the terms of trade will have moved against X. The price of Y will have fallen less than the price of X. It can be seen from the position of the point R' that the smaller (numerically) are the elasticities of A's and B's offer curves the more the terms of trade will move against X. It is possible that the terms of trade move so much against X that, with a constant total money expenditure on X and Y together, the money price of X falls so much that the money price of Y either does not fall at all or actually rises.[3] In this case the increased output of X by group A would cause no improvement or even an actual decline in the share of group A in the national income.

Any changes in the shares of group A and group B in the national income can be seen very simply from Figure 22. In order to compare the incomes of group A and group B we must choose a single measuring rod for both incomes. It does not matter what measuring rod we choose, since it is simply the ratio of group A's to group B's income which we are considering. There are three possible measuring rods. We can measure money income, or real income in terms of purchasing power over Y (i.e. money income divided by the price of Y), or real income in terms of purchasing power over X (i.e. money income divided by the price of X). Let us

[1] This corresponds to line $A_3'B_3'$ in Figure 13 when $A_3'B_3'$ has the same slope as AB.

[2] These two cases correspond to the lines $A_4'B_4'$ and $A_5'B_5'$ in Figure 13.

[3] These would correspond to the lines $A_2'B_2'$ and $A_1'B_1'$ of Figure 13.

measure the incomes of both groups in terms of purchasing power over Y. Group B's income in terms of Y is, of course, group B's output of Y which remains unchanged at $BO = B'O' = AD$. Group A's income in terms of Y is group A's income in terms of X converted into Y at the ruling terms of trade. Before the change in Figure 22 this is equal to AC. For group A has an income in terms of X of AO which can be converted at the initial market prices into AC units of Y. The ratio of group A's income to group B's income is, therefore, $\frac{AC}{AD}$.

After the increase of group A's output to AO', group A's income in terms of Y would be equal to AC' if the terms of trade were unchanged (i.e. γ' parallel to γ). This as we have seen would be the case if the income elasticity of group A's demand for Y were zero, represented by the new offer curve $O' - O_a''$. In this case the ratio of group A's income to group B's income would have risen to $\frac{AC'}{AD}$.

If Y were an inferior good in group A's consumption (i.e. with a new offer curve of the sort $O' - O_a'''$) the terms of trade line γ' would be pulled round in the direction of the arrow from Q''', C' would rise up the vertical axis through A, and the ratio of group A's income to group B's income would be even larger. With a new offer curve of the kind $O' - O_a'$, the terms of trade line would be pulled in the direction of the arrow from Q'. If there were a sufficient pull in this direction, the point C' on the vertical axis through A might be pulled below C. In this case the ratio of group A's to group B's income would be lower than before the increase in the output of X. With a constant money national income, the increased output of X would have raised the money income of group B and lowered the money income of group A.

We can generalize the type of situation discussed in this chapter by allowing for a large number of products. The essence of the situation is that the prices of the products X, Y, Z, etc., will affect the distribution of the national income between groups of citizens, but will not affect the output of the products themselves. For this to be the case we must imagine a large number of factors of production each specialized for the production of a single product. Thus one man is a cobbler, another man a baker, and so on; and one acre of land can produce wheat, another beef, and so on. The cobbler cannot become a baker, and the wheat land cannot be used for grazing. We must imagine further that the ownership of these specialized factors is not evenly spread over the families of citizens in the communities. Thus one family receives its income from shoe-making rather than from the baking of bread or from the raising of cattle; and so on.[1] Our analysis proceeds then on exactly the same lines as in Chapter III except that we now have to allow for the fact that changes in the prices of the products will themselves improve the position of those citizens who are concerned with the production of the higher priced products and will worsen the position of those citizens who are concerned with the production of the lower priced products.

Consider the case of a shift of demand from X to Y in this general case. As we have argued in Chapter III, the direct effect would be a fall in the price of X and a rise in the price of Y. There would then be a series of sympathetic price changes in those products which were close substitutes for, or complements to, X or Y. These price changes would now have repercussions upon the money incomes of the producers of the various products, money income being transferred from the producers of the products which had fallen in price to the producers of the products which had risen in price. These distributional effects require some comments.

First, the effects upon the distribution of real income between the citizens in the community now depends upon the outcome of two sets of forces. The citizens who will gain most are those who (i) produce in more than the national average those products which have risen most in price and at the same time (ii) consume in more than the national average those products which have fallen in price. That is to say, citizens now stand to gain or lose both as producers and consumers. If their income as producers is very specialized (i.e. if it depends exclusively upon the production of one product) whereas their expenditure as consumers is very widely spread (i.e. something like the national average) over all products, then they are likely to be much more closely affected as producers than as consumers by any change in relative prices. But it is the combination of the two influences which now determines how much particular groups will be benefited or hurt by a change in prices.

Second, the effect on the distribution of the national money income between various producers which is caused by changes in the relative product prices may itself now affect the demand for the various products. This may reduce or may magnify the price changes.

[1] It is not necessary to assume that each family receives its income from only one source, but merely that each family receives a higher proportion of its income from some activities than corresponds to the share of those activities in the national average and receives a lower proportion of its income from some other activities than corresponds to the share of those activities in the national income.

Thus suppose that as a result of a shift of demand the prices of *X* and of good substitutes for *X* go down whereas the prices of *Y* and of good substitutes for *Y* go up. The producers of the former group lose, and of the latter group gain, money income. If the latter group spends an exceptionally high proportion of its additional income on *Y* and substitutes for *Y*, while the former group economises mainly by demanding less *X* and substitutes for *X*, then the redistribution of money incomes will intensify the initial shift of demand away from the *X*-group of products on to the *Y*-group of products; this will further intensify the shift of money incomes which will further intensify the shift of demand and the shift of prices, and so on. The price changes may now have to be much more marked than they would have been without the effect on the distribution of incomes. In the opposite case, if the producers of the *Y*-group of products spend an exceptionally high proportion of any additional income on the *X*-group of products, and *vice versa*, the price changes may be much less marked than they would have been in the absence of the effects on the redistribution of incomes. Price changes and the redistribution of incomes itself will now be moderate because those who gain in price spend more on those who have lost, while those who have lost cut back their demand for the products of those who have gained.

Exactly the same sort of considerations must be borne in mind in the case of a change of relative prices due in the first instance to an increase in the supply of one product, *X*. We have already discussed in Chapter III (pp. 61 and 67) the sort of changes in relative prices which this change may bring about in the absence of repercussions upon the distribution of money incomes. We must now bear in mind that (i) the money incomes of the producers of *X* will have gone up (or down) according as the money price of *X* has gone down less (or more) than in proportion to the increase in its supply and (ii) the money incomes of other producers will have gone down (or up) according as the prices for their products have gone down (or up).

These shifts in the distribution of money incomes must be considered from the two points of view which we have just examined. First, the final effects on the real standards of living of different groups will depend upon whether they produce the goods which have gone up or down in price and whether they consume the goods which have gone up or down in price. Second, the initial redistribution of money incomes may cause shifts in demand. These will intensify the initial changes in distribution, if those who have lost spend less on the products of those who have lost while those who have gained spend more on the products of those who have gained. The opposite pattern of demand will mitigate the initial change in the distribution of incomes, since the gainers would increase the demand for the products of the losers and *vice versa*.

But if we assume that citizens are much more similar as consumers than as producers, we can concentrate our attention on the way in which the price changes which we have already examined in Chapter III are likely directly to affect the distribution of money incomes between the various groups in the economy. The further repercussions would be of secondary importance.

CHAPTER V

CONSTANT COSTS

In the last chapter we examined a case in which changes in the prices of the products might affect the distribution of income but not the outputs of the various products. In this chapter we will examine a case which gives exactly the opposite result: a change in the prices of the products may now affect the outputs of the various products but not the distribution of incomes.

For this purpose let us assume:

(i) that there is only one factor of production, namely, labour, all workers being equally skilled in all occupations. Alternatively we may assume that while there are other factors, such as land, they are in such plentiful supply that there is no economic scarcity of them at all. Any producer can hire any amount of land which he wants at a zero or negligible rent. Labour is the only factor for which he must pay; and

(ii) that this factor, labour, can and does move freely and without cost from one occupation to another in search of the highest money reward, the other non-monetary advantages and disadvantages being the same for a worker in all occupations.

Since we are assuming constant returns to scale (assumption 7 on p. 27), a given state of technical knowledge (assumption 6, p. 27), a constant money national income (assumption 10, p. 28), and a constant working population (assumption 4, p. 26), we now have constant money costs of production for each product. With a constant money national income and a constant working population, we must have a constant money wage per worker equal to the money national income divided by the number of workers. For in competition with each other workers will move freely from lower to higher paid occupations until the wage earned is the same in every occupation; and since there are no other factors of production wages will absorb the whole national income. With constant returns to scale and with given technical knowledge there will be a given and constant output per worker in each occupation, and thus the money cost of production of each product will be given and equal to the money wage rate of a worker divided by output per worker of that product.

In a fully competitive equilibrium each product must be selling at its cost of production. If this were not so, producers would be moving in to produce more in those occupations in which the price of the product was above the money wage cost; and they would be moving out of, and so reducing output in, those occupations in which the price of the product was below its cost of production.

In these circumstances it is extremely easy to illustrate geometrically what would happen if there were only two products, X and Y. In Figure 23 we illustrate the situation for a series of workers'

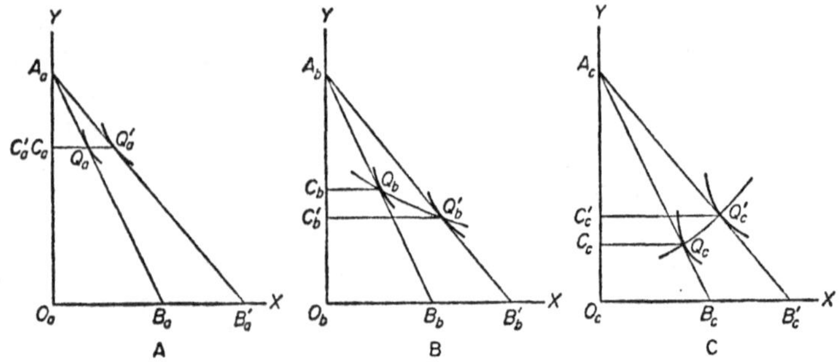

Figure 23

families, A, B, C, etc. Each worker receives the same money income which has a purchasing power over O_aA_a $(=O_bA_b = O_cA_c)$ which is the output per worker of Y and over O_aB_a $(= O_bB_b = O_cB_c)$ which is the output per worker of X. For each worker receives the same money wage and the money price of each product is equal to its wage cost, so that each worker receives a wage which has a purchasing power over Y (or X) equal to a worker's output of Y (or X).

The lines AB which are the same for each worker show the budget-constraint line for each working class family. Each moves on its budget constraint line until it is purchasing at Q that combination of X and Y which brings it to its highest indifference curve. In Figure 23 we illustrate the situation in which family A has a high demand for Y, family B an intermediate demand for Y, and family C a low demand for Y. The total community's demand for Y will be $O_aC_a + O_bC_b + O_cC_c + \ldots$ and for X will be $C_a\,Q_a + C_bQ_b + C_cQ_c + \ldots$.

We can easily construct a picture for the whole economy from the individual pictures given in Figure 23. This is done in Figure 24. The length OA measures the total amount of Y which the community could produce if all workers produced only Y, so that $OA = O_aA_a + O_bA_b + O_cA_c + \ldots$ from Figure 23. Similarly OB measures the total amount of X which the community could produce if all workers produced only X. The community can produce any combination of X and Y on the line AB. Each worker who moves from the production of Y to the production of X will reduce the output of Y by an amount equal to O_aA_a, and will increase the output of X by an amount equal to O_aB_a, in Figure 23. OC in Figure 24 represents $O_aC_a + O_bC_b + O_cC_c \ldots$ of Figure 23 and shows the amount of Y which, given the needs and tastes of all the individual working-class families, society will choose to consume. Similarly, CQ in Figure 24 equals the sum of $C_aQ_a + C_bQ_b + C_cQ_c + \ldots$ of Figure 23.

It is now very easy to see what will be the result of a change of taste or of an increased supply of one of the products.

Suppose first that in a given equilibrium situation tastes change and consumers demand more Y and less X. The immediate effect

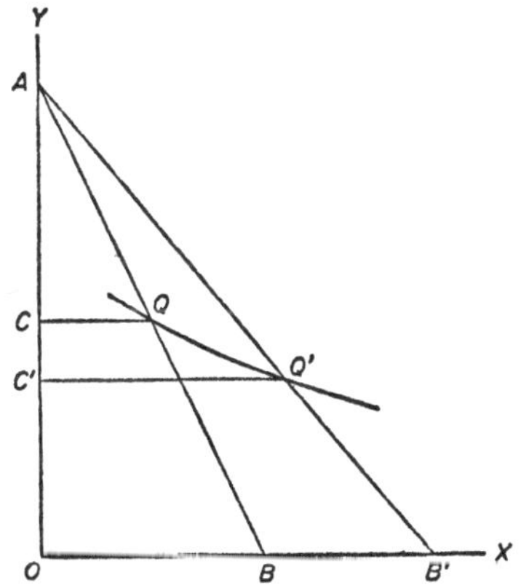

Figure 24

will be to drive up the money price of Y and to reduce the money price offered for X. But workers will then move from the production of X in which a loss is now made to that of Y which has now become exceptionally profitable. This will reduce the supply of X and raise the supply of Y until the previous price relationship which corresponds to costs of production has been restored. The final result will be simply that with the change of tastes some or all of the points $Q_a, Q_b, Q_c \ldots$ move North-West up the lines $A_aB_a, A_bB_b, A_cB_c, \ldots$ in Figure 23; and, in correspondence with these changes in demand the community's production point Q moves North-West up the community's production possibility line AB in Figure 24. The change of demand will ultimately have caused a change of outputs without any change in prices or in the distribution of income.

The effects of a change in productivity is also easily illustrated on Figures 23 and 24. Suppose that the output per head of X increases from O_aB_a to $O_aB'_a$ in Figure 23. The cost and so, in any new equilibrium, the price of *X* falls in a corresponding proportion. The individual budget-constraint lines of Figure 23 and the production possibility line of Figure 24 all change in the same way: the length *OA* remains constant but the length *OB* increases in the ratio of the increased output per head of *X* to *OB′*.

Each individual family will now have the same money income as before and will be faced with the same money price for *Y* but a lower money price of *X*. What happens to the demands for *X* and *Y* depends, therefore, simply on the price-consumption curves of the various families (cf. pp. 42–45 above). In Figure 23 family A is assumed to have a price elasticity of demand for *X* (numerically) equal to one; after the fall in price the same amount is spent on *X* as before ($A_aC_a = A_aC'_a$). Family B has a price elasticity of demand for *X* (numerically) greater than one; more is spent on *X* after the fall in price ($A_bC_b > A_bC'_b$). Family C has an elasticity (numerically) lless than one ($A_cC_c < A_cC'_c$).

It is interesting to observe from Figure 23 that in the present case in which the increased output of *X* can have no effect on the distribution of money incomes or on the price of *Y*, every individual family must be benefited by the increased productivity in the production of *X*. Each family has the same income, the same price of *Y*, but a ower price of *X* in the Shops. *Q′* is on a higher indifference curve than *Q* in every case in Figure 23. This result is to be contrasted with the cases examined in the last two chapters where particular families might be hurt by a fall in their money incomes or a rise in their cost of living resulting from increased productivity in one line of production.

By summing up all individual demands shown in Figure 23 one can get, in the present case where there is no effect on the distribution of incomes or the price of *Y*, a straightforward community price-consumption curve for *X*. This is shown in Figure 24 where $CQ = C_aQ_a + C_bQ_b + C_cQ_c + \ldots$ and $C'Q' = C'_aQ'_a + C'_bQ'_b + C'_cQ'_c + \ldots$. The movement from *Q* to *Q′* shows the movement in the community's demand for *X* and *Y* when the national income and the price of *Y* remain unchanged but the price of *X* falls. Once again there is no change in the distribution of income; prices are set at constant levels equal to costs of production; and it is the supplies of the products *X* and *Y* which are adjusted by the flow of labour from unprofitable to profitable occupations until supplies are adjusted to demands.

This analysis can easily be generalized to cover the case where there are many products, *X*, *Y*, *Z*, etc. Each worker as before has a money income equal to the money national income divided by the number of workers; the cost of each product will be equal to the money wage rate divided by output per head of that product; in competitive equilibrium supplies will shift until prices are equal to costs for all products; supplies will thus have adjusted themselves to demands at given incomes and given money prices.

Any shift of demand from one product to another will tend to raise the price of the latter and to lower the price of the former. But this will cause changes of supply until the final result is simply reduced output of the former and increased output of the latter sufficient to satisfy the new demands at the old unchanged prices.

Any increase in output per head in any one occupation will cause a corresponding fall in the cost and, in competitive equilibrium, in the price of that product. With unchanged money incomes and prices for other products the net effect will depend upon the price elasticity of demand for the product whose cost has fallen.

If this elasticity is (numerically) greater than one, then more will be spent on this product and less on other products in general. But while less labour will in this case be devoted to the production of other products in general, nevertheless within this general group of other products there may be a particular product which is a complement to the product whose price has fallen and this particular complementary product may be in greater demand than before. In this case the production of some other products must have fallen still more markedly.

If the price elasticity of demand for the product whose cost has fallen is (numerically) less than one, then less resources will be devoted to its production and more labour will be devoted to the production of other products in general. But this does not mean to say that each and every other product will be increased in supply. There may be a product or group of products which are particularly close substitutes for the product whose cost has fallen. These, being supplied at an unchanged cost, are likely to be bought in smaller amounts. This means that the output of some other products will go up all the more.

But the fundamental conclusion for our present case is a very simple one. Prices will be set on the cost side by the technical productivity of labour in the various occupations. Whatever happens to changes in tastes or changes in productivity, there will be no permanent effect upon the distribution of incomes among the individual citizens; but the outputs of the various products will be adjusted until the supply of each product is equal to the demand for it at given and unchanged individual money incomes and at prices equal to the technically given costs.

CHAPTER VI

INCREASING COSTS (i) COMPARATIVE ADVANTAGES

In the last two chapters we have examined models in which *either* (i) the factors of production were so specialized in the production of particular products that a change in demand could cause no transfer of factors between different occupations, so that prices changed but outputs remained constant, *or else* (ii) the factors of production were not specialized at all in the production of different products but could move so easily from one line of production to another that outputs changed without any change in prices. We shall now turn to the intermediate cases in which different factors can move between different lines of production but for one reason or another have certain partial advantages or disadvantages in particular lines of production. In these intermediate and more realistic cases a change of demand will, as we shall see, cause partly a change in prices and partly a change in outputs. There are many reasons why this intermediate situation may arise.

In the first place suppose that labour were the only scarce factor of production, but that different men had different aptitudes. Mr A is a cobbler but could become a baker. Mr B is a baker but could become a cobbler. But productivity as a cobbler relatively to productivity as a baker may be higher in Mr A's case than in Mr B's case because of the different aptitudes of the two men.

Consider the numerical example given in Table III. We assume that there are only two products X and Y, that labour is the only scarce factor, but that each worker owing to his particular innate aptitudes has his own particular productivity in each line of production. Table III shows the position of Messrs A to K in the economy. Column (i) shows each worker's daily output of X; column (ii) shows his output of Y; and column (iii) shows his output of Y relatively to his output of X. In Table III the workers are arranged in order according to the level of their productivity in Y relatively to their productivity in X. As we go down the table the figure in column (iii) rises continually. Which product each of these workers will choose to produce will depend upon the prices offered for products X and Y.

Suppose that initially, as is illustrated in columns (iv) and (v), the demands for X and Y were such that the price of X (P_x) were

\$1.5 and the price of *Y* (P_y) were \$1.0. Any worker whose productivity in *Y* was exactly 1½ times his productivity in *X* would be able to earn the same in either industry, since the shortfall in his productivity in *X* would be exactly balanced by the higher price offered for *X*. (\$1.50 = 1·5 × \$1.0). But any worker whose productivity in *Y* was less than 1½ times his productivity in *X* would choose to produce *X*, while any worker whose productivity in *Y* was more than 1½ times his productivity in *X* would choose to produce *Y*. Looking down

	Productivity in *X*	Productivity in *Y*	Productivity in *Y* ÷ productivity in *X*	$\frac{P_x}{P_y} = 1\cdot5$	Individual incomes with $P_x = \$1\cdot50$, $P_y = \$1\cdot0$	$\frac{P_x}{P_y} = 2\cdot5$	Individual incomes with $P_x = \$1\cdot75$, $P_y = \$0\cdot70$
	(i)	(ii)	(iii)	(iv)	(v)	(vi)	(vii)
					\$		\$
A	24	4	$\frac{1}{6}$	Output of $X = 118$	36	Output of $X = 138$	42
B	20	4	$\frac{1}{5}$		30		35
C	16	4	$\frac{1}{4}$		24		28
D	30	10	$\frac{1}{3}$		45		53
E	16	8	$\frac{1}{2}$		24		28
F	12	12	1		18		21
G	20	40	2	Output of $Y = 123$	40		35
H	4	12	3		12	Output of $Y = 83$	8
I	4	16	4		16		11
J	5	25	5		25		18
K	5	30	6		30		21
				Total	300		300

Table III

column (iii) we see that the dividing line will come between Mr F and Mr G. Messrs A to F will produce *X* and Messrs G to K will choose to produce *Y*, the total outputs of *X* and *Y* will thus be 118 and 123 units respectively (column iv). The money incomes which each worker will now earn in his chosen occupation are shown in column (v), being simply the output of each worker in his chosen occupation multiplied by the price of his output. In our numerical example the total money national income adds up to \$300.

It is to be observed that the workers choose their jobs not according to their absolute advantages in producing *X* or *Y*, but according to their 'comparative advantages' in their productivity in the two industries. Thus Mr G can produce an absolutely larger output of *X* (20 units) than can either Mr C (16 units), Mr E (16 units) or Mr F (12 units). Yet Mr G chooses to produce *Y* while Messrs C,

E, and F produce X. The point is that Mr G has an absolute advantage over Messrs C, E, and F in both lines of production, but he has a greater absolute advantage in producing Y than in producing X. It is column (iii) which measures the comparative, as contrasted with the absolute, advantage of each worker in producing Y rather than X; and it is according to this scale that they will choose their jobs. Of course, those workers whose absolute productivity is high (or low) will receive larger (or smaller) incomes. In column (v) it can be seen that Mr G earns \$40 a week, while Messrs C, E, and F earn only \$24, \$24, and \$18 a week respectively. Absolute productivity will affect the distribution of incomes; comparative productivity will determine the allocation of jobs.

Suppose now that there is a shift of demand from Y to X so that the price of X goes up and of Y goes down. Suppose (column (vi) that this change in demand is such as to cause the price of X to become $2\frac{1}{2}$ instead of $1\frac{1}{2}$ the price of Y in the final equilibrium after any consequential changes in supplies of X and Y have occurred. Any worker whose productivity in Y is less than $2\frac{1}{2}$ times his productivity in X would now choose to produce X. The dividing line in column (iii) now comes between Messrs G and H instead of between Messrs F and G. The total output of X is increased by 20 (the output of Mr G in X) and the total output of Y is decreased by 40 (the output of Mr G in Y). The total output of X thus goes up from 118 to 138 and of Y goes down from 123 to 83 (column (vi)).

If, as we are assuming, the total national money income remains unchanged at \$300, then the price of X must rise from \$1.5 to \$1.75 and the price of Y must fall from \$1 to \$0.70 (approximately).[1] We can then see what the new distribution of incomes between the individual workers will be by multiplying the outputs of each worker by the new price of his output. This is done in column (vii). All those who were producing X before and after the change (Messrs A to F inclusive) will have gained in money income in the ratio of the rise in the price of X from \$1.5 to \$1.75. All those who were producing Y before and after the change (Messrs H to K inclusive) will have lost in money income in the ratio of the fall in the price of Y from \$1.00 to \$0.70. Mr G was threatened by a similar fall in his income; but he was able to avoid the greater part of this fall by moving to the production of X in which, with the higher price of X relatively to Y, his comparative advantage now lies. His income falls only from

[1] We know that in this case $X = 138$ and $Y = 83$. For the national income to remain constant at \$300 we must have $138\ P_x + 83\ P_y = 300$. Moreover, we are assuming $\frac{P_x}{P_y} = 2{\cdot}5$. From these two equations we have $P_x = \$1{\cdot}7525$ and $P_y = \$0{\cdot}701$.

\$40 to \$35. It would have fallen to \$28 if he had stayed in his old job.

We can see then that in this sort of case a rise in the demand for *X* relatively to that for *Y* will (i) cause some increase in the output of *X* and fall in the output of *Y*, (ii) cause some rise in the price of *X* and fall in the price of *Y*, (iii) cause a redistribution of income in favour of those whose comparative advantage in *X* is very marked at the expense of those whose comparative advantage in *Y* is very marked, and (iv) will enable those producers of *Y* whose comparative advantage in *Y* is not very marked to offset the threat to their

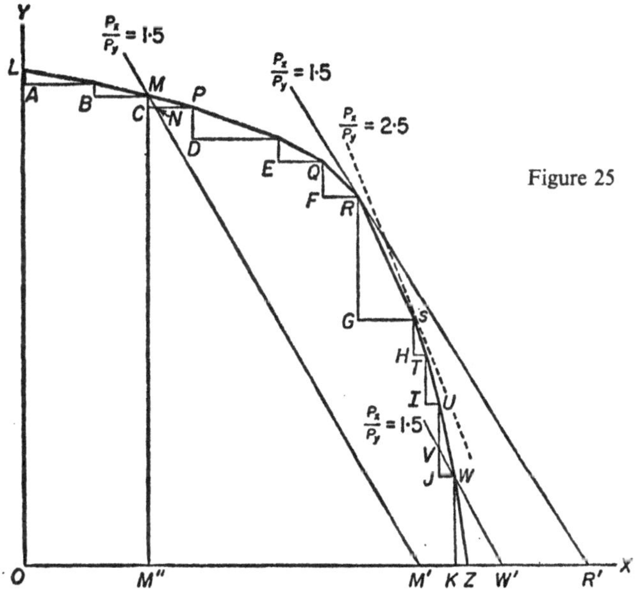

Figure 25

incomes by moving across to the production of *X*. The movement of Mr G from the production of *Y* to that of *X* by increasing the output of *X* and reducing the output of *Y* will, of course, cause the prices of *X* to rise, and of *Y* to fall, by less than they would otherwise have done. Thus it helps not only to maintain Mr G's personal income, but also to reduce the shift of income from the Messrs H to K to Messrs A to F. We have a case which is intermediate between those of Chapter IV and of Chapter V.

This situation can be depicted geometrically as is done in Figure 25.

Let us start at the bottom of Table III. Let $KZ = 5$, the output of *X* which Mr K could produce, and $KW = 30$, the output of *Y* which Mr K could produce. Let $JW = 5$, the output of *X* which Mr J could produce, and $JU = 25$, the output of *Y* which Mr J could produce. And so on up the table. The result is that *OZ* measures the total amount of *X* that the community could produce if all workers concentrated on the production of *X* while *OL* represents the community's output of *Y* if all workers produced only *Y*. The points *W*, *U*, *T*, *S*, etc., represent other intermediate possible combinations of output. Thus *W* represents the case where Mr K alone moves from the production of *X* to that of *Y* so that the community, starting with an output solely of *X* of *OZ*, gives up *KZ* of *X* and acquires *KW* of *Y*. *U* represents the case where Mr K and Mr I have moved to the production of *Y*; and so on.

So far in Figure 25, as throughout our discussion of Table III, we have assumed that each worker can work only at one job. On this assumption (which may for institutional reasons be a realistic one) the stepped line *ZKWJUITHS*, etc., represents the best possible combinations of *X* and *Y* which can be produced. If everyone produces *X* we shall be at the point *Z*; Mr K can then slacken off in the production of *Z* until we are at the point *K*; he can then transfer to the production of *Y* and by exerting himself more and more in that line can move the output from *K* to *W*. And similarly up the stepped line for Messrs J, I, H, etc. But it would be more in keeping with our strict assumption that there are no indivisibilities or elements of lumpiness in the system (assumption 7 on p. 27) to suppose that a worker can divide his time in any desired proportions between two or more jobs. For example, Mr K can spend $\frac{1}{4}$ of his time producing *X* and $\frac{3}{4}$ of his time producing *Y*; and so on. In this case Mr K's production points on Figure 25 are not confined to the points along the step *Z* to *K* and *K* to *W*, but are spread along the straight line *ZW*. By spending $\frac{1}{4}$ of his time on the production of *X* and $\frac{3}{4}$ of his time on the production of *Y*, he will produce $\frac{1}{4}$ of *KZ* and $\frac{3}{4}$ of *KW*; his production point will be $\frac{3}{4}$ of the way up the straight line from *Z* to *W*. And similarly for Messrs J, I, H, G, etc. In this way the best possible combinations of output of *X* and *Y* for the community as a whole are shown by the kinked line *ZWUTSR . . . L*.

The relative prices of *X* and *Y* can be depicted by the slope of price lines in Figure 25. Thus when the price of *X* is $1\frac{1}{2}$ times the price of *Y* $\left(\frac{P_x}{P_y} = 1 \cdot 5\right)$, then one unit of *X* can be bought in the market for every $1\frac{1}{2}$ units of *Y* that are sold. This is depicted by a straight line sloping downwards from left to right with a slope of $1\frac{1}{2}$ down ($1\frac{1}{2}$ units of *Y* given up) for 1 along (1 unit of *X* gained). On Figure 25 three price lines with this slope are shown going through *M*, *R*, and *W*. Suppose Mr C were producing *Y*; he would be producing *CM* of *Y* which would be worth only *CN* of *X*; but he could produce *CP* of *X*, so that he would shift from the production of *Y* to that of *X*. Conversely, Mr J could produce *JW* of *X* which would be worth only *JV* of *Y*, while he could produce *JU* of *Y*, so that he would produce *Y* rather than *X*.

The point *R* is clearly the critical dividing point with the price line $\frac{P_x}{P_y} = 1\cdot5$. Mr G will now produce *Y*, because he can produce an amount *GR* which, since the price line through *R* passes to the right of *S*, has a greater value in terms of *X* than *GS*, the amount of *X* which he could produce. Conversely, Mr F will produce *FR* of *X* which, since the price line through *R* passes above the point *Q*, has a greater value in terms of *Y* than the amount of *Y* (*FQ*) which he could produce himself. This point *R* is the combination of outputs which maximizes the national income at the current price ratio of $\frac{P_x}{P_y} = 1\cdot5$. This can be seen in the following way.

Consider the point *M*. The community's output of *X* is OM'' and of *Y* is $M''M$. But at the price slope $\left(\frac{P_x}{P_y} = 1\cdot5\right)$ passing through *M*, $M''M$ of *Y* is worth $M''M'$ of *X*. Thus the value of the national income in terms of *X* is $OM'' + M''M'$ or OM'. Similarly, the value in terms of *X* of the output combination *W*, at the price slope $\frac{P_x}{P_y} = 1\cdot5$, is OW' and of the output combination *R* is OR'. The national income is maximized by moving along the kinked line *ZWUTSRQ*, etc., until one comes to the price line which is farthest to the right. With the price slope $\frac{P_x}{P_y} = 1\cdot5$ this is clearly at *R*, where the price line passes to the right of *S* and above *Q*. With a price slope $\frac{P_x}{P_y} = 2\cdot5$ the point which reaches the price line farthest to the right is clearly *S*, where the price line with slope $\frac{P_x}{P_y} = 2\cdot5$ passes to the right of *T* and above *R*. The rise in the price of *X* relatively to the price of *Y* from 1·5 to 2·5 will have caused an increase in the output of *X* of *GS* and a fall in the output of *Y* of *GR*.

But it might perhaps happen that when relatively little *X* and much *Y* is produced at *R*, the demand price for *X* relatively to the demand price for *Y* would be high, namely $\frac{P_x}{P_y} = 2\cdot5$. Whereas when relatively much *X* and little *Y* is produced at *S*, the demand price for *X* relatively to the demand price for *Y* might be low, namely $\frac{P_x}{D_y} = 1\cdot5$. In Figure 25 the broken price line $\frac{P_x}{P_y} = 2\cdot5$ must be imagined as passing through *R* and the continuous price line $\frac{P_x}{D_y} = 1\cdot5$ as passing through *S*, both price lines being now regarded

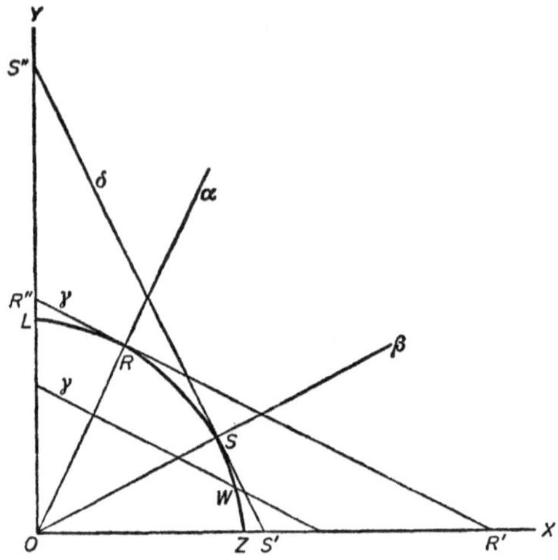

Figure 26

as part of the same demand curve. We can now see the importance of the assumption of divisibility of Mr G's labour. Suppose Mr G had to spend all his time producing either *Y* or *X*. Then at *R* the price of *X* is high so that it pays to shift to *S*; but at *S* the price of *Y* is high so that it pays to shift back to *R*. There would be a continual shift from *R* to *S* to *R* to *S* and so on.

But suppose that Mr G can divide his working time between the productions of *X* and *Y*. He can now move partially from *R* toward *S* along the line *RS*. As he does so *X* becomes more plentiful relatively to *Y* and $\frac{P_x}{P_y}$ falls from $2\cdot5$ towards $1\cdot5$. At some point on the journey of Mr G's output from *R* to *S* the slope of the price line $\frac{P_x}{P_y}$ coincides with the slope of the straight line *RS*. At this point demand is equal to supply; the line of relative cost at the margin of production (namely the slope $\frac{GR}{GS}$) is the same as the slope of the demand price line $\frac{P_y}{P_x}$.

Even so we are not yet out of the wood. If the situation were as we have just described it, Mr G by deciding how much X and how much Y to produce could in fact affect the market prices of X and Y between the ratios $\frac{P_x}{P_y} = 2 \cdot 5$ and $\frac{P_x}{P_y} = 1 \cdot 5$. We should not be in a situation of perfect competition or of perfect potential competition (as defined on pp. 30–32 above), but in a monopolistic situation in which an individual decision-making unit (in this case Mr G) could affect appreciably the price of what he was deciding to put on the market. We can make competitive sense of Table III and Figure 25 only by assuming that A, B, C, etc., do not stand for single individuals but for groups of individuals with competition between the individuals within each group. Thus group G contains a large number of individuals with identical comparative productivities (i.e. each able to produce twice as many units of Y as of X) and a movement from R to S in Figure 25 now represents a shift of the labour of members of this group from the production of Y to that of X.[1] This, of course, also makes much better sense of the assumption of divisibility of G's labour between the productions of X and Y, since the movement from R to S can now take the form of the movement of individuals in group G rather than of the division of one man's work between two occupations.

But why should we assume that there are a very large number of men divided into a small number (A to K) of discrete groups within each of which all members are identical in comparative productivities? Why not simply assume that there are a very large number of men, no two of whom are exactly alike, but with very narrowly graded differences of comparative advantage in the two lines of production? In this case the stepped line *ZKWJUITHS* . . . of Figure 25 would approximate very closely to a smooth curve of the kind shown in Figure 26. That is to say, even if a man could not divide his time between two jobs, the existence of a very large number of men would make the curve a smooth one for all practical purposes. The smooth line *LRSZ* of Figure 26 (which is in fact a line with a vast number of tiny steps in it like *ZKWJUI* . . . *L* of Figure 25)

[1] Columns (v) and (vii) of Table III then show the distribution of the national income between groups and not between individuals.

shows the combinations of X and Y which it is possible to produce by transferring successively from the production of X to that of Y the workers which have the highest comparative advantage in the production of Y. This curve may be called the 'production possibility curve'. Suppose we start at the point W with market prices of X and Y which give market price lines with the slope γ. Then at W the slope of the production possibility curve is steeper than that of the market price line. The rate at which Y can be gained in production by giving up a unit of X is greater than the amount of Y that can be gained by any individual in the market producing X and selling it to purchase Y. The marginal worker will move from the production of X to that of Y. This process will go on until the point R is reached at which the production possibility curve is tangential to the highest market price line with the given slope γ. The national income will be maximized in value at OR' in terms of X or OR'' in terms of Y.

If as a result of a change in tastes the price of X rises relatively to that of Y so that the price line slope swings round from γ to δ, the combination S will be produced at which the slope of the production possibility curve is equal to δ instead of γ. The value of the national income will now be maximized at OS' in terms of X or OS'' in terms of Y.

We can now think in terms of an elasticity of substitution in production between the products X and Y. If there are relatively slight differences in the comparative advantages of different workers, a small change in the ratio of the price of X to the price of Y will cause a large shift of labour between the occupations and a large change in the ratio of the output of X to the output of Y. In this case we may say that the elasticity of substitution is large. We can define the elasticity of substitution between X and Y in production as the percentage increase in the ratio of X produced to Y produced that would be brought about by a one per cent increase in the ratio of the price of X to the price of Y. If a one per cent increase in $\frac{P_x}{P_y}$ caused a two (or half of one) per cent increase in $\frac{X}{Y}$, then the elasticity of substitution between X and Y is $+2$ (or $+\frac{1}{2}$). Now the ratio of $\frac{X}{Y}$ in Figure 26 is shown by the slopes of the lines α and β, while the price ratios are shown by the slopes of the lines γ and δ. If, therefore, a small percentage change in the slopes between γ and δ causes a large percentage change in the slopes between α and β, then the elasticity of substitution is large.

Chapters IV and V can now be seen to be two limiting extremes of the present case, the elasticity of substitution between *X* and *Y* being zero in the case of Chapter IV and infinite in the case of Chapter V. This can be seen in Figure 27.

In case (i) (i.e. Chapter IV) the outputs are fixed at *OL* of *Y* and *OZ* of *X*. The ratio of $\frac{X}{Y}$ is thus fixed and the slopes α and β coincide.

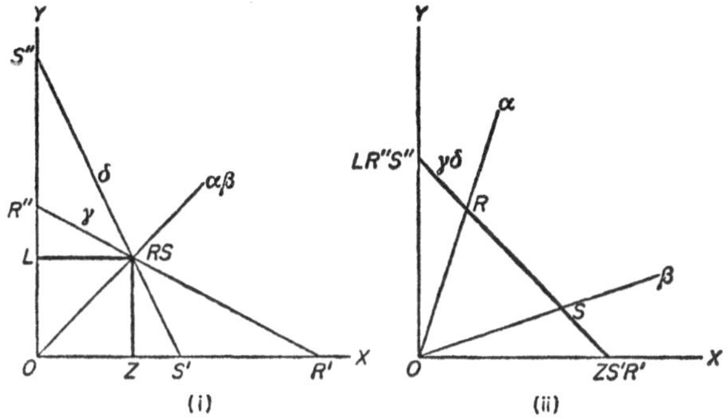

Figure 27

If demand changes, the price slope changes from γ to δ, but the quantity slope remains unchanged at αβ. The elasticity of substitution is zero. In case (ii) (i.e. Chapter V) the outputs are *OL* if all workers produce *Y* and *OZ* if all workers produce *X*, or any combination on the straight line *LZ* as the workers, with no differences in comparative advantages, move between the two industries. A shift of demand will cause the output combination to move from *R* to *S* and the quantity ratio slope to change from α to β; but there will be no permanent change in the relative prices of *X* and *Y* in the market which will be given by the constant cost of *X* in terms of *Y*, i.e. by the slope γ or δ of the production possibility line *LZ*. An infinitely small change in the price ratio will suffice to cause any given required change in the quantity ratio, and the elasticity of substitution between *X* and *Y* is infinite.

We shall proceed in the next two chapters to give further models which will lead to production possibility curves of the intermediate kind shown in Figure 26.

CHAPTER VII

INCREASING COSTS (ii) A FIXED FACTOR

In Chapter IV we considered the case in which the factors of production were completely specialized on producing particular products. In Chapter V we examined the opposite extreme where there was a single factor of production which was completely unspecialized as between different occupations. In Chapter VI we examined one intermediate case in which the factors of production were not completely specialized but had certain comparative advantages in producing various products. In this chapter we shall examine another intermediate case in which there are two factors, one completely specialized and one completely unspecialized.

Suppose then that

(i) there are two products Food (X) and Clothing (Y),

(ii) there are two factors of production, Labour (L) and Land (N), every worker being the same as every other worker and every acre of land being the same as every other acre,

(iii) Y is produced solely with L, but

(iv) X needs for its production both L and N, i.e. Land is needed for Food production and only for Food production whereas Labour is required both for Food production and Clothing production.

As far as the production of Y is concerned the situation is very simple. Since there are constant returns to scale and no changes in technical knowledge, there will be a fixed output of Y per worker employed in the Y industry. The output of Y will go up or down in direct proportion to changes in the amount of labour employed in the Y-industry.

The position in the production of X is, however, now more complicated. The fixed amount of land in the economy has no usefulness except in the production of X and will all, therefore, be available for the production of X. The output of X will vary with the amount of labour left over from the production of Y and available, therefore, to be used with the fixed amount of land to produce X.

We are now confronted with the phenomenon of 'diminishing returns to a single factor'. When there is little labour employed on the land, an additional worker will be able to add a lot to the output.

But as more and more labour is employed on the same amount of land, the amount which can be added to the output by employing yet one more worker will become smaller and smaller. On any given acreage only the most important and productive jobs will be done if labour is scarce; further workers will be set to do the next most important and productive jobs; and so on, until the farm is so crowded that an additional worker could add little or nothing to total output and might indeed simply get in the way of the other workers.

We define the 'average product' of the workers in farming as the total output of *X* divided by the number of workers employed, i.e.

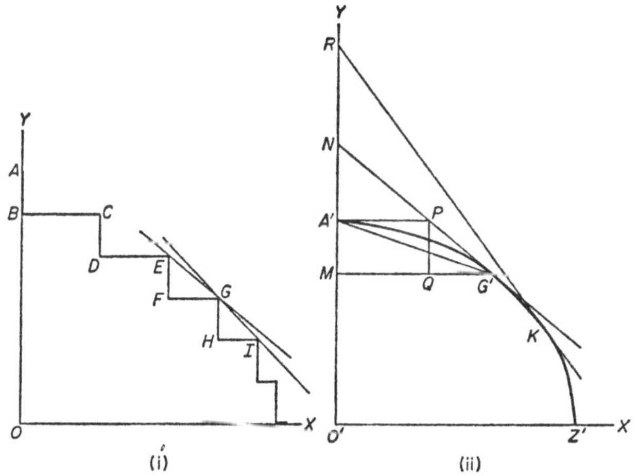

Figure 28

the output per head. We define the 'marginal product' of the workers employed in farming as the addition to the total output of *X* which would be caused by employing one more worker on the constant acreage of land. The proposition which we are making is that as the total amount of labour employed on a given acreage of land increases, so the marginal product of labour in agriculture will fall. Each successive addition to the labour force will add a smaller amount to the output.

We can see at once that the shape of the production possibility curve relating the economy's outputs of *X* and *Y* will be of the general shape shown in Figure 26 of the last chapter. In Figure 28 we measure the amount of *Y* produced up the vertical axis and the amount of *X* produced to the right along the horizontal axis. If all labour were employed in producing *Y*, an amount of *Y* equal to *OA* could be produced. Suppose now that one worker is transferred from Y-production to X-production. The output of Y falls by AB and of X rises by BC. If a second worker is transferred, the output of Y falls by the same amount ($CD = AB$) because output per head in Y is constant; but the output of X rises by a smaller amount than before ($DE < BC$) because of the falling marginal product of labour in X. The transfer of a third worker will decrease the output of Y by the same amount again ($EF = CD = AB$) but will increase the output of X by yet a smaller amount ($FG < DE < BC$). And so on until all workers have been transferred from Y-production to X-production.

If there are a large number of workers so that the steps AB, CD, EF, etc., are each a very small part of the total distance OA, then the stepped line $ABCDEFG$, etc., will approximate very closely to a smooth curve of the kind $A'Z'$ shown in Figure 28 (ii). Compare the point G on (i) with the corresponding point G' on (ii). FG is the amount of X which must be given up to produce EF more of Y, while HI is the additional amount of X that can be obtained by giving up an amount HG ($= EF$) of Y. Where the number of steps is very large the line EGI will be practically a straight line because FG will be very little larger than HI. The slope of this line will show the rate of substitution between X and Y at the point G, i.e. $\frac{FG}{EF}$ or $\frac{HI}{HG}$ which will be practically the same will measure the amount of X which can be obtained for a unit of Y if the production combination at G is being produced. This slope is equal to the slope of tangent to the curve $A'Z'$ at the point G' in Figure 28 (ii). $\frac{G'M}{NM}$ measures the output of X which can be gained (or must be sacrificed) for the sacrifice (or the gain) of a unit of production of Y if the output combination is $O'M$ of Y and MG' of X.

We have so far considered the interconnection between the production of X and the production of Y. Let us now consider the market mechanisms which will determine the prices of X and of Y and the wage of labour and the rent of land in this economy.

As far as the price of Y and the wage rate of labour is concerned, there is a very simple interrelationship. The output per head in Y production is constant and no other factor is involved. Suppose 1 worker can produce 2 units of Y. Then if the price of Y is \$1 the wage of labour must be \$2. If the wage of labour were less than \$2, Y would be selling at a price which was above its costs of production;

more workers would be attracted into the production of *Y*. If the wage of labour were greater than $2, then *Y*-production would be unprofitable and the labour employed in *Y*-production would be reduced.

The position in the *X*-industry is more complicated. Let us suppose that there are a large number of landlords, each owning a certain proportion of the land and each acting as an entrepreneur farmer, hiring labour at the current wage rate to work on his acreage to produce *X*. How much labour will each landlord hire at the current wage rate to produce *X* to sell at the current price of *X*? Each landlord will add to his profit by taking on one more unit of labour if the wage of labour is less than the price at which he can sell the marginal product of labour on his farm. For in that case he will add to his costs the wage of an additional worker which is less than what he adds to his receipts, namely the price at which he can sell the additional product due to taking on the one extra worker. Conversely, he will add to his profit by dismissing one worker if the wage (which he saves) is greater than the price of the marginal product of a worker (which he no longer receives as revenue). He will maximize his profit at the point at which the wage rate is equal to the value of the marginal product of labour.

Number of workers (i)	Total product (ii)	Marginal product (iii) increase in (ii)	Average product (iv) (ii) ÷ (i)	Wage bill (v) (i) × (iii)	Rent of land (vi) (ii) − (v)
1	100	100	100	100	0
2	190	90	95	180	10
3	270	80	90	240	30
4	340	70	85	280	60
5	400	60	80	300	100
6	450	50	75	300	150
7	490	40	70	280	210
8	520	30	65	240	280
9	540	20	60	180	360
10	550	10	55	100	450

Table IV

The position is illustrated numerically in Table IV. In column (i) and (ii) we have a description of the total output of *X* which our landlord-farmer can produce on his given acreage of land with various labour forces. Column (iii) is derived from column (ii) by showing the addition to the output of column (ii) which is caused by taking on one more unit of labour. Thus 4 men produce 340 units, and 5 men 400 units of *X* (column (ii)); in other words adding a 5th worker adds 60 units to output which is shown as the marginal product of the 5th worker in column (iii). The figures are so chosen that the marginal product of labour in column (iii) falls as more workers are employed. The average product of labour (column iv) is simply the total output of column (ii) divided by the total number of workers of column (i). This average product (except for the first worker where the average product and the marginal product are the same) is always greater than the marginal product of column (iii), because the average product takes into account, as it were, the high productivity of the first workers as well as the low productivity of the last worker, whose output measures the marginal product of labour.

How many men this landlord-farmer will employ depends upon the relationship between the money wage rate and the money price that can be received for selling *X*. If the wage of labour were 50 times as great as the price of *X*, then the landlord-farmer would take on 6 men, since (column iii) up to that point the value of the marginal product would be above the wage rate of labour and after that point it would be below it. Paying 6 men each a wage which was worth 50 units of *X*, he would be paying out a wage bill worth 300 units of *X* (column v). Since the total output of 6 men is 450 units (column ii) the payment of a wage bill of 300 units would leave a rent for the landlord of 150 units of *X* (column vi). If the wage rate were reduced or the price of *X* were raised, so that the wage rate was worth only 30 units of *X*, the landlord would employ 8 instead of 6 men. The wage bill would fall from 300 to 240; the landlord's price elasticity of demand for labour is (numerically) less than one, since he pays a smaller total amount of *X* for a larger quantity of labour at a lower price of labour in terms of *X*. The rent would rise from 150 to 280.

The reaction of our present model to a change of demand will be as follows. Suppose we start in equilibrium with a certain money wage rate. The price of *Y* must then be equal to the cost of producing *Y* at this wage rate. A certain amount of labour will be employed on the given amount of land to produce a given amount of *X*. For this to be an equilibrium output the price of *X* must be such as to make the value of the marginal product of the labour employed in *X*-production equal to the money wage rate. This, in accordance with the principles shown in Table IV, will leave a certain rent over for the landlords equal to the difference between the average and the marginal product of the labour force. If the workers' and the landlords' tastes and needs are such that, at these wage incomes and rent incomes and at these prices of *X* and *Y*, they demand *X* and *Y* in the amounts produced, the system is in equilibrium.

Suppose now that their tastes shift and they demand at current incomes and prices more X and less Y. The price of Y and so the money wage rate earned in Y production will fall; the price of X will rise; as a result of the fall in the money wage rate and the rise in the price of X labour will shift into the production of X until the marginal product of labour there has fallen so as to compensate for the fall in the wage rate and the rise in the price of X. In accordance with the principle illustrated in Table IV landlords' rents will go up in terms of X and, since the price of Y has fallen and of X has risen, they will *a fortiori* have gone up in terms of Y. In money terms, if the money national income is constant, money wages will have gone down and money rents will have gone up by the same amounts. The price and output of X will have gone up and the price and output of Y will have gone down.

These changes can be illustrated geometrically in Figure 28. Without any loss of generality we can assume that in Y-production 1 worker produces 1 unit of Y; we are simply defining a unit of Y as that amount of Y which can be produced by 1 worker. We can then measure up the vertical axis in Figure 28 either units of Y or units of L; there is a one to one relationship between them. Suppose now that we start in equilibrium at the point G' in Figure 28 (ii). This means that $O'M$ labour is being employed to produce $O'M$ units of Y. The remaining available labour is MA' (since $O'A'$ is the total amount of Y that could be produced, $O'A'$ must measure the total supply of labour). The labour MA' is employed in the X-industry to produce MG' units of X. Output per head in the X-industry is thus $\frac{MG'}{MA'}$, or the slope of the line $A'G'$. The marginal product of labour in the X-industry is, however, less than this, namely $\frac{MG'}{MN}$ or the slope of the tangent at G' to the curve $A'Z'$. This slope represents (cf. $\frac{FG}{EF}$ in Figure 28 (i)) the amount of X that can be gained by shifting one unit of labour out of the Y-industry into the X-industry. Of the total output of X equal to MG' an amount equal to $G'Q$ is, therefore, paid in wages in the X-industry; $A'M$ $(= PQ)$ is the amount of labour employed in the X-industry and $\frac{MG'}{MN}\left(=\frac{QG'}{PQ}\right)$ is the marginal product of labour in the X-industry; the wage bill in the X-industry is, therefore, $A'M \times \frac{MG'}{MN} = PQ \times \frac{QG}{PQ} = QG'$. The remaining output of X, namely MQ is the rent left over to the landlords.

We can also see from Figure 28 (ii) the distribution of the total national income between wages and rents. Let us measure both wages and rents in terms of Y. Then total wages equals $O'A'$; for this is the total labour force and in equilibrium the wage rate of labour in terms of Y must be its output of Y, namely 1 unit of Y. $A'N$ represents the value of rents in terms of Y; for $A'P\,(= MQ)$ is the total of rents in terms of X and the slope $\frac{A'N}{A'P}\left(=\frac{MN}{MG'}\right)$ represents the rate at which Y can be obtained for X in the market. Thus the ratio of wages to rents is $\frac{O'A'}{A'N}$.

If the demand for X increases, so that the output combination moves from G' to K, then the marginal product of labour and the price of labour and of Y in terms of X falls from the slope of the line NG' to that of the line RK; and the ratio of wages to rents falls from $\frac{O'A'}{A'N}$ to $\frac{O'A'}{A'R}$.

CHAPTER VIII

INCREASING COSTS (iii) DIFFERENCES IN FACTOR PROPORTIONS

In the last chapter we examined a model in which in one industry (Y) only one factor (L) was used, whereas in the other industry (X) two factors (L and N) were used. This is a special case of a more general phenomenon which we shall examine in this chapter, namely the case in which the proportions in which the two factors are employed is different in the two industries.

Suppose then that

(i) there are two factors, land (N) and labour (L),
(ii) there are two industries, one producing Food (X) and one Clothing (Y),
(iii) each industry employs some Land and some Labour, but
(iv) at any relevant wage rate and rate of rent the industry producing Food employs a higher ratio of Land to Labour than does the industry producing Clothing.

We must now imagine certain persons acting as entrepreneurs and organizing competing Firms to produce Clothing or competing Farms to produce Food. These persons may be workers or landowners; but the amount of labour or land employed in any one firm or farm in no way depends upon the amount of labour or land belonging to the entrepreneur himself. Any entrepreneur can take on more land or labour for his firm or farm by hiring it at the current competitive rent or wage rate, and any entrepreneur can hire out at the current market rent or wage rate any of his own land or labour which he does not wish to employ in his own firm or farm.

In our perfectly competitive, stationary economy with constant returns to scale and no changes in technical knowledge there is no risk or uncertainty when equilibrium has been reached. Entrepreneurs will in fact then have a trivially easy job. Anyone can become an entrepreneur if entrepreneurs are earning more than the current wage rate and rate of rent on their own labour and land; any entrepreneur can give up being an entrepreneur if entrepreneurs are receiving less than the market return on their own labour and land. In equilibrium entrepreneurs will receive nothing for being entrepreneurs. Wages and rents make up the only costs of production of *X* and *Y*. If we were to allow for growth, change, risk, uncertainty, economies of large-scale production, and imperfect competition the function of entrepreneurship would become of great importance; but in this volume we can forget about it.

We have already explained (Chapter I, pp. 30–32) that with our present assumptions it makes no difference whether in the production of clothing (or of food) there is a single entrepreneur running a single firm (or farm) and subject to perfect potential competition or whether there is a large number of entrepreneurs running a large number of firms (or farms) which are actually in competition with each other. We imagine then a farmer or farmers hiring labour and land at the current market rates of wage and of rent to produce *X* for sale at the current market price of *X*, and a manufacturer or manufacturers hiring labour and land at current wage and rent rates to produce and sell *Y* at the current price of *Y*. In each case the entrepreneur takes as beyond his own control the market prices of the factors he buys and of the products he sells. We must now consider the marginal product of either factor in terms of either product. The marginal product of labour in terms of *X*, for example, is the amount of *X* that would be added to the existing output of *X* if a farmer took on one more worker on the existing acreage of land. The marginal product of land in terms of *X*, on the other hand, is the amount of *X* that would be added to the existing output of *X* if a farmer took on one more acre of land to be worked by the existing farm labour force. Similarly, there is a marginal product of labour in terms of *Y* and a marginal product of land in terms of *Y*.

We may assume that the marginal product of labour in farming is smaller the larger is the amount of labour already employed per acre. For additional workers will be put on to the successively less productive jobs as they are employed on the same amount of land. We can similarly assume that the marginal product of land in farming is the smaller the larger is the amount of acreage on which a given labour force is already employed. If the density of labour per acre is very high, the additional product due to taking on one more acre is very great; but if the density of labour per acre is very low, not much can be added to output by taking on one more acre of land.

In fact with our assumption of constant returns to scale the marginal products of labour and land in agriculture will depend solely upon the ratio of labour to land already employed in agriculture. If the numbers employed per acre are already very high, not much more can be added to output by taking on one more man;

but a lot can be added to output by taking on one more acre. If numbers employed per acre are very low, much can be added to output by taking on more labour but not much can be added by taking on yet another additional acre.

We can describe this same phenomenon in different language. A farmer takes on land and labour to produce an output of X. This given output of X he can still produce if he takes on more labour and less land. In other words in his productive process he can substitute labour for land. But the more labour he takes on and the less land he takes on the more difficult will it become to produce the same output on an even smaller acreage. As he increases the ratio of labour to land on his farm, the amount of labour that will have to be substituted for an acre of land will become greater and greater. The marginal importance of land (which is becoming scarce) will grow relatively to the marginal importance of labour (which is becoming plentiful). As the ratio of labour to land grows, the marginal product of labour falls and of land grows; and, in consequence, more labour must be taken on to make up for the loss of yet another acre.

These relationships are true in industry as well as in agriculture. In the production of Y the marginal product of L will fall and the marginal product of N will rise as the ratio of L to N employed in the firm rises. The difficulty of substituting yet more L for the loss of one more unit of N will grow as the ratio of L to N rises.

Each entrepreneur in each industry in an effort to maximize his own income will take on more labour to employ with the existing amount of land in his firm or farm so long as the wage rate of labour (which he will thereby add to his costs) is lower than the market price at which he can sell the marginal product of labour (which he will thereby add to his receipts). Conversely, he will dismiss labour if the wage rate which he will save is greater than the market price which he no longer receives for the marginal product of the labour dismissed. Competitive equilibrium thus requires that the wage rate in each industry should be equal to the value of the marginal product of labour in each industry. Similarly competitive equilibrium requires that the rate of rent in each industry should be equal to the value of the marginal product of land in each industry. Only in these conditions will no entrepreneur have any incentive to adjust the amount of labour or land marginally in his enterprise.

But competitive equilibrium also requires that no entrepreneur in any undertaking should be making a net profit or loss. If his total receipts exceeded his total costs, new entrepreneurs would come in to the industry to expand output by taking on more labour and land to produce more of the output. If total costs exceeded total receipts, entrepreneurs already in the industry would be closing down their businesses. We are, therefore, faced with an apparent puzzle. The conditions mentioned in the previous paragraph told us that each factor of production must be paid a reward equal to the value of its marginal product; the conditions mentioned in this paragraph tell us that the total amount paid out to the factors must be equal to the total amount received by the sale of the product. Is there any reason to believe that these two conditions are compatible, that is to say that the total amount received from the sale of output will be just enough (neither too much nor too little) to pay to each factor a reward equal to the value of its marginal product?

The answer is that in conditions of constant returns to scale this will necessarily be so. This proposition is illustrated in Table V. Consider the position in a particular farm which is shown in that table. The farmer is in situation I employing 100 units of *L* and 100 units of *N* to produce 100 units of *X*. Since there are constant returns

		Situation I	Situation II	Situation III
Amounts of factors employed	*L*	100	100	101
	N	100	101	101
Output of *X*		100	$100\frac{1}{4}$	101
Marginal Products of	*L*	—	—	$\frac{3}{4}$
	N	—	$\frac{1}{4}$	—

Table V

to scale, by increasing both *L* and *N* by 1 per cent to 101 he would also increase his output by 1 per cent to 101 (situation III). Suppose, however, that starting in situation I he increases his employment of *N* by one unit without increasing his employment of *L* (situation II). Then the output in situation II will be intermediate between the outputs of situations I and III; in Table V we assume it to be $100\frac{1}{4}$. We can now see that we have by implication assumed that the marginal product of *N* is $\frac{1}{4}$ since between situations I and II, the amount of *L* being unchanged, an increase of 1 unit in *N* has caused *X* to rise by $\frac{1}{4}$ of a unit. But by comparing situations II and III we can now see that our assumptions necessarily imply that the marginal product of *L* is $\frac{3}{4}$; for between these two situations the amount of *N* is constant and an increase of *L* by 1 unit has caused the output of *X* to go up from $100\frac{1}{4}$ to 101, i.e. by $\frac{3}{4}$ of a unit of *X*. If now in situation I we pay each of the 100 units of *L* a wage rate equal to the value of its marginal product, we shall pay in wages the value of $100 \times \frac{3}{4} = 75$ units of X. If similarly we pay each of the 100 units of N a rent equal to the value of its marginal product, we shall pay in rents the value of $100 \times \frac{1}{4} = 25$ units of X. Wages of 75 plus rents of 25 add up to 100, which is exactly equal to the total available output. With constant returns to scale the payment of a reward to each factor exactly equal to the value of its marginal product will absorb exactly the total output, neither less nor more.[1]

We can now consider the general properties of our present simple two-factor two-product economy. In equilibrium the given money income of the community is spent on certain outputs of X and Y at certain prices of X and Y. At these outputs, prices, and money income consumers are satisfied. Labour and land are allocated between the two industries in such a way as to produce these outputs. The money wage rate of labour is the same in both industries and is equal to the value of the marginal product of labour in each industry; and similarly for the money rate of rent per acre of land.

Suppose now that consumers' needs and tastes change and that at the existing incomes of wage earners and landlords and at the existing prices of X and Y \$100 more is spent on Y and \$100 less on X. If the ratio of labour to land employed in the production of Y were the same as that in X, all that would happen would be that more Y and less X would be produced without any change in the prices of X and Y or in the distribution of the national income between wages and rents. We would be in the situation examined in Chapter V. Suppose that in both X and Y 40 per cent of the cost are rents of land and 60 per cent wages of labour. The reduction of \$100 in expenditure on X would represent indirectly a \$40 reduction in the demand for the use of land and a \$60 reduction in the demand for labour, the increase of \$100 in expenditure on Y would represent indirectly a \$40 increase in the demand for the use of land and a \$60 increase in the demand for labour. Land and labour would be transferred in these proportions from X production to Y production, and the output of X would fall by \$100 and of Y would increase by \$100 without any change in the prices of Y or X and without any change in the money wage rate or rate of rent.

[1] The arithmetical argument from Table V is not in fact a strict one. What Table V shows is a case in which the marginal product of land *in situation I* is $\frac{1}{4}$ and the marginal product of labour *in situation II* is $\frac{3}{4}$. But will labour *in situation I* be paid a wage equal to the value of its marginal product *in situation II*? The demonstration in the text relies upon the implicit assumption that this will be so. In fact by taking sufficiently small units of L and N the difference between the ratio of L to N in situations I and II can be made so small that the difference between the marginal products of labour in situation I and situation II becomes negligible.

But the story is very different if there are differences in the ratio of land to labour in the two industries. Suppose that in agriculture much land and little labour is needed because of the technical nature of food production, whereas in manufactures little land and much labour is needed because of the technical nature of clothing production. For example, suppose that the ratio of rents to wages in *X* production in the initial equilibrium is 60:40, whereas in *Y* production it is 20:80. Then at current prices a shift of demand of $100 from *X* to *Y* represents indirectly a decrease of $60 in demand for land in *X* and an increase of $20 in demand for land in *Y*—a net fall in the demand for land of $40 ($60–$20) at the current rent per acre. The shift in demand also means at the current wage rate an increased demand for labour of $80 in the *Y*-industry and a decreased demand of $40 in the *X*-industry—a net increase in the demand for labour of $40. The shift of demand of $100 from the land-intensive product *X* to the labour-intensive product *Y* will have caused indirectly a shift of demand of $40 from land to labour.

There will at the current rates of wages and rents be an excess demand for labour and an excess supply of land. The money wage rate will rise and the money rate of rent will fall. The money cost of *X* will fall and the money cost of *Y* will rise.[1]

Thus in competition the price of *X* will fall and the price of *Y* will rise. If there were no technical possibility of substituting cheaper land for more expensive labour in either industry, this change of prices of *X* and *Y* would go on without any change in the amounts produced until the price of *X* had so risen that consumers were content once more to go on consuming the unchanged amounts of *X* and *Y*. We should be in the situation of Chapter IV where a shift of demand causes a change in prices and in the distribution of income but no change in outputs.

The reason is clear. As long as any less *X* and any more *Y* were produced there would be some unemployed land. For a reduction in the output of *X* releases a large amount of land with each worker released, whereas an increase in the output of *Y* absorbs only a small amount of land with each additional worker employed. But as long as some land were unused, landlords in competition with each other would reduce the rent charged per acre of land. The cost and the

[1] Consider some notional intermediate product *Z* which is produced with the national average ratio of land to labour. When, with a given total supply of *L* and *N*, the wage rate goes up and the rate of rent goes down in such a way that a constant money national income is redistributed in favour of *L*, then the cost of the notional product *Z* will go neither up nor down. In its case the rise in labour cost will be exactly offset by the fall in rent cost. Any product (like *Y*) which is produced with a higher ratio of *L* to *N* will experience some net rise in cost. Conversely *X* will experience some net fall in cost.

price of *X* would thus continue to fall relatively to that of *Y* until the demand was shifted back from *Y* to *X* to an extent sufficient to take up the old initial outputs of *X* and *Y*.[1]

The position would be an intermediate one if it were possible in either *X* or *Y* or in both industries to substitute the cheaper *N* for the more expensive *L* as the money rent per acre fell and the money wage rate rose. In this case in one or both industries a higher ratio of land to labour will be used than was initially the case. The contraction of agriculture will be more largely through the dismissal of expensive labour and/or the expansion of manufactures will be more markedly through the absorption of cheap land. The possibilities of substitution may well be much greater in one industry than another. For example, in agriculture it may be possible to farm very intensively (as in the Netherlands) if land is very expensive relatively to labour or to farm very extensively (as on the Canadian prairies) if land is very cheap relatively to labour. On the other hand, in manufactures a rather fixed ratio of land to labour may be required whatever the relative prices of the factors. This does not affect the main outcome of the process. Whether it be in the *X*-industry or the *Y*-industry does not matter so long as when the price of land falls and of labour rises more land per worker can be used somewhere in the economy. This will enable the output of labour-intensive *Y* to be increased and of land-intensive *X* to be decreased without any unemployed land being left unabsorbed into the economy.

The greater is the ease of substitution between *L* and *N* in *X* and in *Y*, the less will be the rise in the wage rate and the fall in the rate of rent required to reabsorb all factors into employment, and the less, therefore, will be the rise in the cost of labour-intensive *Y* and the fall in the cost of labour-intensive *X*.

We have then again the intermediate case of Chapters VI and VII. A shift of demand from *X* to *Y* will cause some fall in the price of *X*, some fall in the output of *X*, some rise in the price of *Y*, and some rise in the output of *Y*. Prices will change much and outputs little if (i) there are great initial differences in the factor proportions employed in *X* and in *Y*, (ii) it is technically difficult for *X* to contract by releasing what are for it abnormally large amounts of the expensive factor *L*, and (iii) it is technically difficult for *Y* to expand by taking on what are for it abnormally large amounts of the cheap factor *N*.

The argument of this chapter can be expressed more precisely in geometrical terms. Let us first consider one of our industries, the production of *X* with the two factors *L* and *N*. The relationship

[1] Or until rents were zero and labour had become the only scarce factor (cf. Chapter XI, pp. 160–5 below).

between the inputs of the factors (L and N) and the output of the product (X) is illustrated in Figure 29. Along the horizontal axis we measure the amount of L, and up the vertical axis the amount of N, used in the industry. The curve marked $X = 100$ then shows the combinations of L and N which are necessary to produce 100 units of X. This curve slopes down from left to right because, if one has less N, one must have more L in order to produce the same amount of X. The downward slope of the curve becomes gentler and gentler as one moves along it to the right, because the higher the existing ratio of men per acre the more difficult it will become to produce the

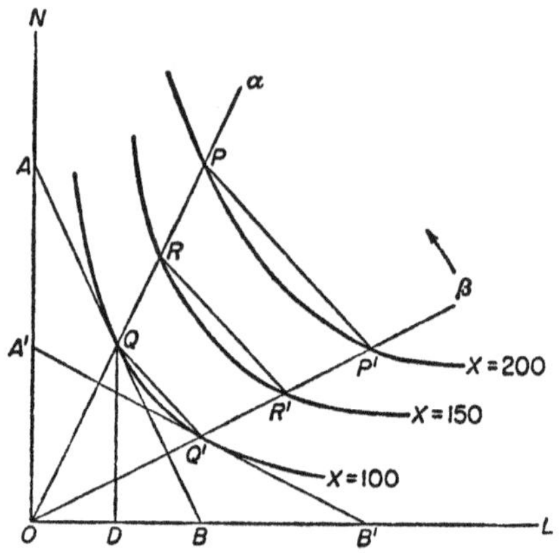

Figure 29

same output with yet more men and less land; the rate at which employment of labour must be increased to make up for the loss of yet one more acre becomes greater and greater as methods become more and more labour-intensive and less and less land intensive. At the point Q OD labour and DQ land are used to produce 100 units of X. The slope of the line α, namely $\frac{QD}{OD}$ measures the ratio of land to labour used in production. The slope of the curve $X = 100$ at Q namely $\frac{AO}{OB}$, represents the amount of land that can be given up for a unit of labour taken on at the margin without changing the total output of X.

There will be whole series of curves such as $X = 100$, $X = 150$, $X = 200$, etc., each of which shows the combinations of L and N needed to produce the stated output of X. These curves may be called 'equi-product curves'. With constant returns to scale once one has drawn one of the curves (e.g. $X = 100$) one can readily derive all the other curves, so that in fact all the production relationships are given by a single equi-product curve of the kind shown on Figure 29. Consider the line $OQRP$. It passes through the curve $X = 100$ at the point Q. Measure along the line OQ extended a length OR, such that $OR = 1\frac{1}{2}$ times OQ. Then the equi-product curve $X = 150$ must pass through R; for at R both L and N are $1\frac{1}{2}$ times as great as at Q; and since there are constant returns to scale a 50 per cent increase in both L and N will cause a 50 per cent increase in X. Similarly if we draw OP equal to twice OQ, the equi-product curve $X = 200$ will pass through P.

Figure 29 also illustrates a second basic feature of these equi-product curves in conditions of constant returns to scale. Draw any other straight line through O such as the line β and let it cut the curve $X = 100$ at Q'. Draw $OR' = 1\frac{1}{2}$ times OQ' and $OP' = 2$ times OQ'. Then by the process of reasoning used in the last paragraph the equi-product curve $X = 150$ will pass through R' and the equi-product curve $X = 200$ will pass through P'. Join QQ', RR', and PP'. These three lines will be parallel to each other. Thus $OR = 1\frac{1}{2}$ times OQ and $OR' = 1\frac{1}{2}\ OQ'$ so that the triangle QOQ' will correspond in all its angles to the triangle ROR'. The slopes of QQ', RR', and PP' are therefore all equal. Now let the line β swing round in the direction of the arrow towards α. The slope of QQ' becomes closer and closer to the slope of the line AB, namely the tangent to the curve $X = 100$ at Q. Similarly, the slopes of RR' and PP' become closer and closer to the slopes of the tangents of $X = 150$ at R and $X = 200$ at P respectively. In the limit as β comes to coincide with α, the slopes of QQ', RR', and PP' which remain equal to each other, coincide with the tangent of the equi-product curves at Q, R, and P. In other words the marginal rate of substitution between L and N is the same at Q, R, and P. As one moves out from O along a straight line such as α, (i) one passes through successive equi-product curves the numbering of which (i.e. the output of X) is directly proportional to the distance from O and (ii) the slope of the equi-product curves remains constant along the line α. The marginal rate of substitution between L and N depends only upon the ratio of L to N. The higher the ratio of $\frac{L}{N}$ the greater the marginal rate at which L must be taken on to make up for one unit of N. The slopes of the tangents at Q', R', and P' will be equal to each other and the slopes of the tangents at Q, R, and P will be equal to each other. But the former will be gentler than the latter.

The equi-product curves can be used to show what ratio of labour to land it will be profitable for a farmer to employ given the wage of labour and the rent of land. This is done in Figure 30. Suppose the wage rate of labour and the rent of land were such that \$100 a month would hire *OB* men or *OA* acres. Then with \$100 the entrepreneur could hire any combination of *L* and *N* on the budget constraint line *AB*. As he hired less land and more labour and moved

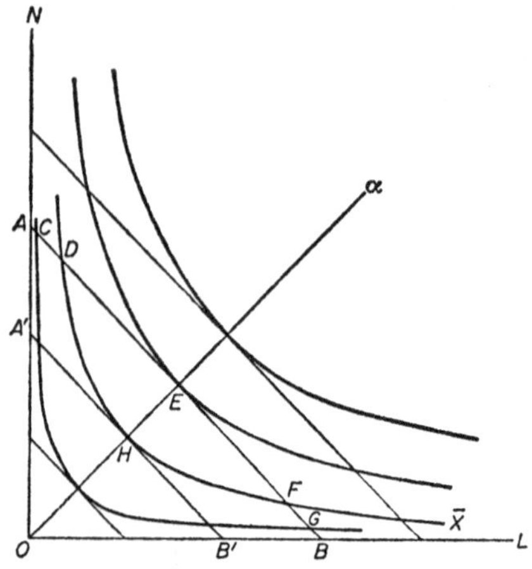

Figure 30

from *A* to *C* to *D* to *E* his output rises; as he hired still less land and more labour and moved from *E* to *F* to *G* to *B* his output falls. For \$100 worth of factors at existing prices *E* is the point which gives him the maximum output. Alternatively we can ask what combination of *L* and *N* at these given prices will enable him to produce a given output at the lowest cost. Consider the equi-product curve marked $\bar{X}$. To produce this with combinations of *L* and *N* at *D* or *F* will cost him \$100—he is on the line *AB*. To produce it with the combination at *H* will cost him less—he will be on the line *A′B′*. Clearly with the relative prices of *L* and *N* shown by the slope of the lines *AB*, *A′B′*, etc., in Figure 30 he will produce with a combination of *L* and *N* given by the slope of α.

Because of the properties of constant returns to scale which we have just examined, we thus know that if the relative prices of *L* and *N* are such as to give a slope equal to the slope of *AB* in Figure 29, then—whatever his scale of operations may be—he will operate somewhere on the line α, i.e. his ratio of labour to land employed will be $\frac{OD}{DQ}$, because it is only on this line that the tangents of the equi-product curves will have the same slope as *AB*. Similarly, if the price of labour fell and/or the price of land rose so that the relative prices of labour and land were represented by the slope of the line *A'B'* in Figure 29, he would operate on the line β, whatever the scale of his operations might be. We have thus a straightforward and unambiguous measure of the elasticity of substitution between *L*

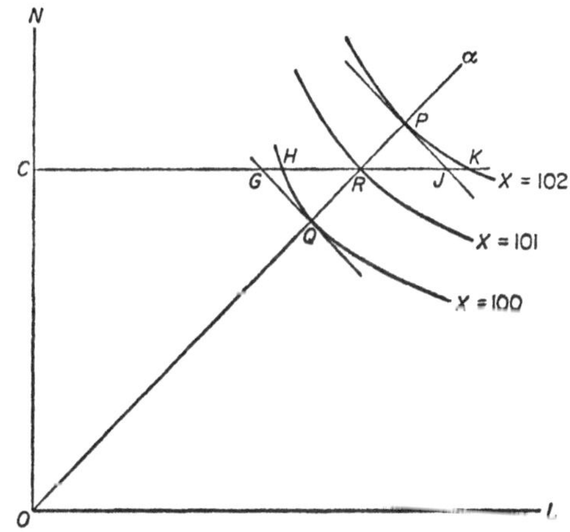

Figure 31

and *N*. It is equal to the percentage change in the ratio of land to labour employed which will be caused by a one per cent change in the ratio of the rate of rent to the rate of wages. It is (numerically) large if a small proportionate change in the slope of the line *AB* causes a large percentage change in the slope of the line α. If a small fall in the price of labour relatively to the price of land, causes a large rise in employment per acre, then the elasticity of substitution between land and labour is (numerically) large. (Cf. pp. 47–50 above.)

Figure 30 gives a complete description of the production relationships in industry *X*. We can deduce from it that the marginal product of labour falls as more labour is used with a given amount of land. This is shown in Figure 31. In that figure we draw equi-product curves for three outputs of *X*, namely 100, 101, and 102 units of *X*.[1] Draw any line through the origin *O* to cut these curves at *Q*, *R*, and *P* and draw a horizontal line through *R* to cut the curves at *H*, *R*, and

[1] Not accurately to scale.

K. Draw the tangents at Q and P to cut the horizontal straight line at G and J. Now $QR = RP$ and the slope of $GQ =$ the slope of PJ because of constant returns to scale. It follows that $GR = RJ$. Therefore $HR < RK$. In other words with a constant amount of N (the height of the horizontal line GK) a smaller additional amount of labour (HR) is needed to raise output from 100 to 101 than is needed (RK) to raise output from 101 to 102. The marginal product of labour will be falling.

In the present case of processes in which only two factors (L and

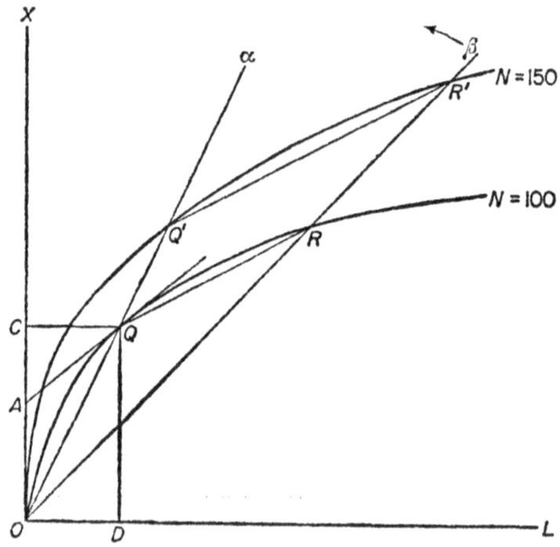

Figure 32

N) are used to produce only one product (X or Y) the productive relationship in any one process can be completely specified in a diagram of the kind used in Figures 30 and 31. Nevertheless even in this case it is useful for some purposes to transform this diagram into one of another kind which is shown in Figure 32. In Figure 32 we measure along the horizontal axis the amount of one of the factors used (e.g. L) and up the vertical axis the amount of the product produced. Suppose that in Figures 31 OC represents 100 units of N. Then by measuring successive amounts of L along CK (namely CG, CH, CR, CJ, CK, etc. etc.) we could read off from the equi-product curves the successive amounts of X which would be produced by larger and larger amounts of L, keeping $N = 100$. We should obtain a curve of the kind marked $N = 100$ in Figure 32.

The slope of the line OQ, namely $\frac{QD}{OD}$, represents output per head or the average product of labour. The slope of the curve $N = 100$ at the point Q $\left(\text{namely the tangent } \frac{AC}{CQ}\right)$ measures what may be called the 'marginal rate of transformation' between the input L and the output X with the amount of the other input N given and constant at 100. This marginal rate of transformation can be thought of in either of two ways. If we consider the additional amount of L needed to produce 1 more unit of X, we may think of it as measuring the marginal cost of X in terms of L. If we consider the additional amount of X that would be produced by taking on one more unit of L, we may think of it as showing the marginal product of L in terms of X. Since the marginal product of labour falls as one employs more and more labour with the given amount of land, the $N = 100$ curve in Figure 32 has been drawn with a gentler and gentler slope as one moves to the right. The marginal rate of transformation between L and X diminishes as one increases L and X.

There will be a whole family of N-curves. If N rises from 100 to 150, then any given amount of L will produce more X. The $N = 150$ curve is above the $N = 100$. With constant returns to scale one can plot the relationship between the $N = 100$ and any other N-curve in the following way. Extend OQ and measure $OQ' = 1\frac{1}{2}\ OQ$. Then the point Q' lies on the $N = 150$ curve; for at Q' there is 50 per cent more L and 50 per cent more X than at Q; but with constant returns to scale to produce 50 per cent more output with 50 per cent more labour one must also have 50 per cent more land. Similarly, draw any other straight line β through O to cut $N = 100$ at R; extend OR to R' so that $OR' = 1\frac{1}{2}\ OR$; then by a similar process of reasoning R' must lie on the curve $N = 150$.

Join QR and $Q'R'$. These two lines are parallel because the triangles OQR and $OQ'R'$ have similar angles. Let β swing round in the direction of the arrow to approach α. The slope of QR approaches the slope of the tangent to $N = 100$ at Q $\left(\text{namely } \frac{AC}{CQ}\right)$ and the slope of $Q'R'$ approaches the slope of the tangent to $N = 150$ at Q'. In other words on any straight line such as α the marginal products of labour will be the same. On such a line, as we have just seen, the ratio of labour to land is unchanged (both have grown by 50 per cent between Q and Q'). The marginal product of labour will depend therefore solely on the ratio of labour to land. When this ratio is low (as at Q and Q') the marginal product of labour is high (the slope of the tangents are steep); when the ratio of labour to land is high (as at R and R') the marginal product of labour is low (the slope of the tangents are gentle). The marginal product of labour will be raised by an increase in the amount of land or by a decrease in the amount of labour in use.

We can use a construction of the kind shown in Figure 32 to show how much labour a farmer will employ with a given amount of land to maximize his profit given the wage rate of labour and the price of his product. This is shown in Figure 33. Suppose that the price of the product *X* and the wage of labour were such that *HB* units of

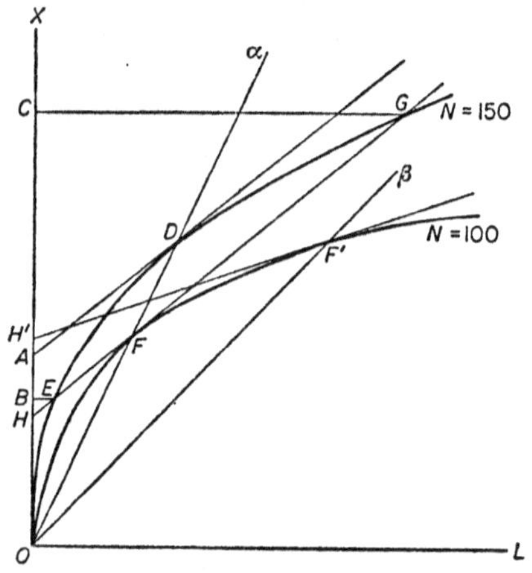

Figure 33

X had the same value as *BE* units of labour. Then one could draw a series of parallel straight lines such as *HG* and *AD* having the slope $\frac{HB}{BE}$. These could be called equi-gross-profit lines. Consider, for example, the point *G* on the line *HG*. A farmer who had an output of *X* equal to *OC* would use *CH* of it to hire an amount of labour *CG* (since *HB* will hire *BE*, *HC* will hire *CG*); and he would have left over a profit in terms of *X* equal to his output *CO* less his wage bill *CH*. In other words starting from any level of employment giving any level of output (such as the point *G*), one can draw through the point *G* a line having a slope equal to the real wage rate $\left(\frac{HB}{BE}\right)$. Where this line cuts the axis *OX* at the point *H*, *HC* will equal the total wage bill and *HO* the total 'gross profit' left over for rent on land. Thus all points on the line *HG* represent a 'gross profit' equal in value to *HO* units of *X*; and all points on the line *AD* represent a 'gross profit' equal in value to *OA* units of *X*.

Suppose that our farmer has 150 units of land. If he employs *BE* units of labour he will produce *OB* and make a profit of *OH*. But at this point the marginal product of labour in terms of *X* is greater than the real wage of labour in terms of *X* (the tangent of the $N = 150$ curve at *E* is steeper than the slope of the line *HG*). If he employs more labour and moves up the *N* curve to *D*, he will increase his gross profit (i.e. revenue less wage bill) to *AO*. Clearly with a given amount of land of 150 he will choose the point *D* at which his $N = 150$ curve is tangential to the highest equi-profit line, *AD*.

One can put the maximizing problem round the other way. Consider on the line *HG* different ways of making the same gross profit *HO*. This can be made at *E* and *G* with 150 units of land or at *F* with 100 units of land. The gross profit per acre will be that much higher at *F* than at *E* or *G*. To maximize profit per acre with a given total profit, the farmer will produce at the point *F* where the equi-profit line *HG* is tangential to the lowest *N*-curve.

All points of equilibrium will thus be on the line *OD* when the real wage rate of labour has the slope of *HG* (= slope of *AD*). When the real wage rate falls it will pay to employ more labour with a given amount of land until the marginal product of labour has fallen to the lower real wage rate. When the real wage rate falls from the slope of *HF* to that of *H'F'*, a farmer with 100 units of *N* will move from the point *F* to *F'* and 'gross profit' will rise from *OH* to *OH'*. We now have a measure of a relationship between *L* and *X* corresponding to the measures of elasticity of substitution which we have previously examined. If a small fall in the real wage rate leads to a large expansion of output with a given amount of land, then we may say that the production relationship is a flexible one. Thus if a one per cent change in the slope of the line *HF* causes a large percentage change in the slope of the line α we may say that the elasticity of transformation between *L* and *X* is large.[1]

We have analysed at some length the geometrical description of the relationships between inputs and outputs in the industry producing *X*. Similar relationships exist in the other industry producing *Y*. We can now put these two production relationships together in order to consider the equilibrium conditions for the whole economy.

[1] In our present simple system of two factors and one output a high elasticity of transformation between *L* and *X* (or between *N* and *X*) implies a (numerically) high elasticity of substitution between *L* and *N* and *vice versa*. But when we come on to more complicated processes it will be useful to have both measures in mind.

In Figure 34 we measure to the left from X along the axis XB the amount of L (L_x) used in the production of X and up from X along the vertical axis XA the amount of N (N_x) used in the production of X. There will then be a series of X equi-product curves such as X_1 and X_2 showing the combinations of L_x and N_x required to produce the outputs X_1 and X_2. Similarly from the origin Y we measure downwards the amount of N (N_y) used to produce Y and to the right the amount of L (L_y) used to produce Y. There are then a series of Y equi-product curves such as Y_1 and Y_2 showing the

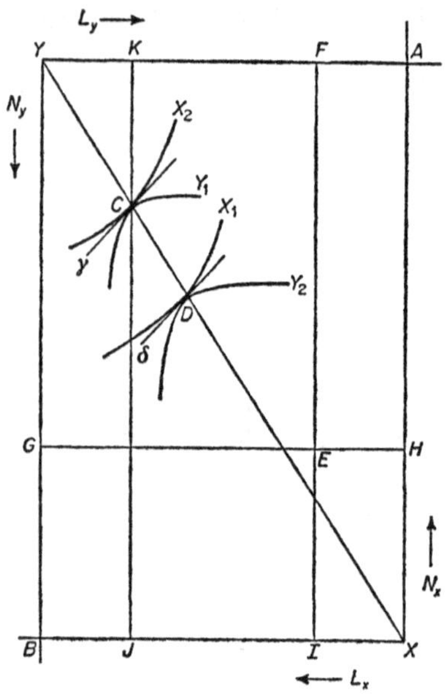

Figure 34

combinations of L_y and N_y required to produce outputs Y_1 and Y_2 of Y. We choose the dimensions of the box in Figure 34 in such a way that YB ($= XA$) equals the total amount of N available in the whole economy and YA ($= XB$) equals the total amount of L available in the economy as a whole. If we then take any point such as E inside the box, we have a complete description of the production arrangements in the economy. At E of the total amount of labour ($YA = XB$) YF is used to produce Y and XI to produce X; and of the total amount of land ($YB = XA$) YG is used to produce Y and XH to produce X. Through E there will pass a Y equi-product curve which will show how much Y is produced with YF labour and YG

land; and similarly through E there will pass an X equi-product curve which will show how much X is being produced.

Consider first any point such as C which is on the diagonal YX. Any point on this diagonal indicates a position in which both the Y industry and the X industry are using labour and land in the national average proportion. At C X is employing $\frac{L_x}{N_x}$ in the ratio $\frac{JX}{JC}$ which equals $\frac{XB}{YB}$ which is the ratio in which labour and land are available in the economy as a whole. Similarly, $\frac{L_y}{N_y} = \frac{YK}{KC} = \frac{YA}{XA} = \frac{\text{total } L}{\text{total } N}$. Through C there will pass an X-equi-product curve (X_2) and a Y-equi-product curve (Y_1). In Figure 34 we have drawn the fluke case in which it happens by mere coincidence that on the diagonal XY at C the slope of the X-equi-product curve is the same as that of the Y-equi-product curve, both being shown by the slope of the line γ.

The slope of the line γ can be taken to represent the price of labour relatively to the price of land. If γ is steeply sloped, then much N must be given for little L as one moves along the line γ; or in other words the price of L is high relatively to the price of N. As we have already shown, the X producers will not want to change the ratio of L_x to N_x if the slope γ is the same as that of the X equi-product curve; and similarly for the Y producers. The point C on the diagonal is in this case one in which both the X and the Y producers will be willing to use L and N in the national average if the relatively rates of wages and rents are in equilibrium at the slope γ.

Whether the point C will be the equilibrium point will depend upon the demand in the economy for X and Y. If the demand for Y were greater and for X smaller, we should move along the diagonal XY from C to D. The output of Y would have gone up from Y_1 to Y_2 and of X down from X_2 to X_1. Since X will have released resources of L and N in the national average and Y will have taken them on in the same proportion, the ratio of L to N will have changed in neither industry. The slopes of X_1 and Y_2 will both be the same at D as those of X_2 and Y_1 at C. The slope of δ is the same as that of γ. Factor prices and so product costs are unchanged. We have a case of constant costs.

But it would be a pure coincidence if both the X and the Y

industry would employ the national average of L to N at the same ratio of factor prices, γ. We consider in Figure 35 the much more probable case where this is not so. At the point C on the diagonal XY the slope of the Y-equi-product curve is δ and of the X-equi-product curve is γ. If both industries used L and N in the national average, the wage rate would have to be very high relatively to the rate of rent to keep the Y producers in equilibrium and it would

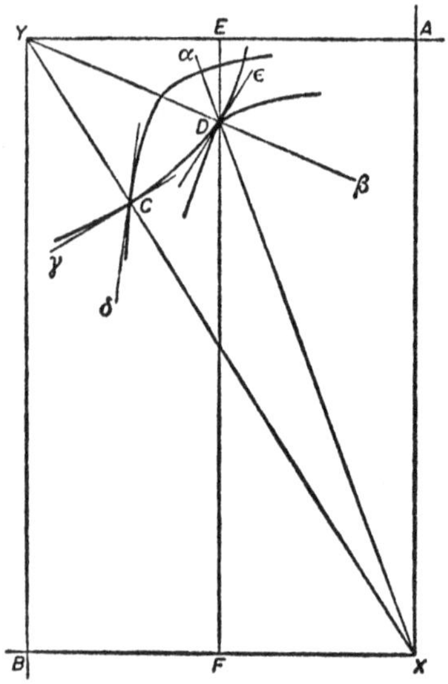

Figure 35

have to be much lower relatively to the rate of rent to keep the X producers in equilibrium. Because of constant returns to scale the X-equi-product curve has the slope γ and the Y-equi-product curve the slope δ at all points on the diagonal XY. From the way in which the X and Y equi-product curves cut each other (as at C) on the diagonal XY, it is clear that they can be tangential to each other only to the North-East of the diagonal XY. This means that all points of equilibrium, at which the slope of the X-equi-product curve and of the Y-equi-product curve are the same must lie to the North-East of the diagonal XY and that the slope of the line showing the relative prices of land and labour must be intermediate between γ and δ.

A possible equilibrium point is shown at D where the relative factor prices are shown by the slope of the line ϵ. At this point the ratio $\frac{N_y}{L_y}$ is equal to $\frac{ED}{YE}$ i.e. it is represented by the steepness of the slope of the line β down from the horizontal line YA. Because of constant returns to scale all Y equi-product curves on the line β will have the same slope as the line ϵ. Similarly at the point D the ratio of $\frac{N_x}{L_x}$ is $\frac{DF}{FX}$, which is equal to the slope of the line α up from the horizontal line XB. Since D is above the diagonal XY, this means that at D X employs a higher ratio of land to labour than does Y.

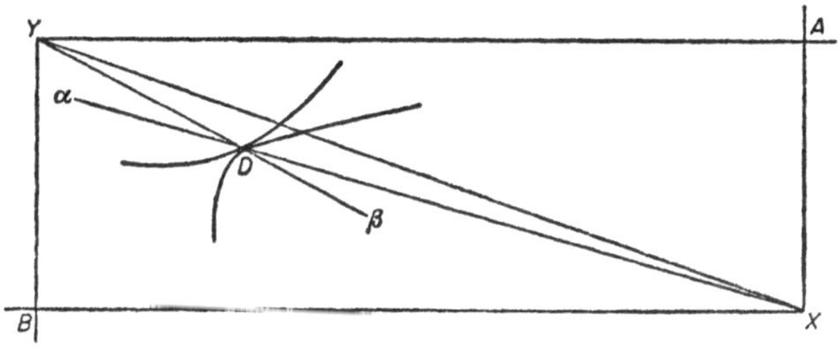

Figure 36

This is not the same thing as saying that for all conceivable prices of L and N the Y industry will be labour intensive and the X industry land intensive. It is possible that techniques of production are such that Y will at every set of factor prices employ a higher ratio of L to N than does Y. But this is not necessarily the case. Suppose (as in fact we have drawn it) that the elasticity of substitution between L and N is much greater in the X industry than in the Y industry. Then at a very low wage X might be more labour-intensive than Y and at a high wage X might be less labour-intensive than Y. If the total supply of labour were great and of land small, the wage rate might have to fall so low that X became the labour-intensive ratio. This is shown in Figure 36 where the shape of the equi-product curves for X and Y are the same as in Figure 35 but the supply of labour is much greater and of land much smaller. It is now apparent that points of equilibrium like D must lie below the diagonal XY. The point is simply that with the low national average of L to N shown in Figure 35 the price of L relatively to that of N must always be high enough to make X the land-intensive industry, whereas with the high national average of L to N in Figure 36 the price of L relatively to that of N must always be low enough to make X the labour-intensive industry.

In Figure 35 D is one possible equilibrium point; but it will be the final equilibrium point only if the needs and tastes of consumers are such as to make them willing to purchase the amounts of X and Y which correspond to the X and Y equi-product curves which pass through the point D. What would now happen if the demand for X were less and for Y greater? This is illustrated in Figure 37. We start at the position D with the ratio $\frac{N_y}{L_y}$ shown by the downward slope of β and the ratio $\frac{N_x}{L_x}$ by the upward slope of α, and with the ratio

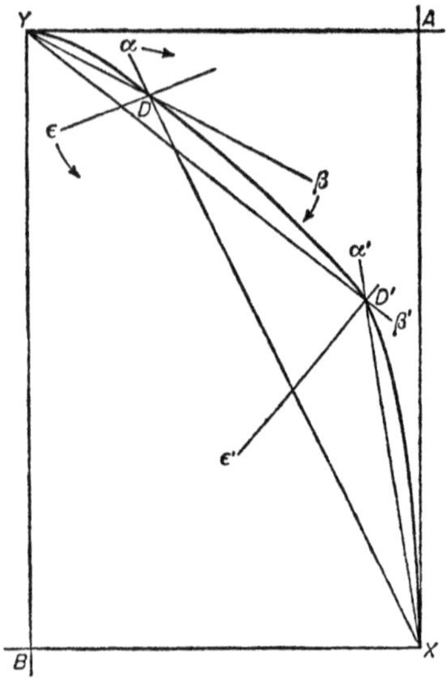

Figure 37

of the price of L to the price of N shown by the upward slope of ϵ. The demand for Y increases and for X falls; $\frac{N_x}{L_x}$ is greater than $\frac{N_y}{L_y}$; X releases a ratio of land to labour above the national average and Y absorbs a ratio of land to labour below the national average; there is an excess supply of land; the price of land falls relatively to the price of labour, and the slope of ϵ becomes steeper, moving in the direction of the arrow from ϵ; as the price of land falls relatively to that of labour both the X industry and the Y industry use a higher ratio of land to labour than before; the α line and the β line swing round in the direction of the arrows; when the slope of ϵ has risen to that of ϵ', the slopes of α and β have changed to α' and β'; the point D' at which α' and β' intersect is, therefore, the only possible point of equilibrium with the new factor price ratio ϵ', because on the line β' lie all the points of the Y equi-product curves with the slope ϵ' and on the line α' lie all the points of the X equi-product curves with the slope ϵ'.

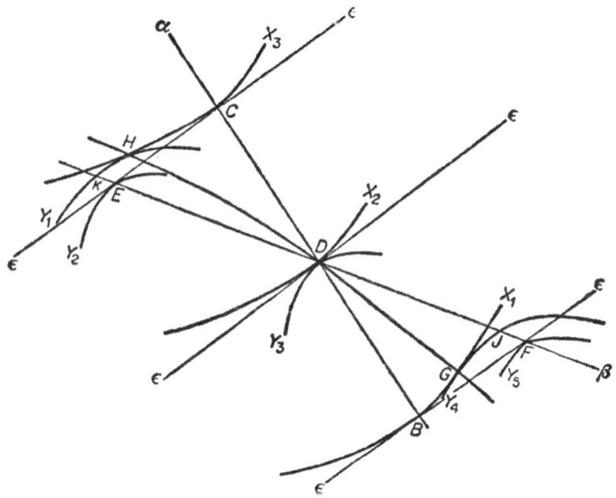

Figure 38

We can thus trace out the line $Y - D - D' - X$ on which all points of competitive equilibrium must lie. As one moves down this line from Y to D to D' towards X (i) more Y and less X is produced, (ii) since Y is more labour intensive than is X, the price of land relatively to that of labour falls, and (iii) as a result of the change in factor prices both X and Y employ a higher ratio of land to labour than before.

We can also show from Figure 37 that in these conditions there will be increasing costs in the sense that as one moves along the line $Y - D - D'$ towards X one will have to give up more and more Y for each additional unit of X produced. This is shown in Figure 38 which is simply a magnification of the part of Figure 37 lying around the point D in Figure 37. At D, then, in Figure 38 we have the intersection of the α and β factor-proportion lines with the X and Y equi-product curves at D both having the same slope, namely that of ϵ. Measure along α on each side of D equal lengths DB and DC ($DB = DC$). Because of constant returns to scale the slopes of the X equi-product curves at C, D, and B will all be the same, namely that of ϵ. Let these ϵ lines cut the line β at E, D, and F respectively. Because of constant returns to scale the Y-equi-product curves at E, D, and F will all have the same slope, namely that of ϵ. The triangles DCE and DBF are equal and, therefore, $ED = DF$. Because of constant returns to scale, therefore, the increases in the output of X between B and D and between D and C are the same, and the decreases in the output of Y between F and D and between D and E are the same (i.e. $X_2 - X_1 = X_3 - X_2$ and $Y_3 - Y_2 = Y_5 - Y_3$).

In between the lines α and β there runs the curve ($Y—D—D'—X$ of Figure 37) on which the Y and X equi-product curves are tangential. Let the X equi-product curve through B (namely X_1) be tangential to a Y equi-product curve (namely Y_4) at G and let Y_4 cut the line β at J. Let the X equi-product curve through C (namely X_3) be tangential to a Y equi-product (namely Y_1) at H and let Y_1 cut the line α at K.

Consider now a shift of demand from Y to X, first from H to D and then from D to G. This represents an equal reduction in the output of X because (since by construction $CD = DB$) the decrease of X from X_3 to X_2 is equal to the decrease from X_2 to X_1. But the shift from D to G represents a smaller increase in the output of Y than does the shift from H to D. We have already seen (since $DF = ED$) that the increase in output of Y from Y_3 to Y_5 is the same as that from Y_2 to Y_3. But the shift from D to G represents a smaller increase in output of Y than this (namely from Y_3 to Y_4) and the shift from H to D represents a larger increase in output of Y than this (namely from Y_1 to Y_3). Thus smaller and smaller increases of Y are obtained for each successive unit decrease in the output of X. We have again a case of increasing cost. If we drew the 'production-possibility curve' for X and Y it would be of the same general form as the curve LZ in Figure 26.

CHAPTER IX

MANY FACTORS AND MANY PRODUCTS

We must now generalize the analysis of the previous chapter to allow for the fact that there are more than two factors of production and more than two products. There are more than one type of land (hilly land and flat land) and more than one type of labour (men capable of heavy physical work and men capable of delicate accurate work). There are a large number of products which are produced for the final consumer. We must now envisage a whole range of industrial processes each of which uses some or all of the factors (L, M, N, etc.) to produce some or all of the products (X, Y, Z, etc.). Some processes will not employ some factors nor produce some products; a steel mill will not employ any hilly land nor produce any milk as a bye-product. But nevertheless we have now to allow for the possibility (which we ignored in the previous chapter) that some processes will produce more than one product as well as employing more than one factor. Thus a sheep farmer employs land and labour to produce wool and mutton.

In our competitive economy there are two sets of conditions which must be fulfilled before the system will be in equilibrium. First, the choice of processes to be employed (i.e. the choice of industries to be set up) and the scale at which each chosen process (i.e. the relative size of each industry) is operated must be such as to make all chosen processes just cover their costs and such as to leave unused no processes which at current prices payable for the factors and receivable from the products it would be profitable to operate. Second, within each firm or farm (i.e. in the case of each single entrepreneur operating any process) it must be impossible to make any further adjustments so as to increase the total profitability of the enterprise.

Some technically feasible processes will never be operated at all because they are unequivocally inferior to other technically feasible processes. Thus consider two processes using L, M, and N to produce X, Y, and Z. Suppose that any given amounts of L, M, and N would be able to produce more X by process I than by process II without producing less Y or less Z (no matter in what proportions X, Y, and Z were produced in process II), then process II would be unequivocally inferior to process I. An entrepreneur could always obtain by process I everything which he could obtain by process II plus something more in addition.

But if we leave out of account all such unequivocally technically inferior processes, the decision whether to set up a new firm in order to introduce or to expand the use of a particular process or whether to close down an existing firm in order to contract or to eliminate the use of a particular process will depend upon the relative prices of the various factors and the various products and upon what may be called the factor-intensity and the product-intensity of each process.

In any given situation with given total supplies of *L*, *M*, and *N* and with the ruling prices of *L*, *M*, and *N*, the national income will be divided between the incomes of *L*, the incomes of *M*, and the incomes of *N*. Suppose 20 per cent of the national income goes to *L*, 50 per cent to *M*, and the remaining 30 per cent to *N*. Then on the average for the economy as a whole costs of production must be 20 per cent *L*-costs, 50 per cent *M*-costs, and 30 per cent *N*-costs. If in any particular process the costs, at ruling prices of the factors, were 40 per cent *L*-costs, 40 per cent *M*-costs, and 20 per cent *N*-costs, we would say that, as compared with the national average, this process was *L*-intensive (because more than the average proportion of its costs were *L*-costs) and was *M*- and *N*-disintensive (because less than the average proportion of its costs were *M*-costs or *N*-costs).

Similarly in any given situation the ruling outputs of *X*, *Y*, and *Z* together with the ruling prices of *X*, *Y*, and *Z* will determine the proportion of the national income which is spent on *X*, *Y*, and *Z*. Suppose of the total national income 20 per cent is spent on *X*, 50 per cent on *Y*, and 30 per cent on *Z*. If in any particular process the receipts from sales, at the ruling prices of the products, were 40 per cent from *X*, 40 per cent from *Y*, and 20 per cent from *Z*, then, as compared with the national average, this process would be *X*-intensive and *Y*- and *Z*-disintensive.

If the prices of *L* and *Z* were very high and of *N* and *X* were very low, then processes which were *L*- and *X*-intensive would be exceptionally unprofitable, while processes which were *N*- and *Z*-intensive would be exceptionally profitable. The former processes would face exceptionally high costs and low receipts while the latter would enjoy exceptionally low costs and high receipts. The former processes would give place to the latter.

As well as the general expansion or contraction of particular processes entrepreneurs will make marginal adjustments within processes in order to make each process as profitable as possible. Such marginal adjustments will be of three kinds. (i) An entrepreneur may find it profitable to change his output programme in such a way as to increase somewhat the output of *Z* at the expense of the output of *X*, while using the same amount of factors and producing the same amount of all other products, provided that the price of *Z* is sufficiently high relatively to that of *X*. (ii) He may find it profitable to change his input programme in such a way as to increase somewhat

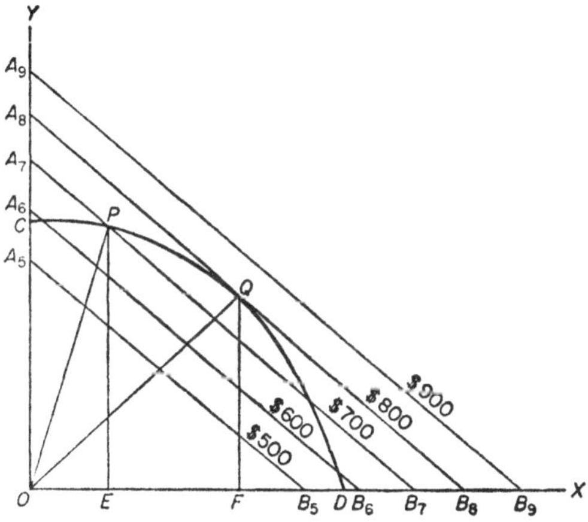

Figure 39

the input of *N* so as to economize the input of *L*, while keeping all his outputs and his employment of other factors unchanged, provided that the price of *N* is sufficiently low relatively to the price of *L*. (iii) He may find it profitable to change his production programme, i.e. to employ somewhat more of input *N* in order to produce more of output *Z*, while keeping his other outputs and inputs unchanged, provided that the price of *N* is sufficiently low relatively to the price of *Z*.

The first of these three types of adjustment has not been considered in earlier chapters of this book. Let us take an example. Consider a mixed farm on which land and labour is used to produce various agricultural products including sheep. Now sheep produce wool and mutton; but, by varying the breed of sheep, the proportions in which wool and mutton can be produced can be varied. If the price of mutton is high and of wool low, a high ratio of mutton to wool will be produced; and *vice versa*. The technically possible variations in the output programme of the farm are illustrated in Figure 39.

We measure along the *X* axis the amount of *X* (wool) produced and up the *Y* axis the amount of *Y* (mutton) produced. Let the curve *CPQD* represent the combinations of *X* and *Y* that can be produced on this farm given the existing employment of the various factors and the existing outputs of all other products. This curve slopes down from left to right because in order to produce more *X* with the given resources one must produce less *Y*; and its slope becomes steeper and steeper as one moves to the right because the greater the ratio of *X* to *Y* which one is producing, the more difficult will it become to produce still more *X* at the expense of *Y*.

One can draw a series of equi-revenue lines, the *AB*-lines of Figure 39, which represent the combinations of *X* and *Y* which it will be necessary to sell in order, at the current prices of *X* and *Y*, to receive a given revenue from the sale of *X* and *Y*. Thus suppose that the price of *X* is such that OB_5 of *X* will sell for $500 and that the price of *Y* is such that OA_5 of *Y* will sell for $500. Then any combination of *X* and *Y* on the line A_5B_5 will sell for $500. The slope of the line A_5B_5 measures the price of *X* relatively to the price of *Y*. If one increases the amounts of *X* and of *Y* sold both in the ratio of 6 to 5, one will obtain a revenue of $600 instead of $500. The combinations of *X* and *Y* necessary to receive $600 are shown on the line A_6B_6 where $\frac{OA_6}{OA_5} = \frac{OB_6}{OB_5} = \frac{6}{5}$. A_6B_6 is parallel to A_5B_5. And so on for the other equi-revenue lines.

In order to maximize his profit our farmer will, at the relative prices of *X* and *Y* shown by the slope of the *AB*-lines on Figure 39, produce *OF* of *X* and *FQ* of *Y*. He will in fact move along the curve *CPQF* until this curve becomes tangential to the highest possible equi-revenue line. For the combination at *P* he will receive $700, but for that at *Q* $800. He will be maximizing his profit only if it is impossible to make any further profitable adjustment of this land between any two of his outputs.

We can derive from Figure 39 a measure of the elasticity of substitution between *X* and *Y* in our farmer's output programmes. This can be measured by the percentage change in the ratio of the output *X* to *Y* which would be caused by a one per cent change in the ratio of the price of *X* to the price of *Y*.[1] If a small percentage change in the slope of the *AB*-lines would cause a large percentage change in the slope of the line *OA*, then the elasticity of substitution between *X* and *Y* in the farmer's output programme is high. If the

[1] This is a partial elasticity of substitution in the sense that we are measuring the farmer's ability to produce more *X* and less *Y* on the assumption that he cannot change his input programme at the same time, i.e. he cannot take on more of the inputs specially useful to produce *X* and less of those specially useful to produce *Y*.

elasticities of substitution between the various pairs of his outputs are in general high, we may call his output programme a flexible one; if they are low, we may call it a rigid one.

Marginal adjustments of the types (ii) and (iii) mentioned above on page 129 have already been mentioned in the previous chapter. Adjustments of type (ii) are illustrated in Figure 40. The entre-

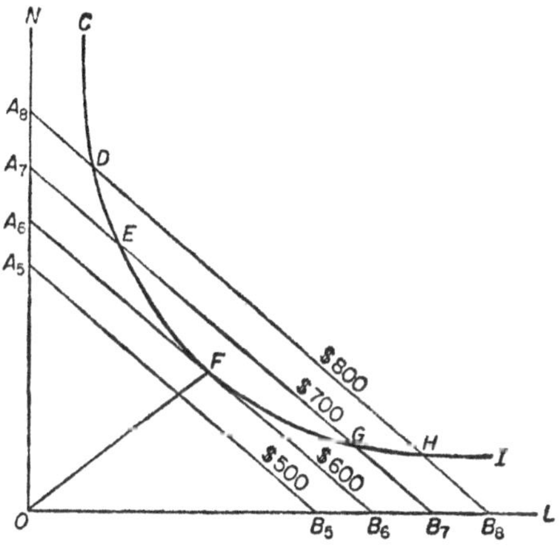

Figure 40

preneur in any given process can vary the amount of N and L he employs to produce a given output of each of his products with a given input of each of the other factors. The curve $CDEFGHI$ describes the combinations of N and L needed for this purpose. We can draw equi-cost lines A_5B_5, A_6B_6, etc., which show, at the ruling prices of N and L, the combinations of N and L which can be purchased for \$500, \$600, etc. The entrepreneur will move down the curve $CDEFGHI$ till he minimizes his L–N costs; this will occur when the curve is tangential to the lowest equi-cost line; at D or H his L–N costs would be \$800, at E or G \$700, and at F only \$600. There is a high elasticity of substitution between L and N if a small percentage change in the slope of the AB lines would cause a large percentage change in the slope of the line OF (cf. p. 115 above).

The entrepreneur will be maximizing his profit only if he is unable to make any further substitutions between any pair of his inputs such as to reduce his costs at current factor prices. If the elasticity of substitution between the various pairs of his inputs are in general high, his input programme is a flexible one; if they are low, it is a rigid one.

Marginal adjustments of type (iii) are illustrated in Figure 41. Our entrepreneur now considers the relationship between any one factor in his input programme (say, *L*) and any one product in his output programme (say, *X*). Given the inputs of all other factors and the outputs of all other products there is a relationship between his input of *L* and output of *X* represented by the curve *OCDEF*. Given the price of *L* and the price of *X* we can draw a series of equi-surplus lines such as A_5B_5. Suppose the price of *X* is such that OA_5

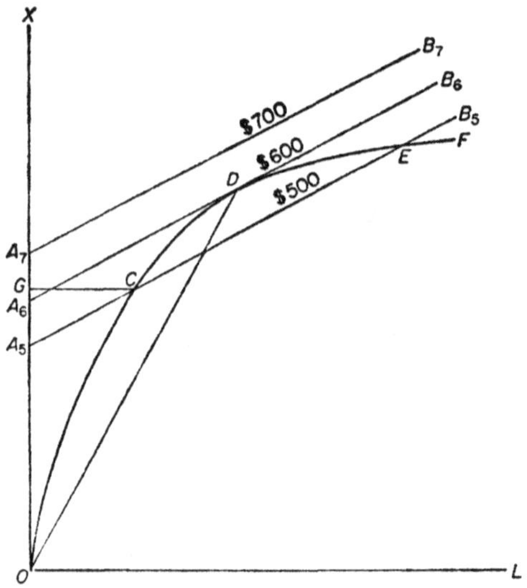

Figure 41

of *X* would sell for \$500; and suppose that the price of *L* is such that *GC* units of *L* have the same value as GA_5 units of *X*. Then any point on the line A_5B_5 represents a surplus of \$500 of the receipts of our entrepreneur from sales of *X* over his purchases of *L*. Similar lines A_6B_6, A_7B_7, etc., can be drawn for surpluses of \$600, \$700, etc., of receipts from *X* over payments for *L*. Our entrepreneur will move up the curve *OCDEF* until it is tangential to his highest equi-surplus line as at *D* in Figure 41; in other words he will employ more and more *L* to produce more and more *X* until the marginal product of *L* in terms of *X* is equal to the real wage rate of *L* measured in terms of *X*. The productive relationship between *L* and *X* has a high elasticity of transformation if a small change in the slope of the *AB*-lines causes a large change in the slope of the line *OD* (p. 119 above).

Our entrepreneur will be maximizing his profit only if he has adjusted his production programme so as to make it impossible to affect his receipts by more than his payments by taking on more or less of any one input to produce more or less of any one output. If in general the elasticities of transformation between his various pairs of inputs and outputs are high, his production programme is a flexible one; if in general they are low, then it is a rigid one.

We shall speak of a flexible process as one in which output programmes, input programmes, and production programmes are flexible, and of a rigid process as one in which these programmes are rigid.

We can now consider how a many-product many-factor system will adjust itself to a change of conditions. We imagine our system to start in an equilibrium situation in which at the ruling prices of the factors and the products it does not pay to contract (or eliminate) or to expand (or introduce) any particular process and in which all entrepreneurs operating particular processes have no incentive to make further marginal adjustments to their output programmes, input programmes, or production programmes. Further we assume that, at the ruling prices of the products and with the ruling distribution of incomes among the owners of the factors of production (corresponding to the ruling prices of the factors of production), consumers demand the amounts of each product which are being produced for the market.

Let us suppose that in this system there is a change of some consumers' needs and tastes which shifts demand away from product *Y* on to product *X*. We have already examined at some length in Chapter II what would be the effect upon the ruling prices of *X* and *Y* and of other products in the market if the supplies of the various products and the distribution of income among consumers remained unchanged. The prices of *X* and of close substitutes for *X* in consumers' demands would go up, while the prices of goods which were complementary in some uses to *X* might fall. On the other hand the prices of *Y* and of goods which were close substitutes for *Y* might well fall, while the prices of goods which were complementary in some uses to *Y* might rise.

Now if the processes which were intensive in the output of *Y* and of the products whose prices had fallen in sympathy with *Y* were *L*-intensive in their inputs and if the processes which were intensive in the output of *X* and of the products whose prices had risen in sympathy with *X* were *N*-intensive in their inputs, attempts to expand the profitable *X*-intensive processes and to contract the unprofitable *Y*-intensive processes would cause an indirect increase in the demand for *N* and fall in the demand for *L*. (A shift of demand from clothing to food would have caused an indirect shift of demand away from labour to land.) In consequence the price of *L* (wage of labour) would fall and the price of *N* (rent of land) would rise.

This would give rise to profits in all other *L*-intensive processes and to losses in all other *N*-intensive processes in the economy; and the former would be expanded and the latter contracted. Suppose there to be some process which is very *L*-intensive in its input but *W*-intensive in its output, while there is some other process which is *N*-intensive in its input but *Z*-intensive in its output. The former process will be expanded so that the output of *W* is expanded, while the latter process is contracted so that the output of *Z* is contracted. The price of *W* falls and of *Z* rises. If in consumers' consumption *W* is a good substitute for other products, the increased supplies of *W* can be readily absorbed. Similarly if *Z* is a good substitute for other products, the decreased supplies *Z* will be readily accepted and demand will be shifted to other products. (In terms of our example, the initial shift of demand from clothing to food lowers the wage rate and raises the rent of land; this lowers the cost of other labour-intensive manufactures like cameras and raises the cost of other land-intensive goods like housing. Labour released from a contraction of clothing production can be more readily absorbed into the system if consumers shift easily to the consumption of labour-intensive cameras when their price falls; and the land required for an expansion of food production can be more readily released from other parts of the system if consumers shift readily away from the consumption of land-intensive dwelling space when its cost rises.)

In general as the prices of factors and of products are affected by these general repercussions throughout the system there will be an expansion of those processes which are intensive in the factors which have fallen in price and in the products which have risen in price and there will be a contraction of those processes which are intensive in the factors which have risen in price and in the products which have fallen in price. These expansions and contractions will serve to make good use of factors which have become relatively abundant, to economize in the use of factors which have become scarce, to increase the supply of products which have become scarce, and to reduce the supply of products which are in relative abundance. The ease of adjustment will clearly be the greater (i.e. will require smaller changes in product and factor prices) (i) the more readily consumers will shift their demands from high priced to low priced products and (ii) the more varied and the more finely graduated are the technically available processes so that processes which use cheap factors can replace those which use dear factors, processses which produce expensive products can replace those which produce cheap products, and processes which use a cheap factor to produce an expensive product can replace those which rely on an expensive factor to produce a cheap product.

It is of interest to note that while the shift of demand from *Y* to *X* will cause the new equilibrium price of *X* to be higher relatively to the price of *Y*, it will not necessarily cause a rise in the absolute money price of *X* and a fall in the absolute money price of *Y*. Suppose that we have only two factors *L* and *N* and that we have seven products *T*, *U*, *V*, *W*, *X*, *Y*, *Z*. Suppose that the ratio of *N* to *L* falls as we move from the production of *T* to that of *U*, from the production of *U* to that of *V*, and so on down the scale to *Z* which is the most *L*-intensive product of all. Suppose that *W* employs a ratio of *N* to *L* equal to the national average. Since *Y* is labour-intensive relatively to *X*, a shift of demand from *Y* to *X* will raise the demand for *N* and reduce the demand for *L*. Since we are assuming a constant money national income and constant supplies of *L* and *N*, this means that the money rate of rent must go up and the money wage rate down. Since *W* employs *L* and *N* in the national average, the rise in the price of *N* will exactly offset the fall in the price of *L* in so far as the cost of *W* is concerned. The money cost of *W* will remain unchanged; but the money costs of *V*, *U*, and *T* will rise in increasing amounts since *V*, *U*, and *T* are increasingly *N*-intensive and the money costs of *X*, *Y*, and *Z* will fall in increasing amounts because *X*, *Y*, and *Z* are increasingly *L*-intensive. In this simple model the final result of a shift of demand from *Y* to *X* would be that the money cost and so the price of *W* remained unchanged, the money costs and so prices of *V*, *U*, and *T* would rise progressively in that order, and the money costs and prices of *X*, *Y*, and *Z* would all fall progressively in that order. The shift of demand from *Y* to *X* would in the end have caused the price of *X* to rise relatively to the price of *Y* by causing the money price of *Y* to fall more than the money price of *X*.

As a result of the shift of demand from *Y* to *X* marginal adjustments will be made within processes similar to the adjustments between processes which we have examined in the proceeding paragraphs. When initially the price of *X* rises and of *Y* falls as the direct result of the increased demand for *X* and of the reduced demand for *Y*, entrepreneurs who are operating processes which produce both *X* and *Y* will have an incentive to adjust their output programmes so that more *X* and less *Y* are produced. If the system of adjustments involved a change in factor prices (for example, in the case we have examined above, a rise in the price of *N* and fall in the price of L),[1] entrepreneurs using both L and N will have an incentive to use more of the cheaper L and less of the more expensive N in their input programmes. At the same time in various processes entrepreneurs will now find it profitable to take on more L to produce X and/or less N to produce Y. In general as the adjustments take place in the economic system entrepreneurs will have an incentive within any process to shift their output programme from lower to higher priced products, their input programmes from higher to lower priced factors, and their production programmes so as to employ more lower-priced factors to produce more higher priced products. The more flexible are the various processes in these three ways, the more readily will it be possible to make the necessary change in the quantities of the products produced with the minimum of change in the prices of the products or of the factors of production.

The more flexible (i.e. sensitive to price changes) are consumers' demand, and entrepreneur's output programmes, input programmes, and production programmes and the greater the range and the more varied and finely graded the product- and factor-intensities of technically known processes, the more readily can the economic system be adjusted to changes in demand without marked changes in product prices or in the distribution of money incomes due to changes of factor prices.

In a many-factor many-product economy there may, however, exist complementarities which may exaggerate the changes in particular prices needed to effect particular adjustments. These relationships may exist (i) in consumers' demand for final products, (ii) in producers' output of products, or (iii) in producers' demands for factors of production. We will consider each of these three possibilities.

(i) Suppose Pens and Pencils to be close substitutes in consumers' demand, but Pens and Ink to be complements in consumers' demand (cf. pp. 52–53 above). Suppose that in the course of some adjustment in the economy (such as the shift of demand from clothing to

[1] In the preceding paragraphs we have shown how the expansion of an X-intensive process and a contraction of a Y-intensive process might have this effect, if the X-intensive process were N-intensive and the Y-intensive process were L-intensive. But an exactly similar effect might result from marginal adjustments within any process. For example, suppose that a rise in the price of X (mutton) and fall in the price of Y (wool) caused an entrepreneur (sheep-farmer) who produced both products to increase the ratio of X to Y produced with a given amount of input of L and N. But if for some technical reason wool-producing sheep required rather more human attention than mutton-producing sheep, the marginal rise in the ratio of X to Y in the sheep-farmers' output programme might, at current prices of L and N, cause him to make a marginal increase in the ratio of N to L in his input programme. Within the process X is N-intensive and Y L-intensive.

food which we have described above) the wage rate of labour falls and of the rent of land rises. Suppose that Pens were labour-intensive and that Pencils and Ink were land-intensive in their production. Authors shift from the use of the more expensive land-intensive Pencils to the use of the cheaper labour-intensive Pens. This releases land needed for food production and gives employment to labour released from clothing production. But unfortunately Ink is needed to go with the Pens and the increased demand for Ink, being land-intensive, in itself accentuates the scarcity of land.

(ii) When the price of one product (*X*) goes up relatively to the others (*YZ*), entrepreneurs will plan to increase the output of *X* relatively to other outputs. If there were only two products, *X* and *Y*, this would mean planning to use a given amount of resources to produce more *X* and less *Y*. When there are three products *XYZ* this means planning to use a given amount of resources to produce more *X* and less *YZ*. But this does not necessarily mean producing less *Y* and less *Z*. If, for example, *X* and *Y* went close together technically in an output programme, it might involve producing somewhat more *Y* to accompany the increased production of *X* and, in consequence, greatly reducing the output of *Z*. In this case *X* and *Y* are complementary elements in the production programme.

Let us take an example. Suppose *X* to be mutton, *Y* wool, and *Z* wheat. A rise in the price of mutton relatively to that of wool and wheat causes an entrepreneur engaged in mixed farming to produce more mutton. But this will involve producing more sheep. It is true that the farmer will attempt to breed mutton-producing rather than wool-producing sheep; but if the technical possibilities of varying the breed are limited, the net result will be a shift from cereal production to sheep farming with a consequential reduction in the output of wheat and increase in the output of mutton, combined however with some increase in the output of wool. Now it might so happen that in the particular adjustment which was needed in the economy, wool was a product of which a smaller rather than a larger supply was required. The fact that *X* (of which a larger supply was needed) was a complement in production to *Y* (of which a smaller supply was needed) would make the adjustment more difficult.

It is to be observed that this penomenon of complementarity in production can occur either within a process or as between two or more processes. If mixed farming is a single process, then the rise in the price of mutton causes our farmer within his single farm to produce more mutton and wool and less wheat. But sheep-farming and cereal-production might be quite different processes. If the former is mutton-intensive while the latter is wheat-intensive, an increased demand for mutton relatively to wheat will cause an expansion of the former and contraction of the latter process. But if the former is also wool-intensive, an indirect result may be an increase in the output of wool which may make the total adjustment of the economy so much the more difficult.

(iii) When the price of one factor (*L*) goes down relatively to the others (*MN*), entrepreneurs will plan to increase the input of *L* relatively to that of the others. If there were only two factors, *L* and *N*, this would mean planning to produce a given output by the employment of more *L* and less *N*. When there are three factors *LMN*, this means planning to produce a given output by using more *L* and less *MN*. But this does not necessarily mean using less *M* and less *N*. If, for example, *L* and *M* went close together technically in an input programme (each plumber must have his boy), it might involve employing more *M* to accompany the increased employment of *L* and, in consequence, greatly reducing the employment of *N*. In this case *L* and *M* are complementary factors of production.

Such a situation could make adjustments more difficult. Suppose that *L* was particular plentiful in a given situation and needed to be absorbed into the economy; but suppose at the same time that *M* was scarce relatively to *N*. The absorption of *L* into the system would have increased rather than have reduced the scarcity of *M* relatively to *N*.

Once more it is to be noted that this relationship of complementarity between factors can occur within or between processes. When the price of *L* falls relatively to *M* and *N*, an entrepreneur operating a particular process may take on less *N* and more *L*, together with some additional *M* to go with the *L*. Or there may be two quite separate processes to produce a given product (e.g. natural and synthetic rubber). The one process may be very *L*-intensive and the other very *N*-intensive. When the price of *L* falls, the former will be expanded and the latter contracted. But the former process may also be somewhat *M*-intensive. In consequence the adjustment which absorbs *L* may at the same time increase an existing scarcity of *M* relatively to *N*.

The two phenomena of complementarity between outputs and complementarity between inputs which we have just discussed can be of great importance in a constant-returns-to-scale production system.[1] Suppose that in the course of some adjustment the prices of some factors and products have fallen and of other factors and products have risen. This will make any process which is intensive in the cheap factors and/or the expensive products especially pro-

[1] See the Note appended at the end of this chapter (pp. 141–6).

fitable and any process which is intensive in the expensive factors and/or the cheap products especially unprofitable.

The former will expand and the latter will contract. With constant returns to scale there is nothing in the technical production function itself to halt the expansion of the former process and the contraction of the latter process; a larger scale of production does not in itself raise costs nor does a smaller scale of production reduce costs. Equilibrium is restored solely by the market effects of the expansion of the profitable process and the contraction of the unprofitable process; the selling prices of the products in which the expanding process is intensive will fall as their supplies are increased and the purchase price of the factors in which the expanding process is intensive will be bid up as the demand for them rises; and conversely with the product and factor prices in the contracting processes. In general these forces will exercise a very powerful influence in adjusting amounts of input and output so as to bring down the exceptionally high product and factor prices and to pull up the exceptionally low product and factor prices.

But it is clear that incidentally they may exercise a powerful leverage in making still scarcer some particular product or factor which has already become scarce or in making still more plentiful some particular product or factor which has already become plentiful. Thus an exceptionally profitable multi-product process may well contain one relatively minor factor which is already scarce and/or one relatively minor product which is already plentiful; and its general expansion will drive up still further the price of that already scarce factor (which is an input-complement with the other main factors) and drive down still further the price of that already plentiful product (which is an output-complement with the other main products).

So far we have considered the possibilities that complementarities in output programmes and complementarities in input programmes may intensify the scale on which some price changes must take place in order to restore equilibrium. There is also the possibility of a similar perverse relationship in a transformation programme which we may perhaps call an 'antipathy between an input and an output'. We may explain the significance of this phenomenon in the following way.

Consider the transformation of L into Y with other inputs and outputs constant. If the price of L falls and/or the price of Y rises more L will be employed to produce more Y and this will tend to keep up the price of L and to drive down the price of Y.

But suppose now that within a multi-product multi-factor process one is considering the employment of L to produce X and Y. The price of *L* has fallen, while the prices of *X* and *Y* have both risen in the same proportion; more *L* is employed; more of *XY* as a whole will be produced; but it is possible that while much more *X* is produced the output of *Y* is actually reduced. In this case there could be said to be an antipathy between *L* and *Y* in the production programme using *L* to produce *XY*. A possible explanation could be on the following lines. *X* is the main product; when more *L* is employed with the other inputs, it means shifting the technique of production in the process on to a form which employed a higher ratio of *L* to other inputs; this change of technique might cause somewhat less of some by-product, *Y*, to be produced. The effect would be to help to maintain the price of *L* through the increased demand for *L*, to help to keep down the price of *X* through the increased supply of *X*, but to intensify the rise in the price of *Y*.

Or suppose that within a multi-product multi-factor process one is considering the production of *X* by means of *L* and *N*. The price of *X* rises while the prices of *L* and *N* both fall in the same proportion; more *X* is produced and more of *LN* as a whole must be employed to produce it; but it is possible that while much more *L* is employed a smaller amount of *N* is needed. There is an antipathy between *N* and *X* in the production programme of producing *X* by means of *L* and *N*. This could be explained by the fact that to increase the proportion of *X* in the total output of the process involved a change in the techniques of production which called for the employment of a smaller total amount of some secondary factor, *N*. As a result the price of *X* would be kept down and the price of *L* would be kept up, but the already low-priced *N* would find that the demand for it was still further depressed.

Antipathies between inputs and outputs are probably of secondary importance. But complementarities between inputs and between outputs may well be important phenomena which make the economic system appreciably more rigid in its adjustment to change than would otherwise be the case. They can constitute important reasons why relatively large changes in relative prices may sometimes be necessary.

We have already noted in Chapter IV (pp. 80–82) another type of market relationship which may intensify the scale of price changes necessary to adjust the economic system to some outside disturbance. If in our example the shift of demand from *Y* to *X* causes a fall in the wage rate and a rise in the rate of rent, and if the ownership of land is unequally divided among the population, there will be a shift in the distribution of income away from those families who live mainly on wage income to those who live mainly on rent income. Either because income per head is higher for the one class than for the other or simply because their needs and tastes are different, this change in the distribution of incomes may, quite apart from any price changes, cause further shifts in demand. It is quite accidental whether these shifts mitigate or accentuate the necessary price changes. If workers consume labour-intensive clothing and landlords land-intensive food, then the shift from wages to rents which would result from an initial shift of demand from clothing to food will accentuate the fall in the demand for clothing relatively to food, which will accentuate the change in the distribution of income, and so on. The other adjustments in the economy will have to be all the more marked to compensate for this perverse income effect upon demand.

Thus adjustment will be easy in an economy in which (i) substitutability is marked between different goods in the pattern of consumers' demands, (ii) processes of production are flexible, (iii) there is a wide and varied range of processes, (iv) complementarities in consumption, outputs, and inputs and antipathies between inputs and outputs are rare, and (v) there are few perverse income effects. On the face of it in the modern economy, with such a wide range of alternative supplies for consumers and so rich a system of technological alternatives, it would seem probable that moderate price changes could lead to extensive changes in the pattern of outputs.

Note to Chapter IX

SUBSTITUTABILITY, COMPLEMENTARITY, TRANSFORMABILITY, AND ANTIPATHY IN THE CASE OF A CONSTANT-RETURNS-TO-SCALE PRODUCTION FUNCTION

Consider first the most straightforward case of Substitutability and Complementarity in consumers' demand with three goods—Pencils, Pens, and Ink. We start in equilibrium; there is a reduction in the price of Pens combined with a reduction in the consumer's money income such that he remains on the same indifference curve; he buys more Pens and less of other goods in general; Pens are substitutes for other goods in general; but if he buys more Ink (to go with the Pens) and a great deal less Pencils, then Ink is said to be complementary to Pens.

Note that there are *four* variables concerned: Pencils, Pens, Ink, and Utility. One variable (Utility) is kept constant in amount; two variables (Ink and Pencils) are allowed to vary in amount but kept constant in price; and one variable (Pens) has its price reduced by a given specified amount. We are in fact minimizing the cost of a given amount of Utility when the price of one input (Pens) changes and the price of the other inputs (Pencils and Ink) remain unchanged.

We may regard the input of Pens, Pencils and Ink as 'producing' the output Utility, or

$$U = F(K, L, M)$$

where U is the amount of Utility and K, L, and M the amount of Pens, Pencils, and Ink consumed. We could write this 'production' function as

$$0 = \phi(U, K, L, M)$$

But we can, of course, have a multi-product production function

$$0 = \phi(W, X, Y, Z, \ldots K, L, M, N, \ldots)$$

where in any process of production the inputs K, L, M, N, etc., produce the outputs W, X, Y, Z, etc. Suppose further that this production function showed constant returns to scale in the sense that if one increased each and every input by 1 per cent and each and every output except one by 1 per cent, then the best that one could do would be to increase this one remaining output also by 1 per cent. Our problem is how to define and handle the ideas of substitutability, complementarity, and similar relationships between these input and output variables.

We can take the hint from the analogy with consumers' demand. In order merely to define our terms we must divide the variables in our production function into three groups—A, B, and C:—

Group A. One or more variable (like Utility in the previous example) must be held constant in amount. The producer's object is then to maximize the quasi-rent or profit earned on this group of inputs or outputs by varying the amounts of the other inputs which he purchases or outputs which he sells at their new given market prices.

Group B. One or more variable (like Ink and Pencils in our first example) must be held constant in price but allowed to vary in quantity. If we are to have the possibility of relationships like complementarity, this group must contain more than one variable.

Group C. One variable (like Pens in our first example) must have its price changed and be allowed to vary in quantity. This is the variable whose relationship with other variables we are defining.

As far as the production function itself is concerned, it is completely arbitrary which variables are put into which Group. Putting the variables into the different Groups is simply a means of defining relationships between the variables. With our constant-returns-to-scale production function, for each set of definitions some variables must be held constant (i.e. Group A must contain some items). Otherwise when the price of the Group C variable was lowered, the process would become profitable if that variable were an input and unprofitable if that variable were an output. If there were constant returns to scale, if no variables were held constant in amount, and if all prices were kept constant at their new level, then in the former case the process would expand indefinitely towards infinity and in the latter case it would contract indefinitely towards zero. Only the existence of the constant variables keeps the process at a positive finite level; but as far as the production function itself is concerned it is wholly arbitrary which variable or variables are kept constant. In fact it will be the market conditions which, taken together with the production function, will determine which variables will alter most in price and which in quantity. If for some outputs the demand was completely inelastic and for some inputs the supply was totally inelastic, then these variables would because of the market conditions be held constant. If for the other outputs the demand was infinitely elastic and for the other inputs the supply was infinitely elastic, then these variables would because of the market conditions be variable in amount but constant in price. Of course, in any given situation the variables do not fall into either one or other of these two extreme market categories. We merely assume that some vary only in price and others only in quantity in order to isolate certain relationships in order to define our terms.

Let us consider certain cases by considering the kind of variables which we put into Groups B and C (and thus by a process of elimination into Group A).

Case (*i*) Suppose that both Groups B and C contain only inputs, Group B containing *KLM* and Group C containing *N*. All outputs and all other inputs are kept constant. The price of *N* falls; more *N* is employed; less is spent on *KLM* as a whole and *N* is an input substitute for *KL* and *M* as a whole; but more of one particular member of *KLM* (say, *M*) may be bought in which case we say that *N* is input-complementary with *M* in respect of *K* and *L*. Note that it is quite possible that if Group B had been made up differently, (say of *IJM* instead of *KLM* with inputs *K* and *L* instead of inputs *I* and *J* now constant in amounts) the input *N* might not now be input-complementary with *M*. If you have to use *N* instead of *K* or *L*, you may need some *M* to 'go with' the *N*. But if you have to use *N* instead of *I* or *J*, you may not need any more *M* to 'go with' the *N*. We express this by saying that *N* is input-complementary with *M* in respect of *K* and *L* but is an input-substitute for *M* in respect of *I* and *J*.

Case (*ii*). Suppose that both Groups contain only outputs, Group B containing *XYZ* and Group C containing *W*. The price of *W* falls; less *W* and more *XYZ* as a whole is produced; *W* and *XYZ* as a whole are output-substitutes; but when *W* (wool) goes down some other output X (mutton) may also go down in which case W is an output-complement of X in respect of Y and Z. Once again whether X and W are output-substitutes or output-complements depends upon the choice of the other members of Group B.

Case (*iii*) Suppose that Group B contains only outputs (XYZ) and Group C an input (L). The price of L falls; more L is employed and as a result more XYZ as a whole is produced. To use Professor Hick's term, L is transformable into XYZ as a whole. But when L goes up, one output (X) may go down while the others (YZ) go up all the more. If L are bulls, X is chinaware and Y and Z are beef and veal, then an increase in L may increase the output of Y and Z but reduce the output of X in this multi-product agricultural-industrial process. L and X may be said to be antipathetic in respect of Y and Z.

Case (*iv*) Suppose that Group B contains only inputs (LMN) and Group C an output (X). The price of X falls; less is produced; and less of LMN as a group is employed. X is transformable into LMN as a whole. But within LMN there may be some factor L which is employed in greater amount when less X is produced, and L may then be said to be antipathetic to X in respect of M and N.

Case (*v*) Group B contains inputs and outputs ($XYMN$) and Group C contains an input (L). The price of L falls; more L is employed; on balance XY must go up and/or MN must fall, or more accurately the sum $P_xX + P_yY - P_mN - P_nN$ must rise, where P_x, P_y, P_m, and P_n are the money prices of X, Y, M, and N respectively, L is on balance transformable into XY and/or input-substitutable with MN. But a particular output (X) may go down in which case L is antipathetic with X in respect of YMN and/or a particular input (M) may go up, in which case L is input-complementary with M in respect of XYN. There are in mixed cases of this kind some interesting relationships between input-complementarity and transformability and between input-substitutability and antipathy.

Thus consider the case in which L and M together produce X and Y within a process in which this sub-activity, as it were, is not very drastically held up by the constant Group A, i.e. by the fact that some other outputs (Z, etc.) must not be produced in greater quantity or that some other factors (K, etc.) cannot be used in greater amount. A fall in the cost of L may then give rise to a very large expansion of the sub-activity in which XY is produced by LM. There will be a very high elasticity of transformability of L into XY (in respect of M) but at the expense, as it were, of a very large increase in employment of M, i.e. at the expense of a high degree of input-complementarity between L and M (in respect of XY).

Or consider another case in which within this sub-activity Y is the main product which can be produced either with one technical method using mainly L or with another technical method using mainly M, but that when it is produced by the one technical means (largely with L) it is produced more or less alone whereas when it is produced by the other technical means (by M) a bye-product X is also produced. Then a high degree of substitutability between L and M (in respect of XY) will mean that as L is used instead of M the output of the bye-product X is reduced. The high degree of input-substitutability between L and M (in respect of XY) is offset by some considerable degree of antipathy between L and X (in respect of YM).

Thus a high degree of transformability may often involve a high measure of input-complementarity; and a high degree of input-substitutability can well be combined with considerable antipathy.

Case (*vi*) Group B contains inputs and outputs ($XYMN$) and Group C contains an output (Z). The price of Z falls; less Z is produced; more XY as a group is produced and/or less MN as a group is employed, i.e. $P_xX + P_yY - P_mM - P_nN$ must fall. Z is on balance output-substitutable for XY and/or transformable into MN. But a particular output (X) may go down in which case Z and X are output-complements in respect of YMN and/or a particular input (M) may go up, in which case Z and M are antipathetic in respect of XYN.

If making ZX by means of MN were a rather independent sub-activity in a whole process, a fall in the price of Z might cause a great contraction in the whole of this sub-activity. There would then be a very high degree of transformability of Z into MN (in respect of X); but if X were a joint-product with Z in this sub-activity, this could imply a very marked degree of output-complementarity between X and Z (in respect of MN).

Or if in this same sub-activity, it was easy to produce X rather than Z but this meant using a rather different technique which required a rather higher ratio of M to N, then a fall in the price of Z might cause a large fall in the output of Z, some increase in the output of X, some increase in the input of M, but a large fall in the input of N. There would be a high degree of substitutability between X and Z (in respect of MN) but this would be combined with some antipathy between Z and M (in respect of XN).

Thus in a multi-output multi-input constant-returns-to-scale production function there are relationships like substitutability and complementarity which depend solely upon the technical conditions of production. Input-substitutability, output-substitutability, and transformability are the rule. If one includes in Group B only one variable, one is bound to find that it is input-substitutable, output substitutable, or transformable with the variable in Group C. It is possible that technical conditions are such that whatever combinations of variables are selected for inclusion in Groups B and C no examples of input-complementarity, output-complementarity, or antipathy could be found. If they are found, they are the exceptional 'perverse' cases.

But it is a nonsense question to ask without further specification whether two variables stand in this 'perverse' relationship to each other or not. The question becomes meaningful only when one specifies which of the other variables are in Group A and which in Group B. One can only say that one variable stands in this 'perverse' relationship with another in respect of the other specified variables included in Group B for the purpose of that particular definition.

The sort of purpose for which one needs to use these definitions in economic analysis is to cope with a question of the following kind: 'Given a once-for-all reduction in the price of, say, L and given the price elasticities of demand for all the outputs (XYZ, etc.) and the price elasticities of supply for all the remaining inputs (M, N, etc.), what will be the ultimate equilibrium quantities in a given productive process which is subject to the motives of profit maximization in conditions of perfect potential competition?' The fall in the price of an input threatens an infinite expansion of the process. But this will be most effectively impeded by the inability to sell those products for which the demand is least elastic or to obtain those inputs for which the supply is least elastic. It may often be helpful to think of a group of such inputs and outputs as being constant in amount and considering the relationships of input and output-substitutability and complementarity and of transformability and antipathy which would in that extreme case exist between L and the remaining variables.

CHAPTER X

CHANGES IN TECHNICAL KNOWLEDGE AND IN FACTOR SUPPLIES

In the previous chapters we have considered various models of stationary competitive equilibria. In the last four of these chapters we have examined how the equilibrium would be affected by a change in consumers' needs and tastes, and we have used these changes on the demand side as means of illustration of the problems of readjustment. But changes on the demand side are not the only changes which can disturb an equilibrium. Changes on the supply side are in fact probably of more importance in the real world. The purpose of this chapter is to examine the way in which a many-factor many-product economy of the type discussed in the last chapter might adjust itself to changes in the conditions of supply.

Changes in supply conditions may take either of two forms. (i) There may be an improvement in technical knowledge—an invention—which enables a greater output to be produced with a given amount of factors of production. (ii) There may be a change in the supply of a factor of production—for example, an increase in the size of the working population. We will examine each of these in turn.

Suppose then that there is an improvement in technical knowledge which enables a particular process to be used to produce more output with a given input. There will then be some percentage increase in output per unit of input which this process could achieve if the compositions of its input programme and of its output programme were unchanged in the sense that an unchanged ratio between its various inputs and an unchanged ratio between its various outputs was maintained.

Suppose, for example, in the process in question unchanged amounts of *L*, *N*, and *M* could now produce 10 per cent more of each of *X*, *Y*, and *Z*. If the money prices of each of the factors of production were unchanged but the money prices of each of the products fell by 10 per cent, then the process would continue just to cover its costs. With productivity up by 10 per cent but selling prices down by 10 per cent the balance between revenue and costs is unchanged. There would be no incentive to expand or to contract the scale of operations of the process, measuring the scale by the amount of factors employed.

But it would not, of course, follow that the entrepreneur would have no incentive to change the composition of his output programme or of his input programme. If the invention had been one which particularly favoured the production of Y within the process, then at unchanged relative prices of X, Y, and Z the entrepreneur might find it profitable to increase the ratio of Y to X and Z in his output programme. For example, an agricultural invention might make it easier to breed wool-bearing rather than mutton-bearing sheep; at unchanged relative prices of wool and mutton farmers would produce a higher ratio of wool to mutton. In this case the invention can be said to be technically biased towards the production of Y (wool) and against the production of X and Z (e.g. mutton).

Similarly, the invention might be such as to make it profitable for the entrepreneur at unchanged prices of the factors of production to take on less of one factor and more of another to produce the 10 per cent greater volume of output. For example, the invention might be one which in particular enabled farmers to economize in the use of one type of labour rather than in the use of other types of labour or of land. In this case at the unchanged prices of various grades of labour and land the farmers would take on less of the one particular grade of labour (L) and more of the other factors (M and N) to produce the 10 per cent larger output. In this case the invention could be said to be technically biased towards the saving of L and against the saving of M and N.

If this process were the only one which existed in the economy, we should now have a complete description of the invention. With our example we could say that it increased overall productivity by 10 per cent and that it was biased in favour of Y production in so far as entrepreneurs at unchanged relative product prices would increase the proportion of sales of Y in their total receipts and that it was biased in favour of L-saving in so far as at unchanged factor prices they would reduce the proportion of purchases of L in their total costs. Another way of putting this same set of definitions (and one which we shall find convenient when we come to consider an economy using many processes) is as follows. The invention is one which would enable the same resources to be used to produce 10 per cent more of every product. If with unchanged factor prices and with all product prices 10 per cent lower, entrepreneurs would in fact choose to use the same factors to produce 10 per cent more of every product, then the invention is a neutral one.[1] But if the price

[1] The fact that with a neutral invention entrepreneurs would be in equilibrium if all factor prices and inputs were unchanged, all outputs were up by 10 per cent, and all product prices were down by 10 per cent does not, of course, imply that

of *L* would have to fall relatively to the price of other factors (or if the price of *Y* would have to fall relatively to the price of other products) to induce the entrepreneurs to go on using the same amount of each factor to produce 10 per cent more of each product, then the invention may be said to be biased towards the saving of *L* (towards the production of *Y*).

But suppose that the process in which the invention takes place is only one among many used in the economy. How are we now to measure the overall increase in the economy's productivity which is caused by the invention and how are we to decide whether on balance for the economy as a whole the invention is biased either for or against the production of a particular product or for or against the saving of a particular factor? Suppose, for example, that the process in question is especially *L*-intensive in its inputs and *Y*-intensive in its outputs. It is, for example, a labour(*L*)-intensive industry producing textiles (*Y*). The invention in this process itself might have no technical bias. That is to say, if all factor prices remained the same and if all product prices fell by 10 per cent, the entrepreneur in the textile industry might have no incentive to change any input or output. But clearly for the economy as a whole this would be a very biased invention since it is above all an invention which enables the same amount of resources to produce more *Y* or the same amount of output to be produced with less *L*. An invention which takes place in a process which is *L*-intensive and *Y*-intensive can, therefore, be said to have a structural bias in favour of saving *L* and producing *Y*.

We have now somehow to combine these notions of technical and of structural bias in order to assess the net overall bias of the invention in the whole economy. We can do this by thinking of the whole economy as if it were one large super-process. Suppose then that there is an invention in the *L*- and *Y*-intensive (textile) industry which would enable the same factors in this industry to produce 10 per cent more of all its outputs. If an appropriate amount of factors of production were moved out of the textile industry into other industries, it would be possible to make use of the special textile invention to obtain a uniform increase in the output of all products in the economy. To take a very simple example, suppose that labour were the only factor in the economy, that an invention raised output per head in the textile industry by 10 per cent, and that initially 20 per cent of the total labour force was employed in the textile industry.

the consumers' markets would be in equilibrium at these unchanged money incomes and these new prices and outputs. That is another matter to which we shall turn in due course.

Then a shift of 1·45 per cent of the total labour force from the textile industry to other industries would enable all output to be raised by the same percentage, namely 1·825 per cent.[1] If we allow for the fact that there are many different factors, we suppose that there is a net transfer of resources from the textile industry to other industries, so as to allow all outputs to go up by the same percentage; but we suppose that the resources of the community are reshuffled among the various processes in the economy in such a way that with the same total resources in the economy as a whole there is the greatest possible equal percentage increase in every output. If, for example, this percentage were 2 per cent, we would say that the particular invention represented an overall increase in productivity for the economy as a whole of 2 per cent. It would enable the given resources of the community, if used in the most effective way, to produce a 2 per cent increase in the output of every product.

Suppose that in these conditions the price of every factor were unchanged and that the price of every product had fallen by 2 per cent. For the economy as a whole receipts would equal costs; the money national income would be unchanged because the same amount of each factor would be receiving the same money price, and money national expenditure would be unchanged because 2 per cent more of each product would be selling at a 2 per cent lower money price. But some processes would be making losses and some profits. In our example, the *L*- and *Y*-intensive textile industry would certainly be making large profits since productivity in that process has been increased by the invention by 10 per cent while product prices have fallen by only 2 per cent. Other processes would almost certainly be unprofitable since productivity has not been raised by any invention but product prices have fallen by 2 per cent. The invention would for the economy as a whole prove to be biased towards the production of *Y* since it would require a fall in the price of *Y* by more than the average 2 per cent to remove any incentive to increase the output of *Y* by more than the average 2 per cent.

To achieve the same 2 per cent increase in all outputs resources would have had to be shifted from the textile industry in which the invention took place to the other industries. What resources were released from the textile industry would depend upon factor-intensity in that industry and upon any technical bias in the invention. If the

[1] The labour force in other industries would go up from 80 to 80 + 1·45, i.e. by 1·825 per cent. The labour force in textiles would go down from 20 to 20 − 1·45, but each remaining worker would produce 10 per cent more output, so that textile output would have gone up by a proportion equal to $\frac{1\cdot 1(20 - 1\cdot 45) - 20}{20}$ or 1·825 per cent.

industry were *L*-intensive then, unless the invention were technically very biased against saving *L*, the resources released from this industry would contain an especially high proportion of *L*. This means that the other industries would have to absorb a higher than average proportion of *L* to other factors for their 2 per cent increase in output. The factor *L* would be made relatively plentiful; and entrepreneurs would in fact be prepared to employ in all industries together (including the textile industry) the same total amount of *L* only if the price of *L* had fallen. The invention would have an overall bias in favour of saving *L*.

If an invention has an overall bias in favour of saving *L*, it must have an overall bias against saving other factors in general. If the price of *L* would have to go down, the price of some other factors would have to go up in order to induce entrepreneurs to spend the same total amount of money on employing the same amount of each factor. But this does not mean that the price of every other factor would have to go up. Among the other factors there may be one (say *M*) which is a very close substitute for *L*. The result might then well be that while the price of *L* and *M* would both have to go down, the price of *N* and of other factors would have to go up in order to give entrepreneurs an incentive to employ the same amount of the factors to produce 2 per cent more of every product after the invention. The invention would be biased in favour of saving both *L* and *M* and against saving *N* and other factors.

Similarly with the products. The invention might in the way which we have explained be biased in favour of the production of *Y*. This would mean the price of *Y* would have to fall by more than the average 2 per cent in order to give entrepreneurs the incentive to increase the output of *Y* by no more than the average 2 per cent. In this case the prices of other products in general would have to rise or at least fall by less than the average 2 per cent. But this does not mean that the price of every other product would have to fall by less than 2 per cent. In our example the process in which the invention took place produced mainly textiles (*Y*) mainly with labour (*L*). There may be some other labour-intensive process producing, say, television sets. The fall in the price of labour as a result of the contraction of the textile industry might be by more than 2 per cent, in which case the cost of producing television sets might fall by more than 2 per cent. To avoid an undue incentive to the production of television sets their prices might have to fall by more than 2 per cent. In this case textiles and television sets are good substitutes for each other on the production side; they need very similar factor-inputs for their production. Although the invention took place only in the textile industry, for the economy as a whole it could have some bias in favour of the production of television sets as well as a marked bias in favour of the production of textiles. It would be biased against the production of the generality of other products.

We now have a working definition of the overall increase in productivity caused by an invention and of its overall bias for and against saving particular factors and for and against the producton of particular products. We must now consider how the economy would adjust itself to an invention. Let us first suppose that there is an invention (or set of inventions) which produces a 2 per cent increase in overall productivity and which is neutral, i.e. without bias either for or against saving any factor or for or against the production of any product. Entrepreneurs would in fact employ the same total amount of each factor to produce 2 per cent more of each product, if each factor price remained unchanged and every product price fell by 2 per cent.

What we now have to ask is whether this situation in which the productive system would be in equilibrium is one in which the market for consumption goods would also be in equilibrium. In fact every citizen's real income would have gone up by 2 per cent. Since there are so far no changes in factor prices, there would be no change in the distribution of money incomes among persons; and since every product price has fallen by 2 per cent, every housewife, no matter what is the composition of her family budget, could purchase 2 per cent more of everything. Now if all income elasticities of demand are unity (cf. pp. 41–42), when real incomes go up by 2 per cent with relative product prices unchanged, then the demand for each individual product also goes up by 2 per cent. In this case then the market for consumption goods would also be in equilibrium. With factor prices unchanged and each product down by 2 per cent (i) entrepreneurs would have an incentive to produce 2 per cent more of each product and (ii) consumers would have an incentive to consume 2 per cent more of each product.

This happy result depends upon the coincidence of three special conditions: first, that all income elasticities of demand are unity;[1] second that the invention is not biased for or against the saving of any particular factor; and third, that the invention is not biased for or against the production of any particular product.

[1] Accurately speaking, this first condition is not quite so strict. It is possible that Mrs A's income elasticity of demand for X is greater than unity but that Mrs B's is less than unity. In this case when the real incomes of Mrs A and of Mrs B both go up by 2 per cent, the total market demand for X may also go up by 2 per cent—Mrs A's by somewhat more and Mrs B's by somewhat less. The argument in the text depends upon the combined market income elasticity of demand, rather than upon each individual consumer's elasticity of demand, being equal to unity.

If income elasticities of demand are not all unity, the increase in real incomes by 2 per cent might cause the demand for some things to go up by more than 2 per cent and for others to go up by less than 2 per cent or—in the extreme case of an inferior good—actually to fall. If the invention is biased in favour of saving labour and against saving land, then this factor alone would cause the wage rate to go down and the rate of rent up, so that the national income would be redistributed against wage earners and in favour of landlords. If the families of wage earners consumed a rather different set of products from those consumed by the families of landlords, this redistribution of money income would cause the demand for some products to rise by more than 2 per cent and for others to rise by less than 2 per cent or even to fall. If the invention is biased in favour of the production of textiles, then the cost price of textiles will have fallen by more than 2 per cent, i.e. will have fallen relatively to the cost-price of other products. This change in relative prices to consumers will cause consumers to shift their demands. If the price of textiles falls heavily relatively to the price of other things and if textiles are good substitutes for a number of other things, then the amount of textiles which consumers will want to purchase may greatly exceed the 2 per cent increase in their output which the fall in the price of textiles is *ex hypothesi* designed to achieve.

We can thus think of adjustment to an invention as taking place in two stages.[1] We start in an 'initial' equilibrium. Then there is an invention. We consider the nature of an 'intermediate' equilibrium, i.e. of the changes in factor prices and of product prices which, in view of the overall biases of the invention, would be necessary to give entrepreneurs the incentive to increase every product by the same percentage as a result of the invention. We then consider whether the consumers' market would also be in balance in this 'intermediate' equilibrium. If not, then we consider the 'final' equilibrium as being the 'intermediate' equilibrium modified by shifts of consumers' demands equal to the differences between the uniform increases in all outputs which occur in the 'intermediate' equilibrium and the amounts which, in view of the changes in the distribution of the national income and of the product prices of the 'intermediate'

[1] These stages are merely a logical device for comparing the initial stationary equilibrium (*A*) with the final stationary equilibrium (*C*) by means of an artificial third equilibrium (*B*)—i.e. what is called the 'intermediate' equilibrium in the text. We compare *B* with *A* and then *C* with *B*, as a means of comparing *C* with *A*. The economy is not to be thought of as moving in time from *A* to *B* and then from *B* to *C*. In this volume we are not concerned with the dynamic process of adjustment, only with the comparison between two final stationary equilibria. The dynamic process of adjustment will be a major topic of a later volume.

equilibrium, consumers would wish to purchase. This final adjustment from the 'intermediate' to the 'final' equilibrium requires the application to the 'intermediate' equilibrium of the analysis which we have developed at length in the previous chapter to consider the effects in the economy of a shift of demand.

It is not possible to give a general account covering all possible cases. But the following is a particular example which may help the reader to apply the method to other particular cases. Consider once again a 10 per cent increase in productivity in an *L*-intensive and a *Y*-intensive industry (e.g. textiles) which would represent a 2 per cent overall increase in productivity for the economy as a whole. This invention is biased in favour of saving *L* and producing *Y*. The 'intermediate' equilibrium will thus be one in which (i) the price of *L* has fallen and of other factors (e.g. *N*) has risen, (ii) all outputs are up by 2 per cent, and (iii) the price of *Y* has fallen by more than 2 per cent while the price of the general run of products has fallen less or not at all. Suppose now that *Y* is a product for which (i) the income elasticity of demand is high and (ii) there are a large range of close substitutes in consumers' demands. Then there will be a large excess demand for textiles, and excess supply of other products in the 'intermediate' equilibrium. It is as if we started in the 'intermediate' equilibrium and were then faced with a large shift of demand away from other products on to textiles. We must now consider the adjustments discussed in the last chapter. *Y*-intensive processes will become profitable and other processes unprofitable; *Y* and close substitutes for *Y* will rise in price so that entrepreneurs rearrange their output programmes in their favour; since the textile industry is *Y*-intensive and *L*-intensive, its expansion will increase the demand for *L* relatively to other factors; the price of *L* will rise again and of other factors fall again as compared with the 'intermediate' equilibrium; input programmes will be remodelled to save *L* and production programmes remodelled to use factors whose price has fallen as compared with the 'intermediate' equilibrium to produce products whose price has risen as compared with the 'intermediate' equilibrium. If the income elasticity of demand for *Y* and the elasticity of substitution between *Y* and other products are both sufficiently high, the re-expansion of the production of *Y* from the 'intermediate' equilibrium may be so great that more resources are employed in the textile industry in the final equilibrium than in the initial equilibrium. Demands will be so shifted on to *Y* that the output of *Y* goes up by more than the 10 per cent increase in productivity in the *Y*-industry and the output of other products in general is actually reduced as a result of the invention. In this case, since the *Y*-industry is *L*-intensive, the demand for *L* will have risen relatively to the demand for other factors as between the 'initial' and the 'final' equilibrium. Income will ultimately have been redistributed in favour of *L* and against the owners of other factors such as *N*.

If, on the other hand, the income elasticity of demand for *Y* were very low (*a fortiori* if *Y* were an inferior good for which the income elasticity of demand were zero) and if the elasticity of substitution in consumers' demand between *Y* and other products were very low, then in the 'intermediate', equilibrium there might be no excess demand for *Y*—possibly even an excess supply of *Y*. The rise in real incomes and the relative fall in the price of *Y* would have stimulated a very small increase in the demand for *Y*. The depression in the demand for, and so in the price of *L*, would in this case be maintained or even accentuated in the 'final' equilibrium. The *L*-intensive *Y*-industry would be greatly contracted.

In between these two extremes is the case where the income elasticity of demand for *Y* and the elasticity of substitution between *Y* and other products were such that consumers spent the same proportion of their incomes on *Y* in the 'final' equilibrium as they did in the 'initial' equilibrium. The same proportion of the same money national income would be being spent on the purchase of factors for the *Y*-industry. Its demand for *L* would be neither expanded nor contracted; and, as far as this major influence was concerned, there would be no ultimate change in the price of *L* or of other factors of production.[1]

So much for the effects of inventions. We turn now to the second type of change on the supply side mentioned at the beginning of this chapter, namely a change in the supply of one of the factors of production. Suppose, by way of example, that there is a once-for-all increase in the supply of *L* (e.g. the number of men of working age). We started in an initial stationary competitive equilibrium. How will this change in the supply of *L* affect this equilibrium?

The immediate effect in our competitive economy would, of course, be that the excess supply in the labour market would cause the money

[1] It is interesting to note that if the owners of *L* spend an abnormally high proportion of their income on *Y* this accentuates whichever movement in the price of *L* would have taken place for other reasons. Thus suppose that in the final equilibrium the *Y*-industry is expanded and the demand for *L* is raised as compared with the initial equilibrium. Then the shift of income from the owners of other factors to *L* will intensify the increase in the demand for *Y* and so in the demand for *L*. But if in the final equilibrium the demand for *L* had been lower than in the initial equilibrium, the shift of income from the owners of *L* would have accentuated the reduction in the demand for *Y* and so in the demand for *L*. Conversely if the owners of *L* spend an abnormally low proportion of their income on *Y*, an increase in the incomes of *L* will damp down the demand for *Y* and so for *L*; and a decrease in the incomes of *L* will stimulate the demand for *Y* and so for *L*.

wage rate to fall. We are assuming that the total money national income remains constant so that the fall in the money price of a factor of production, labour, allows more employment to be given in the economy as a whole. The fall in the wage rate will make all *L*-intensive processes particularly profitable and these will be expanded. This expansion of *L*-intensive processes will cause (i) an increase in the supply of those products in which these processes are intensive (in our previous example, if the textile industry is labour intensive then a fall in the price of labour (*L*) will cause an expansion in the output of textiles—*Y*) and (ii), in a many-factor economy, an increase in the demand for any particular factors in which the *L*-intensive processes are also intensive (for example, if the textile industry which is intensive in *L* is also intensive in *M*, being especially disintensive in *N*, etc., the expansion of the textile industry will lead to a particularly heavy increased demand for *M*).

Thus the first effects of the fall in the money wage rate will be to increase the supply of products like *Y* and to increase the demand for factors like *M* which are complementary to *L*. The price of *Y* will fall and of *M* will rise. The ease of absorption of the increased supply of *L* into the system will thus depend, *inter alia*, upon the ease with which increased supplies of *Y* can be absorbed into the consumers' market. If a small fall in the price of *Y* relatively to other products causes a large shift of consumers from other products on to *Y*, then much *L* can be absorbed into an expanded textile industry (*L*- and *Y*-intensive). Similarly, the scope for the expansion of this industry depends upon the ease with which, when its price goes up, *M* can be released from other uses to go with the *L* in the textile industry. The increased demand for *M* will raise the price of *M*; this will make other *M*-intensive processes unprofitable and will lead to their contraction.

Thus the prices of *Y* and of good substitutes for *Y* in consumers' demand will fall; the price of some close complements with *Y* in consumers' demand may be driven up; the price of *L* and of other factors which are close substitutes for *L* will fall; and the price of a factor such as *M* which is complementary to *L* will rise. These price changes will cause other processes which are intensive in the products whose prices have fallen and in the factors whose prices have risen to become unprofitable; and it will cause other processes which are intensive in the products whose prices have risen and in the factors whose prices have fallen to become profitable; the former will contract and the latter expand. There will be a whole series of repercussions of this kind, each helping to absorb relatively plentiful factors—and in particularly *L*—and to produce the relatively scarce products.

These adjustments between processes will be supplemented by adjustments within processes. Within each process entrepreneurs will have an incentive to increase their employment of the cheap factors—and in particular of *L*—to take the place of the relatively more expensive factors, to shift their outputs from the cheaper to the more expensive products, and to take on more of the cheap factors—and in particular of *L*—to produce more of the expensive products.

The greater the substitutability between products in consumers' demands, the greater the range of variety of available processes for expansion and contraction, the greater the flexibilities of each process, the less important are complementarities in consumers' demands and the less important are complementarities between inputs, complementarities between outputs, and antipathies between inputs and outputs in the productive system, the smaller will be the changes in relative prices both of products and of factors which are needed to absorb a given amount of additional *L* into the system.

It is of interest to consider what may have happened to the absolute level of factor prices and of product prices. The increased supply of *L* with unchanged amounts of the other factors will mean that there are more factors in general to be hired and that there are more products in general being produced for sale to consumers. With a constant total of money expenditure on products and of money incomes to factors the general level of factor prices and of money prices must both have fallen. It is possible that every money price in the economy will have fallen absolutely and that changes in relative prices will take place only by some prices falling more than others.

Consider first the money prices of the factors. If all the conditions in the economy are favourable to the ready absorption of *L* into the system, a very small fall in the price of *L* relatively to other factor prices will be required. In this case the proportion of the constant money national income going to *L* will rise; a 10 per cent increase in *L* can be absorbed by, say, only a 5 per cent fall in the money wage rate; the total money wage bill will rise because the increase in the quantity of *L* employed outweighs the fall in the price per unit of *L*; out of a constant total money income less is left over to go to the unchanged amounts of other factors; their money prices will also have fallen, though by less than the 5 per cent fall in the price of *L*, some relative fall in the price of *L* being required to absorb more *L* into the system. In this case the price of every other factor might have fallen. But this is not necessarily the case. If there were in a many-factor economy some particular factor which was a close complement to *L* in many uses, its money price might have gone up, in which case the price of all the other factors would have fallen all the more.

In the opposite case in which conditions make it very difficult to absorb L into the system a 20 per cent fall in the price of L might be needed to absorb a 10 per cent increase in the amount of L; the total money wage bill received by L would fall; more of the constant money income would be left over to go to all the other factors so that L would receive a lower proportion of the total income; and the general level of all factor prices other than L would have to rise. In this case all other factor prices might rise. But this is not necessarily so because among these other factors there might be one which was a particularly close substitute for L and the price of such a factor might fall in sympathy with the price of L; but this would mean that the other factor prices rose all the more.

In the case in which all factor prices without exception fell it is very probable that all product prices would also fall. If every process produced only a single product, this would necessarily be so. For since the cost of every factor was lower, the cost of producing every product would be lower; and in the new equilibrium, therefore, since prices must equal costs, every product price would be lower.[1] But in the case in which the absorption of L into the economy is difficult and large changes in relative prices are necessary it is quite probable that some product prices will actually rise. For example, in the case in which the prices of some factors go up absolutely there may well be a rise in the costs and so in the prices of those products which rely for their production particularly on these more expensive factors. If labour and land were the only two factors in the economy and if an increased supply of labour could be absorbed into the economy only if the wage rate fell very sharply, a smaller proportion of the constant money national income would go to wages and a higher to rents. The money rent per acre would rise; and the cost-price of products which were sufficiently land-intensive in their production would also rise, while the cost-price of very labour-intensive products would fall sharply.

[1] This is not absolutely certain if a process produces two or more products. Consider labour and land used to produce sheep which provide wool and mutton. The prices of labour and land are both lower so that the cost of a sheep is lower. But suppose that the technical possibilities of producing a different ratio of wool to mutton are very limited, and that changes in other industries (e.g. the increased outputs elsewhere of a substitute for wool and of a complement for mutton) have greatly reduced the demand for wool and increased the demand for mutton. Then the lower cost of a sheep may be covered by a much lower price of wool combined with a somewhat higher price of mutton.

CHAPTER XI

FIXED TECHNICAL CO-EFFICIENTS

In the two previous chapters we have discussed the economic system as if it were composed of a number of separate and independent processes within each of which there is the possibility of some marginal adjustments in the pattern of inputs and outputs. There are engineering works and dairy farms; in the engineering works some adjustments can be made in the proportions in which different engineering products are produced and in the proportions in which different factors are employed; in the dairy farms some adjustments can be made between the proportions in which butter and cheese are produced or in which land and labour are employed; but an engineering works remains an engineering works and a dairy farm a dairy farm.

This is in fact a realistic and useful way of regarding the economic system and we shall continue often to employ it in the remaining chapters of this work. It will, however, already be clear to the attentive reader of the last two chapters that the problems involved in expanding one process and contracting another are very similar to those involved in making an adjustment of the inputs and outputs of a given process. In this chapter we shall consider a method of analysis which makes no distinction between adjustments as between processes and adjustments within processes.

The method consists in supposing that no adjustments within processes are possible. Each process consists of a method of production whereby a given amount of each factor is needed to produce a given amount of each output; in any one process some inputs and some outputs may, of course, be zero—the dairy farm produces no steel; the scale of operation of the process may be varied, but in this case every input must be increased by the same percentage and every output will be thereby increased by the same percentage. There are, however, a large number of processes, some of which differ rather slightly from each other. For example, there may be many 'dairy farm' processes: one may produce much butter and little cheese with much labour and little land; a second may produce little butter and much cheese with much labour and little land; a third may produce much butter and little cheese with little labour and much land; a fourth may produce little butter and much cheese with little labour and much land; and so on, with a number of intermediate processes. In this model it is not possible, for example, to make a completely smooth and continuous adjustment of the ratio of labour to land used in dairy farming, using within the single dairy farming process gradually less and less men and more and more acres to produce the same output. There are a limited number of distinct dairy-farming processes, one using a higher and fixed ratio of men per acre, a second a lower but fixed ratio of men to an acre, and so on. What in the last two chapters we treated as a continuous substitution of factors within a process now itself becomes a choice between different processes with different but fixed factor intensities. Every process has fixed technical co-efficients, i.e. fixed ratios of inputs to outputs. All adjustment in the production system is a matter of expansion and contraction or introduction and elimination of technically rigid processes. If, however, the number of available processes is sufficiently great and their nature sufficiently varied, the result will be approximately the same. What was, for example, a substitution of land for labour within a process itself becomes a choice between two distinct processes which differ slightly in their factor proportions.

Let us then start with the situation considered in Chapter VIII in which there are only two products *X* and *Z*, only two factors *L* and *N*, and only two processes one of which uses *L* and *N* to produce *X* and the other of which uses *L* and *N* to produce *Z*. But unlike the situation considered in Chapter VIII we assume now that these two processes are rigid in the sense that in each process the ratio of *L* to *N* used is rigidly fixed. Table VI gives a simple numerical example of a situation of this kind. The *X*-industry is an *N*-intensive industry

	Number of units of factor required to produce 1 unit of		Total supply of factor available for employment
	X	Z	
L	1	2	1500
N	2	1	1500

Table VI

requiring 2 units of *N* and 1 of *L* to produce 1 unit of *X*; the *Z*-industry is *L*-intensive requiring 1 unit of *N* and 2 units of *L* to produce 1 unit of *Y*. These fixed technical co-efficients together with the available supplies of the factors of production shown in the right-hand column of Table VI can be depicted diagrammatically in Figure 42.

In this figure the line *AE* shows the combinations of *X* and *Z* which could be produced if *N* were superabundant and production were restrained only by the limited supply of *L* of 1500 units as shown in Table VI. In this case if all the *L* were used to produce *X*, *OE* or 1500 units of *X* would be produced; if all the *L* were used to produce *Z*, *OA* or 750 units of *Z* would be produced; and by moving the labour from *X* to *Z* any combination of *X* and *Z* on the line *AE* could be produced. (Cf. p. 85 above.) Similarly if *L* were superabundant and production were restrained only by the limited supply of *N* of 1500 units as shown in Table VI, the line *DC* would indicate

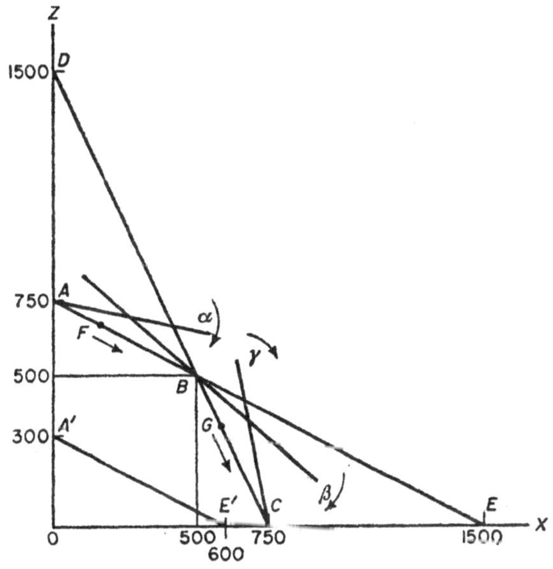

Figure 42

the combinations of *X* and *Z* which it were possible to produce. If all the 1500 units of *N* were used to produce *X*, *OC* or 750 units of *X* would be produced; if all *N* were used to produce *Z*, *OD* or 1500 units of *Z* would be produced; and, as far as *N* is concerned, any combination of *X* and *Z* on the line *DC* could be produced.

But in fact neither *L* nor *N* are superabundant; the available supplies of both must be taken into account. In fact this means that the production possibility boundary will take the form of the kinked line *ABC* in Figure 42. The reason for this and the way in which the system will work can best be explained by assuming that all the citizens in the economy start with an extremely strong demand for *Z* and weak demand for *X*, that their tastes and needs gradually change so that their demand for Z becomes weaker and weaker and their demand for X stronger and stronger until in the end their demand for Z is very weak and for X is very strong. During this process of shifting demand we will watch in terms of Table VI and Figure 42 what happens to

(i) the amounts of X and Z produced,
(ii) the prices of X and Z,
(iii) the amounts of L and N employed, and
(iv) the prices of L and N.

Suppose then we start with such a heavy demand for Z that only Z is produced. We start at the point A in Figure 42. To produce this 750 units of Z, 1500 units of L and 750 units of N are required. This uses up all the 1500 available units of L but leaves unemployed 750 out of the 1500 available units of N. There is an excess supply of N and the price of N falls to zero in the market. The price of L is such as to absorb the whole of the national income as wages for the suppliers of L.

Although no X is being produced there are nevertheless two prices of X which are relevant to the situation. The first of these is given by the slope of the line AB. The slope of this line represents the cost of X in terms of Z. So long as N remains in excess supply only the labour constraint on production is operative; and, as Table VI shows, 1 unit of L is required to produce 1 unit of X but 2 units of L are required to produce 1 unit of Z. The L-cost of Z is twice that of X. If, therefore, the price offered for Z fell below twice the price offered for X, entrepreneurs would move labour from Z production to X production. The slope of the line AB shows how much Z must be given up to obtain 1 unit of X; it is the cost of X in terms of Z. The second price of X which is relevant at the point A is the demand price which consumers would in fact offer for X at that point. This is illustrated by the slope of the line α. This slope is gentler than the slope of the line AB, which means that the demand price offered for X is lower than its cost of production. On the line α the amount of Z offered for 1 unit of X is less than the amount of Z which must be given up to produce 1 unit of X on the line AB. With our numerical example, on the line AB the cost of 1 unit of X is $\frac{1}{2}$ of a unit of Z; the slope of the line α is something less than $\frac{1}{2}$ of unit of Z for each unit of X.

We start then at the point A with the slope of α gentler than that of the line AB. A shift of tastes from Z to X simply moves the slope of α in the direction of the arrow. People would pay a somewhat higher price for a first unit of X. Nothing happens, however, until the slope of α falls to that of *AB*. At this point the demand price for a first unit of *X* has risen to equality with the cost of *X* as determined by the single scarce factor *L*. Any further shift of demand from *Z* to *X* would tend to lower the slope of α below that of *AB* (i.e. raise the price of *X* above its cost). This would be met by a decrease in the production of *Z* and increase in the production of *X* at the constant cost as shown by the slope of *AB*. Shifts of demand from *Z* to *X* are now shown by shifts of the equilibrium point of supply and demand, such as *F*, in the direction of the arrow from *A* towards *B*.

As this happens the *X*-industry is growing and the *Z*-industry contracting. But this is reducing the excess supply of *N*, since—as Table VI shows—for every unit of *L* transferred from the *Z*-industry to the *X*-industry $\frac{1}{2}$ unit of *N* is released from the *Z*-industry but 2 units of *N* are absorbed into the *X*-industry. This process is indicated on Figure 42 by the fact that the line *DC* is becoming closer and closer to the line *AE* as the point *F* moves down the line *AE*. A point may be reached—it is reached in our example at the point *B*—at which the shift from *Z* production to *X* production has just absorbed the excess supply of *N*. At this point *B* the size of the two industries is such that there is full employment of both the factors *L* and *N*. The condition for this to be possible is a very simple one, namely that the total available supply of *N* relatively to the total available supply of *L* should be in between the ratio of *N* to *L* needed in the *X*-industry and the ratio of *N* to *L* needed in the *Z*-industry. In Table VI the total supply of *N* is equal to the supply of *L*; the ratio of *N* to *L* required in the *X*-industry is 2 and in the *Z*-industry is $\frac{1}{2}$. In this case there is some combination of *X* output and *Z* output which will give an average demand for *N* relatively to *L* in between 2 to 1 and 1 to 2 and equal to the national average of the supplies of the factors of 1 to 1. If the total supply of *N* were less than $\frac{1}{2}$ times the supply of *L*, then there would be an excess supply of *L* even if only the *L*-intensive product *Z* were produced. If the total supply of *N* were more than 2 times the supply of *L*, then there would be an excess supply of *N* even if only the *N*-intensive product *X* were produced. This latter possibility is represented on Figure 42 by the shift of the line *AE* to *A′E′* which would occur if the total supply of *L* in Table VI were 600 instead of 1500 units. In this case *L* would be the only scarce factor in all circumstances and we would be back at the constant costs of Chapter V with the line *A′E′* in Figure 42 representing the production possibility curve.

But in our numerical example the line *DC* does cut the line *AE* at the point *B*. When the demand has shifted sufficiently to *X* to cause the equilibrium point *F* to reach the point *B* we are faced with a new situation. We reach the point *B* with the price of *X* in terms of

Z given by the slope of the line AB (i.e. by the cost of X in terms of Z as determined solely by the L-costs of production) and with the price of N zero and of L so high as to absorb the whole national income. The point B is reached when 500 units of Z and 500 units of X are being produced.[1] If in response to a further increase in the demand for X 501 units of X were produced, this would require 1002 units of N and 501 units of L; this would leave 498 units of N and 999 units of L to produce Z; but the production of Z needs only 996 units of L to go with the 498 units of N available for Z-production; L would now be in excess supply and its price would fall to zero; but if the price of L is zero and the price of N absorbs the whole national income, the cost of X in terms of Z is no longer $\frac{1}{2}$ unit of Z but will have risen to 2 units of Z because, as Table VI shows, X-production requires twice as much N as Z-production per unit of output; and the slope of the cost-price line would now be given by the slope of the line BC.

What in fact happens as demand shifts from Z to X is that the point F reaches the point B at the low price of X in terms of Z given by the slope of the line AB. Further shifts of demand from Z to X do not at first cause any further change in outputs but raise the price of X in terms of Z. The increased demand for N-intensive X and the decreased demand for L-intensive Z indirectly increases the demand for N and decreases the demand for L. The price of N rises above zero and of L falls below the level which would absorb the whole national income. The rise in the price of N and the fall in the price of L raises the cost of N-intensive X relatively to that of L-intensive Z, and the cost-price line moves from the slope of AB to that of, say, the slope of the line β. As the demand for X grows, this process continues and the slope of the price cost line β swings round in the direction of the arrow with the price of N rising and that of L falling.[2] When the demand for X has so grown that the slope of β

[1] The 500 units of Z absorb 500 units of N and 1000 units of L, while the 500 units of X absorb 1000 units of N and 500 units of L. In total, therefore, 1500 units of N and of L are required, which equal the total supplies of the factors.

[2] The cost-price of $X = 2\ P_n + 1\ P_l$ and the cost price of $Z = 1\ P_n + 2\ P_l$. Therefore $\frac{P_x}{P_z} = \frac{2\ P_n + P_l}{P_n + 2\ P_l} = \frac{2\frac{P_n}{Pl} + 1}{\frac{P_n}{P_l} + 2}$. Therefore, $\frac{P_n}{P_l} = \frac{2\frac{P_x}{P_z} - 1}{2 - \frac{P_x}{P_z}}$. This is the formula which gives the price of N relatively to the price of N at the point B, i.e. when $\frac{P_x}{P_z}$ lies between $\frac{1}{2}$ and 2. When $\frac{P_x}{P_z} = \frac{1}{2}$, $P_n = 0$. When $\frac{P_x}{P_z} = 2$, $P_l = 0$. When $\frac{P_x}{P_z} = 1$, $\frac{P_n}{P_l} = 1$.

is equal to the slope of *BC*, then the price of *L* will have fallen to zero and the whole costs of *X* and of *Z* are *N*-costs. *L* is on the verge of being in excess supply.

Further shifts of demand now move the equilibrium point along the line *BC*. Any further tendency for the demand price for *X* to rise would raise the price of *X* above its costs as determined now by the *N*-costs of production of *X* and *Z*. The scarce factor *N* would be shifted from *X*-production to *Z*-production with the excess supply of *L* growing greater and greater. At *C* only *X* is produced. Any further increase in the demand for *X* can only mean now that the price which consumers would pay for 1 unit of *Z* as shown by the slope of the line γ falls below its *N*-cost of production as shown by the slope of the line *BC*. Further shifts of demand from *Z* merely shift this notional price line in the direction of the arrow from γ.

We have considered this, the simplest case of choice between, and combination of, two rigid processes at considerable length because it well illustrates certain general principles. The process of adjustment to shifts of demand fell into two distinct categories. At the points *A*, *B*, and *C* changes in demand caused no changes in outputs but only changes in prices of products and/or factors. Between these points were straight line segments *AB* and *BC* where shifts of demand caused no changes in the prices of products or of factors but only changes in outputs and employments. This is an esssential feature of the situations which arise with fixed technical co-efficients. But if there are a large range and variety of rigid processes, the number of points and the number of interconnecting straight lines can be greatly increased, until the kinked line such as *ABC* becomes practically equivalent to a smooth curve on which the price adjustments and quantity adjustments are both occurring simultaneously. The main purpose of the rest of this long chapter will be to show how the introduction of different varieties of alternative rigid processes can have this sort of effect.

But so far in this chapter we have applied to the simplest two process model of Table VI and Figure 42 only the effects of shifts of demand. Before we elaborate it by introducing more processes it may be useful to apply very briefly to this simplest model the analysis of inventions and of changes in the size of the population which we have already discussed in Chapter X.

Let us start then with the effect of an invention on the system. In Figure 43 we show (i) a technically neutral invention, (ii) an invention technically biased solely in favour of the production of *Z*, and (iii) an invention technically biased solely in favour of saving *L*. In all three cases the lines *AE* and *DC* are the same as in Figure 42, based upon the arithmetical example of Table VI, so that we start from the same production possibility curve ABC. In (i) we suppose that the amounts of labour and of land required to produce both X and Z are reduced by 9 per cent. As a result the amounts of output which could be produced by any one of the factors if it were concentrated on the production of any one of the outputs is increased by 10 per cent.[1] In Figure 43 (i) the lines AE and DC move outwards to $A'E'$ and $D'C'$ in such a way that OC' is 10 per cent longer than OC, OE' 10 per cent longer than OE, OA' 10 per cent longer than

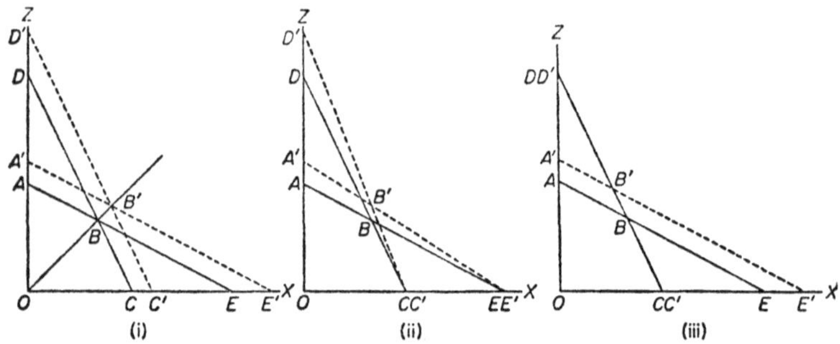

Figure 43

OA, and OD' 10 per cent longer than OD. In case (ii) the invention is confined to the Z-industry. OC and OE remain unchanged but OA is lengthened by 10 per cent to OA' and OD by 10 per cent to OD'. In case (iii) the amount of L saved per unit of output is 9 per cent in both industries but there is no change in the requirements of N in either industry. As a result OA and OE are both lengthened by 10 per cent while OD and OC remain unchanged. In each case the new production boundary is $A'B'C'$.

There would be little point in applying to these cases the criteria which we have applied in the more general case in the previous chapter (pp. 147–53) to enquire whether the structure of the economy is such that these technical biases give rise to a total bias in the invention for or against the production of either commodity or

[1] Let X = total output and L = total labour so that $\frac{X}{L}$ = output per head. If L goes down by 9 per cent while X remains unchanged, output per head = $\frac{X}{0{\cdot}91L} = \frac{1{\cdot}1X}{L}$, so that output per head has risen by 10 per cent. In this numerical example we are not using the rough approximation to which reference is made in the footnote on pages 38–39.

for or against the saving of either factor.[1] But there is an illuminating way of considering the same sort of issues, namely by comparing the full-employment points *B* and *B'* in each of the three cases of Figure 43. Let us suppose that demand conditions are such that in each case both before and after the invention the equilibrium reached is at the full employment point (*B* before and *B'* after the invention). For this purpose we are in fact assuming only that at the points *B* (and *B'*) the demand is such that the demand price for those amounts of *X* and *Z* will lie between the limits of the slope of *AB* and *BC* (*A'B'* and *B'C'*). If there is a large difference between these two slopes (i.e. if there is a large difference between the factor-intensities of the two industries), this, as a glance at Figure 43 will show, is by no means an improbable assumption. Let us then compare *B'* with *B* in each of the three cases of Figure 43.

In case (i) *B'* will lie on the straight line *OB* extended. In other words the new full-employment position will be one in which both outputs increased by 10 per cent when the output per unit of input increases for each factor in each industry. The ratio of *N* to *L* will still be 2 in the *X*-industry and $\frac{1}{2}$ in the *Z*-industry, although 9 per cent less *N* and less *L* is needed in each industry to produce the same output. The only way in which to get 1500 units of *N* and 1500 units of *L* employed remains, as before, to employ 1000 units of *N* and 500 units of *L* (1000 : 500 = 2 : 1) in the *X*-industry and 500 units of *N* and 1000 of *L* (500 : 1000 = 1 : 2) in the *Z*-industry. With employment unchanged outputs will rise in each industry by 10 per cent.

If all income elasticities of demand were unity, all prices would in fact also remain unchanged. Each factor in each industry would earn the same amount of money; every price would fall by 9 per cent; with this 10 per cent increase in real incomes everyone would demand 10 per cent more of each product and so the markets for *X* and *Z* would be cleared. If, however, demands were such that there were a greater demand than this for *Z* and a smaller for *X*, the price of *Z* would fall less than 10 per cent and of *X* by more than 10 per cent. Provided, however, that the variation in relative prices

[1] The criteria used in the previous chapter assumed that in order to induce entrepreneurs to produce a given set of outputs (or to employ a given set of factors) a unique set of product prices (or of factor prices) was required. But in the present case at the full-employment point *B* a whole range of relative product prices within the limits of the slopes of *AB* and *BC* and a whole range of matching factor prices from zero to enough to absorb the whole national income are compatible with the full-employment output. The criteria used in the previous chapter could be re-phrased (referring to limits of possible relative prices rather than to unique relative prices) to cover our present case; but the effort would hardly be worth while.

kept within the limits set by the slopes of $A'B'$ and $B'C'$, the outputs would remain unchanged at B' but the fall in the price of N-intensive X relatively to the price of L-intensive Z would cause some absolute fall in the price of N and rise in the price of L.

In case (ii) the ratios of N to L in each industry once again remain unaffected at 2 to 1 in the X-industry and 1 to 2 in the Z-industry, because the amount of input required to produce a unit of Z falls by the same proportion (9 per cent) for both inputs. By the process of reasoning used at the beginning of the last paragraph but one, we can see that in this case also the volumes of employment in each industry must remain unchanged if there is to be full employment of both factors. Therefore the output of X remains unchanged and the output of Z rises by 10 per cent. B' is 10 per cent vertically above B.

Suppose in this case that all price elasticities of demand for Z were equal to unity. Then equilibrium would be maintained without any change in factor incomes. This can be seen in the following way. Out of a constant money income everyone would spend the same total amount on Z when its price fell and the same total amount on X. The money price of X would be unchanged and the money price of Z would fall by 9 per cent while its output went up by 10 per cent. With unchanged factor prices the costs of X would be covered (no change in price or cost) and the cost of Z would be covered (prices down by 9 per cent and costs down by 9 per cent because of the invention). If, however, price elasticities of demand for Z were on the average (numerically) greater than one, more in total would be spent on Z whose price would go down by less than 9 per cent and less would be spent on X whose price would go down somewhat. This further shift of demand from N-intensive X to L-intensive Z would cause some rise in the price of L and fall in the price of N.

In case (iii) of Figure 43 the maintenance of full employment for both factors requires an absolute reduction in the output of X and a large increase in the output of Z. The reason for this can be seen in the following way. We start at B with 1000 units of N used to produce X and 500 units of N used to produce Z. Suppose that there is no change in the use of N. Then the effect of the invention would be simply to cause 9 per cent of the available L to be unemployed, since the invention takes the form of economizing 9 per cent of the L previously required to go with the N in each industry. The only way to re-absorb the now excess supply of L is to transfer some N and L from the N-intensive X-industry to the L-intensive Z-industry. For every unit of N so transferred four times as much L will be required in the Z-industry as will be released from the X-industry. In terms of Figure 43 (iii), the invention has made L in excess supply at the point B; $A'E'$ is not acting as a restraint on production. We now transfer N from the X-industry to the Z-industry moving along the straight line BB'. As we do so BB' and $A'E'$ converge. At B' we have taken up all the slack L and there is full employment of both factors again.

The market mechanism by which this works can be conceived in the following way. The invention at B simply saves L and causes L to be redundant. The price of L falls and of N rises. This lowers the cost price of L-intensive Z and raises the cost price of N-intensive X. Consumers buy more of the cheaper Z and less of the more expensive X. The Z-industry expands and the X-industry contracts, thereby raising the average ratio of L to N in employment. This goes on until the unemployed L is re-absorbed.

Figure 43 (iii) can also be used to illustrate the case in which we are not dealing with an invention but with an increase in the size of the available working population. If L were the number of workers in the economy, the shift of the line AB to $A'B'$ could be due either to an invention which saved 9 per cent of the labour needed for any given output in either industry or else to an increase of 10 per cent in the size of the total labour force without any change in the technical labour requirements of either industry. We start at B. An excess supply of labour now arises because there is an increase in the available labour supply from 1500 to 1650. This causes a fall in the wage rate; a fall in the cost-price of labour-intensive Z and a rise in the cost-price of N-intensive X; the Z-industry expands and the X-industry contracts until we reach the point B' at which the unemployed workers are again fully employed in the expanded labour-intensive industry.

An increase in the supply of L with the supply of N constant will thus have caused a decrease in the supply of X and an increase in the supply of Z. Is there any meaning in these conditions to the idea of the marginal product of L, i.e. to the addition to output caused by a small increment of L applied to the same amount of N? And, if so, is there any reason to believe that the price of L will in competitive equilibrium still be equal to the value of the marginal product of L? The answer to both these questions is in the affirmative.

First, then, what do we now mean by the marginal product of L? Let us consider how much the output of X must be reduced to release N so as to absorb more L into the L-intensive Z industry. On the numerical assumptions which we are making (see Table VI) we show in Table VII how 3 more units of L could be absorbed into the productive system. If the output of the X-industry is cut down by 1 unit this will release 2 units of N and 1 unit of L for the Z-industry. But with the 2 units of N in the Z-industry 4 units of L will be employed, so that there is a net increase in the total employment of L of 3 and an increase in the output of Z of 2 units. An additional employment of 3 units of L will thus raise the output of Z by 2 units and reduce the output of X by 1 unit. We can, therefore, regard the additional output due to an additional unit of L employed with the same amount of N as being $\frac{2}{3}$ of a unit of Z *less* $\frac{1}{3}$ of a unit of a unit of X. This is the marginal product of L.

The value of the marginal product of L is the price which could be obtained for this marginal product and this is $\frac{2}{3} P_z - \frac{1}{3} P_x$ where P_z and P_x are the money prices of a unit of Z and of X. But in equilibrium the price of Z will equal the cost of Z; and since a unit

		X-industry	*Z*-industry	Total
Change in Employment	N	−2	+2	0
	L	−1	+4	+3
Change in output		−1	+2	—

Table VII

of Z requires 2 units of L and 1 unit of N for its production, the cost of a unit of Z will be $2 P_l + P_n$, where P_l and P_n are the money prices of units of L and N. Similarly $P_x = P_l + 2 P_n$. The value of the marginal product of L in competitive equilibrium $= \frac{2}{3} P_z - \frac{1}{3} P_x = \frac{2}{3} (2 P_l + P_n) - \frac{1}{3} (P_l + 2 P_n) = P_l$. In other words, even with fixed technical co-efficients, in competitive equilibrium the value of the marginal product of any factor will be equal to its price.

We can now elaborate in various ways the very simple two-factor two-product two-process model on which we have so far concentrated in this chapter. The really important elaborations are those which take the form of introducing more than two processes. But before we introduce a third process let us consider the introduction of a third factor M into each of our two processes. Suppose that Table VI were modified by the introduction into each industry of a third factor M, one unit of which was needed to produce one unit of X or one unit of Y and suppose that 900 units of M were available in the community. Table VIII shows these new conditions which are illustrated in Figure 44. In Figure 44 as in Figure 42, the lines AE and DC show the restraints on the production of X and Z set by the available supplies of L and N. We now have a third restraint set by the available supply of M. OH measures the amount of Z and OJ the amount of X which could be produced by the 900 units of M if there were no shortages of the two other factors. The production possibility curve now takes the form of the kinked line $AKPC$.

Between *A* and *K* both *M* and *N* are in excess supply; the cost of *X* in terms of *Z* is set by the slope of the line *AK* which represents the relative *L*-costs of production; the whole national income is paid out to *L*. At *K* both *L* and *M* are fully employed but *N* is still in excess supply. As the demand for *X* increased further, the price of *X* would rise relatively to *Z* and the price of *M* would rise from zero and the price of *L* would fall. When the price of *X* in terms of *Z*

	Number of units of factor required to produce one unit of *X*	*Z*	Total supply of factor available for employment
L	1	2	1500
M	1	1	900
N	2	1	1500

Table VIII

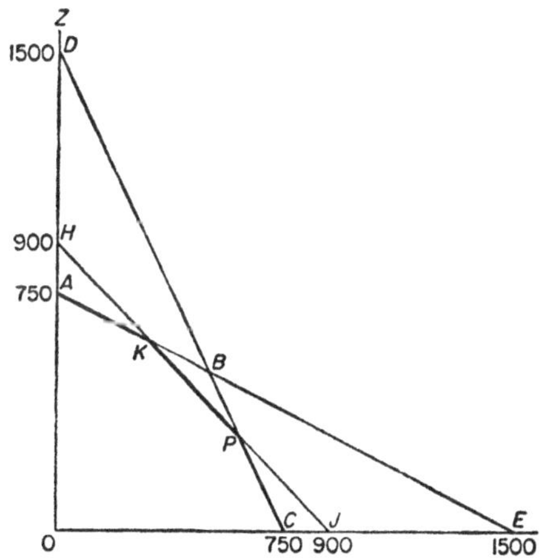

Figure 44

had risen to the slope of the line *KP*, the price of *L* would have fallen to zero and the whole national income would be paid out to *M*. Further increases in demand for *X* would move the equilibrium outputs down the line *KP* at a price ratio equal to the slope of *KP*, i.e. of the *K*-costs of production. At *P* we would get a second point at which prices would change without any change of output until the price of *M* as well as of *L* had fallen to zero and the cost of *X* had risen to the slope of *PC*, i.e. the *N*-costs of production. The introduction of the third factor has introduced a third straight-line segment into the production possibility curve.[1] But the situation is still an extremely unreal one because with only two processes it is impossible for more than two of the factors to be fully employed at the same time (*L* and *M* at the point *P* or *M* and *N* at the point *K*).

Much more important is to elaborate the original two-factor two-product two-process model by introducing a third process producing a third product (say, *Y*). The situation might be as depicted in Table IX. *X* is now the most *N*-intensive and *Z* the most *L*-intensive product with *Y* taking an intermediate position. Full employment

	Number of units of factor required to produce one unit of output of			Total supplies of the factors
	X	*Y*	*Z*	
L	1	1	2	2000
N	2	1	1	2000

Table IX

of both factors can be obtained by producing a mixture of *X*, *Y*, and *Z* which uses the two factors *N* and *L* in the ratio in which they are available in total supply for employment in the economy. This, as before, is possible only if the ratio of the total supplies of the two factors lies in between the extreme ratios in which they are needed in the most *N*-intensive use and in the most *L*-intensive use. This condition is satisfied in Table IX where the two factors are available in the ratio 1 to 1 (i.e. 2000 units of *N* to 2000 units of *L*) whereas they are required in the ratio 2 to 1 in the most *N*-intensive industry producing *X* and only in the ratio ½ to 1 in the most *L*-intensive industry producing *Z*.

In the example given in Table IX outputs of 500 each of *X*, *Y*, and *Z* would give full employment to all three factors. The requirements of *N* would be 1000 units to produce *X*, 500 units to produce *Y*, and 500 units to produce *Z*, a total of 2000 units; and the requirements of *L* would be 500 units to produce *X*, 500 units to produce *Y*, and 1000 units to produce *Z*, a total of 2000 units. But this is not

[1] This is true only if the total supplies of *M* are neither too large nor too small. If the total supply of *M* were so great that *HJ* in Figure 44 passed to the North-East of *B*, then *M* would be in excess supply for all possible outputs of *X* and *Z*. If the total supply of *M* were so small that *HJ* passed to the left of *A* (and/or of *C*), then the factor *L* (and/or *N*) would be in excess supply for all possible outputs.

now the only possible set of outputs which gives full employment. If the outputs of *X* and *Z* both went down by 1 unit, this would release 3 units of *N* (2 from the *X*-industry and 1 from the *Z*-industry) and 3 units of *L* (1 from the *X*-industry and 2 from the *Z*-industry); and these 3 units of *N* and 3 units of *L* would just suffice to produce 3 units of *Y*. In other words, so long as all three products were still being produced, it would be possible always to maintain full employment of all three factors if 1 less (or more) unit of *X* and 1 less (or more) unit of *Z* were produced for every 3 units by which the output of *Y* were raised (or lowered).

The position is illustrated geometrically in Figure 45. We measure

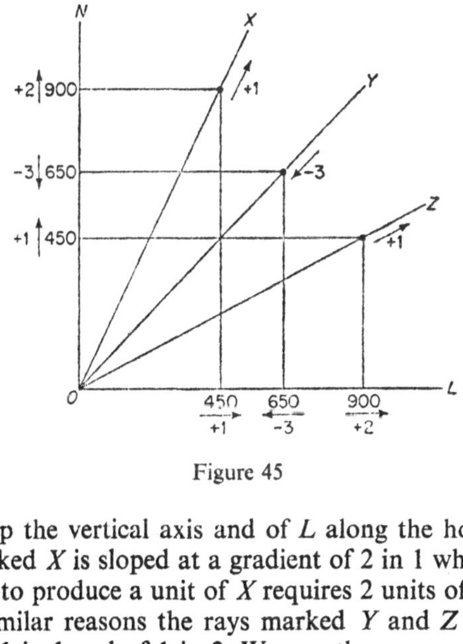

Figure 45

units of *N* up the vertical axis and of *L* along the horizontal axis. The ray marked *X* is sloped at a gradient of 2 in 1 which represents the fact that to produce a unit of *X* requires 2 units of *N* and 1 unit of *L*. For similar reasons the rays marked *Y* and *Z* are sloped at gradients of 1 in 1 and of 1 in 2. We can then measure units of *X*, *Y*, and *Z* along the three rays marked *X*, *Y*, and *Z* respectively. We start in a position in which there is full employment of both factors. This is shown in the figure with outputs of 450 units of *X* (needing 900 units of *N* and 450 units of *L*), 650 units of *Y* (needing 650 units each of *N* and of *L*), and 450 units of *Y* (needing 450 units of *N* and 900 units of *L*). Together this employs the available 2000 units of *N* and 2000 units of *L*. If for every 3 units contraction along the *Y* ray there is an expansion of 1 unit along both the *X* and *Z* rays, then the total demands for *N* and for *L* will remain unchanged, as can be seen from Figure 45.

The productive system is still a pretty inflexible one. If full employment is to be maintained, there is only one possible pattern of change in outputs, namely a change of 1 unit of *X* and of *Z* for every change in the opposite direction of *Y* by 3 units. There is one degree of freedom. But suppose now that there were four single-product industries *W*, *X*, *Y*, and *Z* with only the two factors, *N* and *L*. We should now have two degrees of freedom in the sense that we could decide independently upon certain changes in outputs of, say, both *X* and *Y*. This would result in certain definite changes in the demands for *N* and *L*. But there would still be two industries, namely *W* and *Z*, whose outputs could still be altered both absolutely and relatively to each other so as to release (or absorb) the amounts of *N* and *L* which were needed (or made redundant) by the predetermined changes in the outputs of *X* and *Y*. The greater are the number of single-product industries relatively to the number of factors of production to be employed, the more flexible is the system, in the sense that full employment of both factors (and thus a positive value for each factor price) is compatible with a greater variety of patterns of consumption of the products.

Let us suppose that we start in equilibrium with full employment of the two factors *N* and *L* in an economy with a number of products (*W*, *X*, *Y*, and *Z* in descending order of *N*-intensity). Suppose then that there is a shift of demand onto *W* the most *N*-intensive product away from some or all of the other products. This will increase the demand for *N* and reduce the demand for *L*. The price of *N* will rise and of *L* will fall. This will raise the cost price of *W* in terms of *X*, of *X* in terms of *Y*, and of *Y* in terms of *Z*. Demand may shift back somewhat from the now expensive *W* onto the other products, thus relieving somewhat the excess demand for *N* and excess supply of *L*. But, equally important, demand will shift down the line from *X* to the cheaper *Y* and from *Y* to the cheaper *Z*. These shifts of demand will also relieve the excess demand for *N* and the excess supply of *L*. According to the degree of substitutability (and possibly of complementarity) between the various products in the consumers' demands a new pattern of demand for *W*, *X*, *Y*, and *Z* can emerge which with some rise in the price of *N* and some fall in the price of *L* will continue to give full employment to both *N* and *L*. There is no longer only one single pattern of demand which will achieve this result.

So far we have confined our attention to the choice between processes when each process produced only one product and where each product was produced by only one process. But neither of these restrictions is necessary or realistic. A process may produce more than one product and different processes may produce these products in different proportions. Moreover, a given output may be produced by a number of processes of which one needs a different proportion of factor inputs to the other.

Suppose then that there are two processes which differ only in that process I produces a large amount of Y and a small amount of X while process II produces a small amount of Y and a large amount of X. For example, a farmer with a given cost in terms of labour and land and with given outputs of other products can keep either (process I) 1000 sheep which produce 2000 units of wool (Y) and 1000 units of mutton (X) or (process II) 1000 sheep which produce 1000 units of wool and 2000 units of mutton. The situation is depicted in Figure 46. For a given total expenditure and with a given

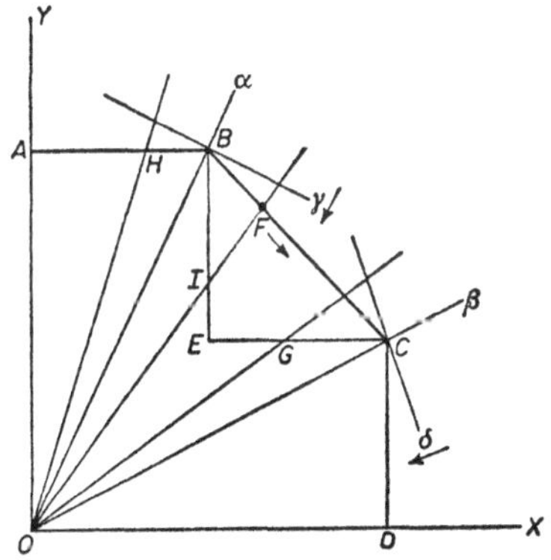

Figure 46

output of other products he can produce either the output combination of X and Y at B or the output combination at C.

Now it might at first sight appear that his production possibility curve is the stepped line $ABECD$. If an output ratio with the slope of the line α is required, he keeps the Y-producing flock and produces at B; if an output ratio with the slope of the line β is required, he keeps the X-producing flock and produces at C. But if an output combination with the slope of the line OH is required, he must produce at B and throw away HB units of X. This is true. It might also appear that if output combinations with the slopes of the lines OI or OG are required, he must produce in the first case at B and throw away BI units of Y and in the second at C and throw away GC units of X. But this is not true.

The farmer can mix his flock. Starting from the point B if he reduces his Y-producing flock by one sheep and introduces one X-producing sheep, he will from the sheep given up lose 2 units of

Y and 1 unit of *X* but he will gain from the new sheep 1 unit of *Y* and 2 units of *X*. Thus if he moves by gradual steps from keeping only 1000 *Y*-producing sheep to keeping only 1000 *X*-producing sheep he can move down the line *BC*, losing 1 unit of *Y* for every 1 unit of *X* gained. Only when he reaches the point *H* and has given up all his *Y*-producing sheep can he make no further adjustments of this kind.

His production possibility curve is in fact the kinked line *ABFCD*. The market mechanism will work in the following manner. We can represent the price of *Y* relatively to the price of *X* by the slope of price lines such as γ and δ in Figure 45. If, as in the case of γ, the price of *Y* is higher than the price of *X*, then it will pay the farmer

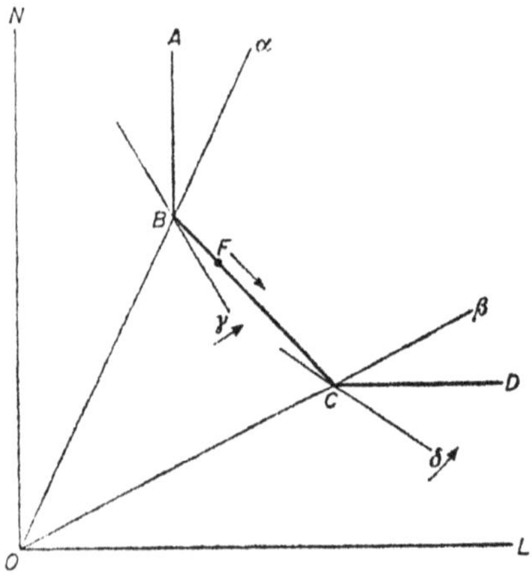

Figure 47

to keep only *Y*-producing sheep. Suppose the market demand for *Y* falls and for *X* rises. The price line γ swings round in the direction of the arrow. When the price line has the slope *BC* (i.e. the price of *Y* is equal to the price of *X*) it is equally profitable to keep *Y*-producing or *X*-producing sheep. If the price of *Y* fell any further the farmer would shift from *Y*-producing to *X*-producing sheep. He now moves along the line *BC* in the direction of the arrow from *F* as the demand shifts. We are on a segment of the curve when outputs change and prices remain constant. When the output reaches the combination *C*, then any further shift of demand from *Y* to *X* simply causes the price of *X* to rise relatively to that of *Y*. The price line swings round in the direction of the arrow from δ.

A similar analysis can be carried out in terms of the substitution of one factor for another. Suppose now that there were two processes

(I and II) of which I used much N and little L but II used little N and much L, but which were the same in every other respect (i.e. used the same amounts of other factors and produced the same amounts of all products). This situation is depicted in Figure 47. The producer can use 2000 units of N and 1000 units of L (as at the point B) or 1000 units of N and 2000 units of L (as at the point C) for an otherwise identical result. His equi-product curve is now the kinked line $ABFCD$. He can operate at the point B; if he employs more N he has no effect on his output and he moves vertically up his equi-product curve BA. He can operate at the point C; if he employs more L he does not affect his output but moves horizontally along CD. But between B and C he can move along the sloped line BC by varying the proportions in which he uses the two processes. Starting at B he can give up 2 units of N and 1 unit of L from process I and replace this with 1 unit of N and 2 units of L in process II. He obtains the same result with 1 unit less of N and 1 unit more of L, until at the point C he has entirely replaced process I with process II.

If N is very plentiful relatively to L so that the price of N is lower than that of L, it will pay the producer to produce with the combination of N and L at the point B. If N becomes less plentiful at first the price of N rises and the price line γ swings round in the direction of the arrow. When the price of N equals the price of L, the two processes are equally profitable. Decreased supplies of N will now simply mean that process I is contracted and process II expanded as quickly as the price of N tends to rise. The combination of N and L moves in the direction of the arrow from F. At the point C volumes of employment are again rigid and the price once more moves in the direction of the arrow from δ as the supply of N increases.

Finally in Figure 48 we show the case in which there are two processes which are in all other respects the same (i.e. produce the same amounts of other products and employ the same amounts of other factors) except that in process I (as at the point B) a small amount of L is employed and a small amount of Y produced whereas in process II (as at the point C) a large amount of L is employed and a large amount of Y produced. The productivity curve is now the kinked line $ABCD$. One can produce at B and throw away some of the output, thus moving vertically down the line BA. One can produce at C and take on more L without making any use of it, thus moving horizontally along the line CD. But between B and C one can move along the line BC by mixing the processes. By giving up a small amount of process I and using that amount of process II which will replace process I as far as other inputs and outputs are concerned, one can take on a little more L to produce a little more Y.

From A to B the marginal product of L is infinite; one can have more Y without taking on any more L. From B to C the marginal product of L is equal to the upward slope of the line BC; by taking on one more unit of L one can add a positive finite amount to the output of Y. From C to D the marginal product of L is zero; one cannot add anything to the output of Y alone simply by taking on more L.

If the price of Y is low relatively to that of L (as with the price line γ), it will pay only to use process I. As the price of Y rises or of L falls, the price line γ will swing round in the direction of the arrow from Y. When the price of L in terms of Y has fallen to the slope of

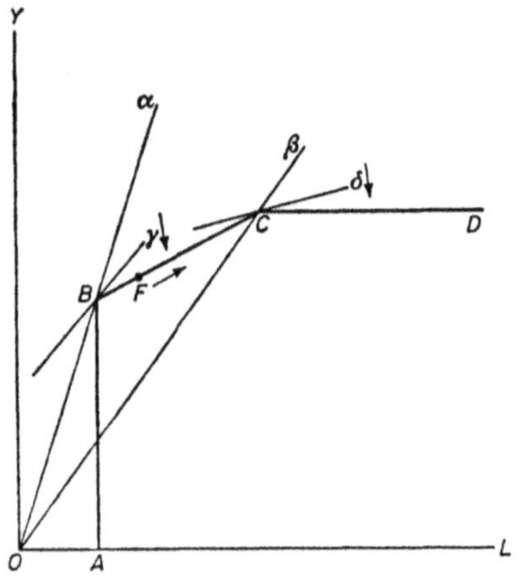

Figure 48

BC, both processes are equally profitable. As the scarcity of Y now increases or of L decreases, the equilibrium combination now moves along the line BC in the direction of the arrow from F without any change in prices until the point C is reached. At this point any further increased scarcity of Y or decreased scarcity of L will cause the price of L in terms of Y to fall again as is shown by the direction of the arrow from δ.

In Figures 46, 47, and 48 we showed only the cases of choice between two processes. But there may, of course, in each case be more than two possible alternative processes. Choice between three processes is shown in Figure 49. The line $ABCD$ in Figure 49 (i) reproduces $ABCD$ of Figure 46; in Figure 49 (ii) it reproduces $ABCD$ of Figure 47; and in Figure 49 (iii) it reproduces $ABCD$ of Figure 48. In each case we have introduced between the two processes on the lines α and β a third process on the new line ϵ.

Consider Figure 49 (i). Suppose that the new production combination is at *E*. Then process ϵ will never be used. At the point *F*, which is obtained by a combined use of processes α and β in the way in which we have already examined, more *X* and more *Y* can be obtained than at *E*. The process ϵ is technically dominated (cf. pp. 127–8 above) not by a single alternative process, but by an average combination of other processes. If at the other extreme, the new process produced an output combination at *G*, then the process α would never be used. Process α would be technically dominated by process ϵ which would produce more *X* and more *Y* than α. In this

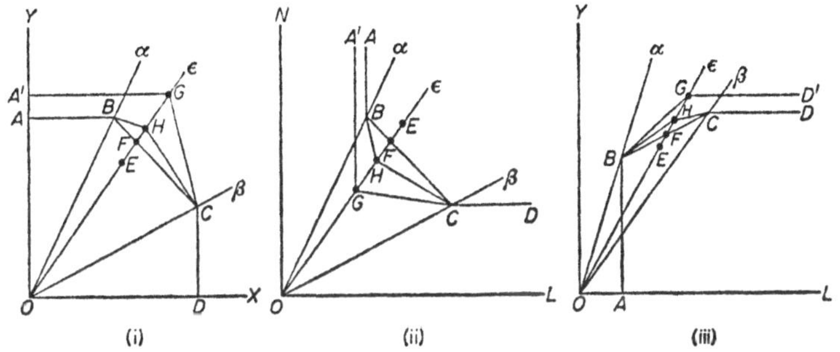

Figure 49

case the production possibility curve would be *A′GCD*. But if the new production combination were at the point *H* the production possibility curve would become *ABHCD*. On the principles which we have examined above, at *B* only process α would be used, between *B* and *H* both process α and ϵ would be used, at *H* only process ϵ would be used, and between *H* and *C* both processes ϵ and β would be used. The greater the number of processes, the more nearly would the line *ABHCD* approach a smooth curve.

Figure 49 (ii) adds to Figure 47 the possibility of a third process ϵ which achieves the same result with a ratio of *N* to *L* intermediate between processes α and β. If the combination of *N* and *L* needed on ϵ is *E*, then the process is dominated by a combination of process α and β. To employ the combination of *N* and *L* at *E* requires more *N* and more *L* than the point *F*. If the combination of *N* and *L* needed on ϵ is *G*, then ϵ dominates α since at *G* less *N* and less *L* is needed than at *B*. The equi-product curve becomes *A′GCD*. If the combination of *N* and *L* needed on ϵ is at *H*, then the equi-product curve becomes *ABHCD*.

Figure 49 (iii) adds to Figure 48 the possibility of a third process which achieves an output per unit of input $\left(\frac{Y}{L}\right)$ intermediate between the process α and β, other outputs and inputs being given. If the output and input combination were at E, process ϵ would be dominated by an average of processes α and β. If it were at G, process ϵ would dominate process β, since more Y would be produced with less L than at C and the production curve would become $ABGD'$. If, however, the point on ϵ were at H, then the production curve would become $ABHCD$.

Let us by way of a final exercise revert to the case in which there are two factors (L and N) and two products (X and Y). Let us assume again that all processes use both factors but produce only one product; but let us now consider the case in which there are three processes, one for the production of Y but two for the production of X. The situation is illustrated numerically in Table X. Process I for the production of X needs 1 more unit of N but $\frac{1}{2}$ less

	Number of units of factor required to produce 1 unit of *X* By process I	*X* II	*Y*	Total supply of factors available for employment
L	$\frac{1}{2}$	1	1	1000
N	3	2	1	1500

Table X

units of L than does Process II. If N is very cheap relatively to L, X will be produced by Process I; but if L is cheap relatively to N, then X will be produced by Process II. When the price of N is one half of the price of L, Processes I and II have the same cost. (When $P_n = \frac{1}{2}P_l$, then $\frac{1}{2}P_l + 3P_n = P_l + 2P_n$.) It follows that when the price of N is less than one half that of L, X will be produced by process I; when the price of N is more than one half that of L, X will be produced by process II; and when the price of N is equal to one half the price of L, X may be produced by either or both of the processes.

The result is shown geometrically in Figure 50. If X were produced by process II we could draw the line AE_{II} which would show the restraint imposed on the production of X and Y by the fact that there were only 1000 units of L available for the two industries. Similarly the line DC_{II} would show the restraint imposed on the production of X and Y by the fact that there are only 1500 units of

N available for the two industries. If process II were the only process available for the production of *X*, then the line $AB_{II}C_{II}$ would be the production possibility curve; and the analysis would proceed exactly as in the case of Figure 42 (pp. 160–65 above).

Similarly if process I were the only process available for the production of *X* we could draw the lines AE_I and DC_I and AB_IC_I would be the production possibility curve.

Let us see now what happens when both processes are available for the production of *X*. Suppose a very high demand for *Y*. We

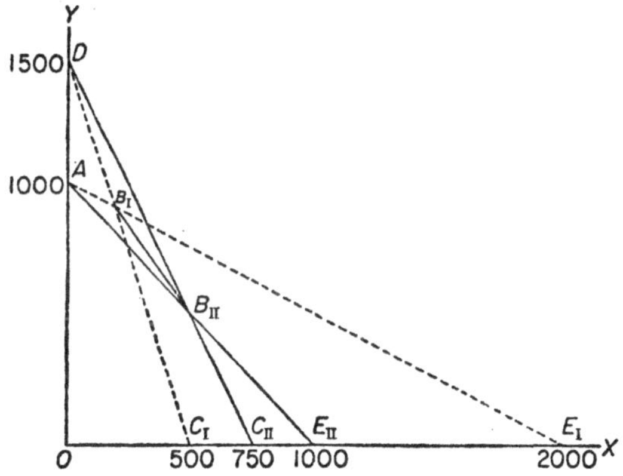

Figure 50

start at the point *A* when only *Y* is being produced and the output of *Y* is limited by the availability of 1000 units of *L*. *N* is in excess supply and its price is zero. As the demand for *X* grows we shall move along the line AB_I. Process I will be used for the production of *X* so long as *N* is in excess supply and its price is zero. At B_I there is full employment of *L* and *N* with the use of process I for the production of *X*. Any further rise in the demand for *X* will raise the price of *X* and raise the price of *N*. When the price of *N* has risen to one half the price of *L* then, as we have seen, processes I and II become equally profitable for the production of *X*.

At this point any further rise in the demand for *X* will cease to raise the price of *N* relatively to that of *L* but will increase the output of *X* at the expense of *Y*. An increase in the demand for *N*-intensive *X* will, of course, tend to raise the price of *N*. But as soon as this happens there will be a tendency to switch over from process I to process II in the *X* industry. Inspection of Table X shows that by producing 2 units less of *X* by process I one releases 1 unit of *L* and

6 units of N and that by producing 5 units more of X by process II one absorbs 5 units of L and 10 units of N. Thus to produce net 3 more units of X in this way one would need net 4 more units of L and 4 more units of N. But these could be provided by reducing the output of Y by 4 units. In other words at B_I in Figure 50 one can obtain 3 units of X for every 4 units of Y given up, if at the same time one switches from process I to process II, obtaining the 3 more units of X by producing 5 more by process *II* and 2 less by process I. This is in fact what will happen from point B_I when the price of N has risen to one half the price of L. Any further increase in the demand for X will (i) expand the output of X but (ii) by tending to raise the price of N above one half that of L will contract process I and expand process II in the X industry. We shall in fact be moving along the straight line $B_I B_{II}$, giving up 4 units of Y for every additional 3 units of X produced.[1] What in fact is happening is that the extremely L-intensive Y-industry and the extremely N-intensive process *I* in the X-industry are both being contracted in order to provide resources of N and L in an intermediate ratio for the expansion of process II in the X-industry. (Cf. pp. 172–73 above where the X and Z industries release resources for the intermediate Y-industry.)

When we reach the point B_{II} process I has been completely replaced by process II. Any further increase in the demand for X raises the price of X and so the price of N. This goes on until the price of N absorbs the whole national product and the price of L becomes zero. Any further increase in the demand for X now moves the equilibrium point down the straight line $B_{II}C_{II}$ with L in excess supply and with the cost of X and Y set in terms of N.

The introduction of process I has thus changed the production possibility curve from $AB_{II}C_{II}$ to $AB_I B_{II} C_{II}$. The greater choice of processes has made the production possibility curve approximately more closely to a smooth curve.

To summarize this long chapter, we can if we so wish imagine the whole productive process to be made up of a large number of very varied, but rigid production processes. Each individual process has a different ratio of inputs and/or of outputs. The economy starts in equilibrium. There is then some change as, for example, a small increase in the size of the working population (an increase in L). This tends to reduce the price of L and all L-intensive processes are stimulated. This may have many other effects. One L-intensive process may be very Y-intensive in its output which will cause Y to

[1] It can be seen from Table X that when the price of N is equal to $\frac{1}{2}$ the price of L ($P_n = \frac{1}{2}P_l$), then the cost of $Y = P_n + P_l = \frac{3}{2}Pl$. The cost of X by process I $= \frac{1}{2}P_l + 3P_n = \frac{4}{2}P_l$ and by process II $= P_l + 2P_n = \frac{4}{2}Pl$. Thus the cost of Y is $\frac{3}{4}$ of the cost of X, so that in the market 4 units of Y exchange for 3 units of X.

become relatively plentiful and cheap. As a result products which are good substitutes for *Y* in consumers' demands may also tend to fall in price, while complements to *Y* tend to rise in price. If there are many factors of production, some *L*-intensive processes may be very *M*-intensive and their expansion may tend to raise the price of *M*. Thus some factor prices will tend to go down and some up and some product prices will tend to go down and some up. Processes will expand (or be introduced) which are intensive in products whose price has gone up and in factors whose price has gone down; and processes will contract (or be eliminated) which are intensive in products whose price has gone down and in factors whose price has gone up. In the end a new equilibrium is reached in which the slightly enlarged amount of *L* is fully employed with the same amount of the other factors and in which, while the general level of output has gone up, the output of one or two particular products may have gone down. If there is a sufficient variety of alternative processes, we can treat the adjustment as if it were based on continuous substitution and transformation between factors and products.

In any case we can regard the factor *L* as being paid a price equal to the value of its marginal product. When 1 more unit of *L* is introduced into the economy some processes expand and some contract in the way which we have examined, until the same amount of the other factors is employed with 1 more unit of *L*. The value of the marginal product of *L* is, therefore, (*a*) the sum of the increases of outputs of those processes which have expanded, each output being multiplied by its price, less (*b*) the sum of the decreases of outputs of those processes which have contracted each output being again multiplied by its price. But in perfect competition (*b*) is equal to the value of the factors which have left the contracting processes and (*a*) is equal to the value of the factors which have moved into the expanding processes. It follows that (*a*) less (*b*) is equal to the value of the additional factor, i.e. to the price of the additional 1 unit of *L*[1]. So the price of *L* in competitive equilibrium is equal to the value of its marginal product even in the case in which the economy is composed of a finite number of rigid processes.

1 Valuing inputs and outputs at their initial prices, the above is an exact calculation except insofar as previously unused processes become profitable as a result of the fall in the wage rate. At the initial prices the value of the outputs of such processes might be less than the cost of their inputs. But since we are concerned only with small changes in *L* and, therefore, in prices, such processes must initially have been on the margin of profitability, so that our calculation does not misrepresent the true state of affairs.

CHAPTER XII

ECONOMIC EFFICIENCY AND THE DISTRIBUTION OF INCOME

We have now completed our analysis of the stationary perfectly competitive equilibrium that is compatible with the extreme assumptions enumerated in Chapter I. It will be the purpose of later volumes to remove those assumptions and observe the effect of their removal upon the economic problems of society. As we have pointed out, many of the ultimate objectives of economic policy which we enumerated in our Introduction (pp. 14–17) cannot be discussed at all realistically until the assumptions of Chapter I have been relaxed. But there is one possible clash between ultimate objectives which our stationary equilibrium can illustrate—namely, the clash between 'economic efficiency' and 'distributive justice'—a clash which remains basic to decisions about economic policy in the real world in which the strict assumptions of Chapter I are no longer relevant. Let us define an inefficient situation as one in which it would be possible to make one citizen better off without making any other citizen worse off. We may then express the clash between 'economic efficiency' and 'distributive justice' by saying that in the conditions laid down in Chapter I a policy of strict *laissez-faire* will generate competitive forces which will eliminate all economically inefficient situations, but that such a policy may at the same time result in a very undesirable distribution of income among the individual citizens.

In this volume we have in effect been making the tacit assumption that the market forces will, on the explicit assumptions made in Chapter I, always bring the economy to a stationary equilibrium in which supply equals demand in every market and in which there is, therefore, no incentive on the part of any buyer or seller to change any price or any quantity of anything which is being bought or sold. It is, however, conceivable that the time-lags and speeds of response of market adjustments are such that the economy will never come to rest in its stationary equilibrium, but will, for example, perpetually fluctuate around it in a 'trade cycle'. We hold over to a later volume an investigation of the dynamic features which the processes of market adjustment must have in order to ensure that a stationary equilibrium is in fact reached. What we intend to demonstrate at this stage of our argument is simply that no stationary equilibrium can be reached except at an efficient economic situation because the market forces of competition will certainly be such, on the explicit assumptions of Chapter I, as to move the system away from any inefficient situation. In short, our present proposition is that if the economy reaches its stationary equilibrium, then, on the explicit assumptions of Chapter I, it will be in an efficient situation in the sense that it would be impossible to make one citizen better off without making any other citizen worse off.

That this is so can best be appreciated by considering the main forms of possible inefficiency and by seeing in each case why a stationary competitive equilibrium would be incompatible with each such inefficiency. We shall proceed then to show that the system can be in stationary equilibrium only if (1) Trade in Products is Optimized, (2) Production is Maximized, (3) Production is Optimized, (4) Trade in Occupations is Optimized, and (5) Effort is Optimized.

(1) THE OPTIMIZATION OF TRADE IN PRODUCTS

Our perfectly competitive economy will never find a stationary equilibrium in which it would be possible for one citizen by trading more (or less) with another citizen to be made better off without the other being made worse off. Suppose that for Mrs B 1 more unit of X would exactly compensate for having 1 less unit of Y, but that for Mrs A 1 less unit of X would be exactly compensated by having $\frac{1}{2}$ more units of Y. These are the conditions in which a change in trade between Mrs A and Mrs B can make Mrs A better off without making Mrs B worse off; for if Mrs A gave up 1 unit of X to Mrs B in return for 1 unit of Y, Mrs B would be equally well off while Mrs A would be better off. But this situation could not persist in a competitive equilibrium. Mrs B would be in equilibrium only if the price of X were the same as the price of Y, since a unit of X has the same marginal value to her as a unit of Y. But if this were so, Mrs A would not be in equilibrium; she would have an incentive to increase her consumption of Y at the expense of her consumption of X, since 1 unit of X costs the same as 1 unit of Y but has only $\frac{1}{2}$ the importance to her as a unit of Y at the margin of her consumption.

(2) THE MAXIMIZATION OF PRODUCTION

If it were possible to increase the output of one product without reducing the output of any other product, then clearly the system would be an inefficient one in the sense that it would be possible to make someone better off without making anyone else worse off. We will assume that each individual firm or farm is efficient in the sense that it could not produce more of any one product without either producing less of some other product or using more of some factor of production.[1] But there remains the essentially economic question to ensure that the various factors and products are shuffled around the various firms and farms so that it is not possible to increase the output of one product without decreasing the output of some other. There are three ways in which such a reshuffling of factors and products might be able to increase the output of one product without decreasing the output of any other

First, suppose that the marginal product of the factor *L* were 1 unit of *X* in farm A but 2 units of *X* in farm B. Then a shift of 1 unit of *L* from farm A to farm B would result in a net increase of 1 unit of *X* of output. But clearly this situation could not persist in a competitive system; since the marginal product of labour in farm B is twice that in farm A, farmer B would be prepared to bid up the price of *L* above the level which farmer A would be prepared to pay. Labour would be attracted by the forces of competition from A to B.

Second, it might be possible by using more *L* and less *N* in farm A producing *X* and less *L* and more *N* in firm B producing *Y* to increase the output of *X* without reducing the output of *Y*.[2] Consider the case shown in Table XI. If 1 unit of *L* moves from B to A and

		Farm A	Firm B
Marginal Product of	*L*	2 units of *X*	1 unit of *Y*
	N	1 unit of *X*	1 unit of *Y*

Table XI

1 unit of *N* from A to B, the output of B remains unchanged but the output of A goes up by 1 unit of *X*. But this situation is incompatible with a competitive equilibrium. For Firm B to be in equilibrium the price of *L* must be equal to the price of *N*, since marginal products are the same. In this case, however, Farm A will not be in equilibrium but will find it profitable to employ a higher ratio of *L* to *N* since the marginal product of *L* is twice that of *N* while the price of *L* is the same as the price of *N*.

Third, it might be possible for Farm A, without any change in its

[1] But see the footnote at the end of Chapter XIV (p. 220).

[2] In this example *L* may naturally be taken to represent labour and *N* land. But the analysis would be exactly the same if *L* were one form of labour and *N* another. If *L* had a comparative advantage (see Chapter VI) in *X*-production and *N* in *Y*-production, the analysis in the text would still apply.

inputs of factors to re-arrange its output programme so as to produce 2 more *X* for each 1 unit of *Y* given up. At the same time it might be possible for Farm B to produce 1 more unit of *Y* for each unit of *X* given up. In this case if Farm A produced 2 more *X* and 1 less *Y* while Farm B produced 1 less *X* and 1 more *Y*, there would be a net increase in total output of 1 unit of *X* with no change in the output of *Y*. But this situation could not continue in a competitive equilibrium. Farm B would be in equilibrium only if the price of a unit of *X* were the same as the price of a unit of *Y*. But if this were so farmer A would have an incentive to produce more *X* and less *Y*, since if the prices of *X* and *Y* were the same he could earn more by producing 2 more units of *X* and 1 unit less of *Y*.

(3) THE OPTIMIZATION OF PRODUCTION

If trade is optimized and production maximized, it is impossible to make one consumer better off without making another worse off by redistributing existing outputs among consumers and it is impossible to produce more of one product without producing less of another; but it might still be possible to make one consumer better off without making another worse off by producing more of one product and less of another. For example, suppose that the marginal product of *L* is 1 unit of *X* and 1 unit of *Y* but that for Mrs A the loss of 1 unit of *X* could be compensated by the gain of ½ unit of *Y*. Mrs A could be made better off without anyone else being made worse off, if 1 unit of *L* were shifted from *X*-production to *Y*-production and Mrs A were given 1 more unit of *Y* and 1 less unit of *X* to consume. But this situation could not persist in a competitive equilibrium. Since the marginal product of *L* is the same in *X*-production as in *Y*-production, there would be no incentive to shift *L*, only if the price of *X* were the same as the price of *Y*. But if this were so, Mrs A would not be in equilibrium; she would have an incentive to purchase less X and more *Y*, since their prices are the same while *Y* is twice as important to her as *X* at the margin of her consumption.

The argument in the preceding paragraph is strictly correct only if the owner of the factor *L* has no preference for using it in *X*-production rather than in *Y*-production. If, however, *X*-production provided pleasant employment and *Y*-production unpleasant employment, while Mrs A could be made better off by having the marginal product of *L* in *Y* rather than *X*, the owner of *L* would be made worse off. The argument can, however, be readily extended to cover this point. The owners of *L* will in competitive equilibrium obtain a higher wage in *Y* than in *X* to compensate for the extra unpleasantness of the job. In competitive equilibrium the marginal cost of Y will be higher than the marginal cost of X by an amount sufficient to pay the owners of L the higher wage in Y. The market will, therefore, not give Mrs A the chance of obtaining for each 1 unit of X given up 1 additional unit of Y, but only 1 additional unit of Y less what is needed to compensate L for the move. If Mrs A prefers this smaller amount of Y to one unit of X, she can be made better off without the owner of L being worse off; and in this case the market will provide her with the incentive to make the change.

(4) THE OPTIMIZATION OF TRADE IN OCCUPATIONS

If the owners of factors which are equally efficient in all uses have nevertheless different attitudes towards the pleasantness or unpleasantness of the different uses for their factors, it might be possible through an exchange of occupations for one owner to be better off without any one else being worse off. If office-worker A prefers working out of doors and farmer B prefers working in an office, then both could be better off without any change in any output if they exchanged their jobs. But clearly the economy could not be in equilibrium in this inefficient situation. Mr A would be in equilibrium only if the wage paid for his office work were higher than the wage paid for a farm worker; but in this case Mr B would certainly not stay on the farm.

(5) THE OPTIMIZATION OF EFFORT

It might be possible for one citizen, Mr A, to be better off, without making anyone else worse off, by working less (more) and enjoying more (less) leisure while he enjoyed less (more) consumption of the products of work. Suppose that Mr A by working 1 hour less would reduce total output by 1 unit of X. The loss of real income imposed on the community would be 1 unit of X. Suppose that Mr A would be better off if he worked 1 hour less but consumed 1 less unit of X. Then it would be possible to make him better off without anyone else being worse off. More generally, suppose that he would be better off if he worked 1 hour less and reduced his own consumption by something which at the competitive prices which were the same for all citizens in the economy had the same value as 1 unit of X. Once again Mr A could be better off without making anyone else worse off. He would prefer the extra hour's leisure to the consumption of the equivalent of 1 unit of X, and the same value of commodities would be available for consumption by the other citizens. But if Mr A is paid an hourly wage equal to the value of his marginal product, he will be paid an hourly wage equal to the price of 1 unit of X. To the extent that it is possible for him to choose the amount of effort which he will provide, he will, therefore, always have an incentive to vary the amount of effort so long as it is possible for him thereby to be better off without anyone else being worse off.

We may thus conclude that our *laissez-faire* competitive stationary economy will be efficient in the sense that it will never come to rest in any situation in which it would still be possible to make one citizen better off without making any citizen worse off. But it is of the utmost importance to realize what this does not mean. Suppose we start from an inefficient situation (situation I) in which it is possible to make some people better off without making anyone else worse off. The forces of competition will enforce adjustments on this situation until some other situation (situation II) is reached in which it is no longer possible to make anyone better off without making someone else worse off. But this does not mean that no one will be worse off in situation II than in situation I. The fact that it is *possible* for some to be better off while no one is worse off in situation II than in situation I does not mean that *in fact* no one will be worse off in situation II than in situation I. The process of competitive adjustment from the inefficient situation I to the efficient situation II may have very marked effects upon the distribution of income; some citizens may gain a very great deal while others suffer some net loss.

An example may help to make the distinction clear.[1] Consider an economy in which there are only two factors of production—land and labour, in which all the land is owned by a small number of citizens who may also work but live to a large extent on their rents, and in which the vast majority of the population rely for their livelihood solely on the wages of labour. We continue the assumption that the total money income and expenditure of the community is constant at a given fixed level. Suppose that we start with some Governmental regulation or trade union arrangement whereby a minimum money wage rate is fixed at a level higher than that which would result from the unimpeded forces of competition. Labour is more expensive relatively to land than it would otherwise be. For all the reasons and in all the ways which we have examined at length in the previous chapters a lower ratio of labour to land is employed than would otherwise be the case. There is full employ-

[1] The case considered in Chapter IV (p. 77) has in fact already provided one good example of a possible clash between economic efficiency and distributional justice. We showed there the conditions in which a good harvest while it would certainly benefit the manufacturers (Group B) might hurt the farmers (Group A). It would clearly be inefficient for the farmers to get together and organize a bad harvest; but it might be in their own interests to do so.

ment of land but some labour is unemployed because at the regulated wage rate the demand for labour is unduly restrained. We may imagine our society to have an extended family system. In each family one out of four of the potential workers is involuntarily unemployed and is maintained out of the earnings of the remaining three workers.

This is an inefficient economic system. The marginal product of labour is still positive. If the unemployed workers did work, they would add something to the community's output. Since their unemployment is involuntary, it would be *possible* thereby to make everyone a bit better off without making anyone worse off.

If the minimum-wage regulation were removed, employment would be expanded. Competition would cause the money wage rate to fall. With a constant total money income the wage rate would fall relatively to the rate of rent. More labour would be employed per acre in all the ways which we have examined. Employment and output would increase. An equilibrium could be found of an efficient kind in the sense that, starting from that new equilibrium, it would be impossible to make anyone better off without making anyone else worse off.

But this does not mean to say that no one would be worse off in the final efficient equilibrium than they were in the inefficient wage-regulated situation. If the economic system is a rigid one in which substitutions of various kinds are difficult to make, then there may have to be a very large fall in the money wage rate and a considerable rise in the money rate of rent in order to absorb the unemployed labour into employment. The total real income of the working class might fall considerably, in which case the real income of the landlords would go up by more than the total increase in output. To take the very extreme case, in a very over-populated economy the marginal product of labour might actually fall to zero before full employment was reached. With the limited supply of other factors there might be no useful occupation that could be found for the final members of the community who sought employment. In this case for economic efficiency the wage rate should be zero. As a factor of production there is no shortage of labour. It is in excess supply. To make the most of productive resources entrepreneurs should treat labour as if it did not need to be economized at all. Its price should be zero. The only snag to this arrangement would be that the whole of the national income would go to the landlords.

This extreme example brings vividly to light the fact that the price of a factor of production, such as the rent of land or the wage of labour, plays a dual role: first, it acts as a measure of the scarcity of a factor and is thus a good signal of how far it should be economized;

second, it acts as a means of distributing income among the owners of the factors.

In the extreme example which we have just examined (but which may not be completely divorced from the situation to be found at present in some overpopulated underdeveloped countries) the clash between this double function of factor prices is most marked. A large part of economic policy consists of a judicious choice of measures which preserve a tolerable distribution of income without damaging too much the use of prices as guides to the efficient use of resources. The most complete way to deal with the clash is, no doubt, to affect fundamentally the distribution of the ownership of property. If, in our example, land were evenly owned by all citizens, prices could be used for the pursuit of economic efficiency without deterimental effects upon the distribution of income. What the representative citizen lost through a fall in his wages he would make up by a rise in his rents. Or if all property were owned by the State and the rents received by the State were used to pay social benefits to all the citizens, the same would be true. What the representative citizen lost through a fall in his wages he would make up by a rise in social benefits.

But there are other less extreme forms of policy which will affect the distribution of incomes at the loss of some economic efficiency. A tax on land-intensive products the revenue from which is used to subsidize labour-intensive products would indirectly reduce the demand for land and raise the demand for labour, but at the expense of some distortion of the pattern of production. There would be a tendency to produce too few land-intensive and too many labour-intensive products. A more direct measure would be to tax the incomes of the rich landlords and to use the revenue to pay social benefits to the poorer members of society. This might have little adverse effect upon economic efficiency other than to disturb somewhat the balance between work and leisure for those whose incomes were taxed—and even this effect might be avoided by confining the tax to incomes from rent.

The choice between policies depends, however, upon so many considerations which are avoided by the strict and unreal assumptions of Chapter I that we shall not pursue these matters further at this stage. We shall return to them in due course when we have made allowance in our economic system for more of the things that happen in the world of reality.

Note to Chapter XII

THE GEOMETRIC REPRESENTATION OF CONDITIONS FOR ECONOMIC EFFICIENCY

The discussion in this chapter of the Optimization of Trade in Products, the Maximization of Production, and the Optimization of Production can be illustrated by geometric constructions which we have used already in earlier chapters.

(1) *The Optimization of Trade in Products*

In Figure 51 (constructed on the same general principles as Figures 19, 20 and 21) we measure from the point A to the left along the horizontal axis (and upwards along the vertical axis) Mrs A's consumption of X (and of Y). Similarly Mrs B's consumption of X

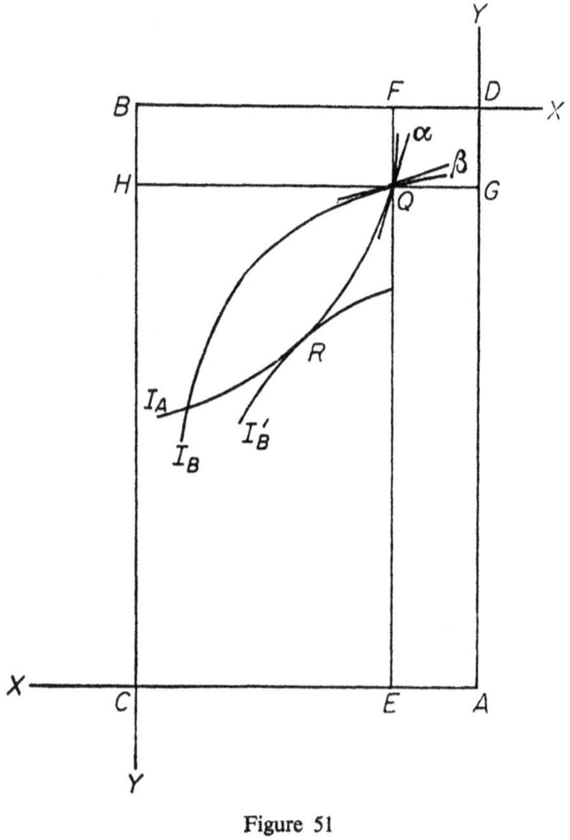

Figure 51

(and of Y) are measured horizontally to the right (and vertically downwards) from the point B. Figure 51 thus represents a case where together Mrs A and Mrs B are consuming an amount of X equal to AC and of Y equal to AD. The point Q would represent the case in which Mrs A was consuming AE of X and AG of Y while Mrs B was consuming BF of X and BH of Y. Through the point Q there will pass an indifference curve for Mrs A (marked I_A) and an indifference curve for Mrs B (marked I_B). Q is an inefficient point; if Mrs B gave up some of her X in exchange for Y and so moved to the point R, she would be better off (on a higher indifference curve I'_B) without Mrs A being worse off (on the same indifference curve I_A). Moreover the point Q is incompatible with perfectly competitive equilibrium. Mrs A could be in equilibrium at Q only if the market price of X in terms of Y were equal to the slope of the line α, while Mrs B could be in equilibrium at Q only if the market price ratio were equal to the slope of the line β. R, being a point at which the slope of I_A is the same as the slope of I'_B, is an efficient point and one which is compatible with competitive equilibrium.

(2) *The Maximization of Production*

(i) In Figure 52 we consider the possibility of increasing the total output of X by shifting some of the factor L from farm B to farm A. From point A we measure horizontally to the left (and vertically upwards) the amount of L employed (and of X produced) in farm A. We then draw (cf. Figure 41) the curve $AQRM$ showing the production of X by L in farm A. Similarly from point B horizontally to the right (and vertically downwards) we measure the amount of L employed (and of X produced) in farm B; and we draw the curve $BMHQ$ showing the production of X by L in farm B. The point Q represents a situation in which farm A is using AE of L to produce QE of X, while farm B is using BF of L to produce FQ of X. A total of L equal to AC is being used to produce a total of X equal to AD.

Q is an inefficient point. If GE of L were transferred from farm B to farm A, A's output would rise by a relatively large amount from QE to GR while B's output would fall by a relatively small amount from QF to HJ, giving a net increase in X of HR. The point Q is also incompatible with perfectly competitive equilibrium, since the marginal product of L is represented by the slope of the line α for farm A and by that of β for farm B, being higher for A than for B. L would be attracted from B to A.

The distribution of a given amount of L between A and B which gives the maximum output of X can be found in the following way. Move the axis $BJDL$ upwards away from the axis $AEGCL$ until the two production curves ($AQRM$ for A and $BMHQ$ for B) touch, but no longer cut each other. This would be so when *BJDL* had been raised to *B'J'D'L'*. At *R* the slopes of the two production curves (i.e. the marginal products of *L*) are the same in both farms. *AD'* is thus the largest output of *X* that can be obtained by distribu-

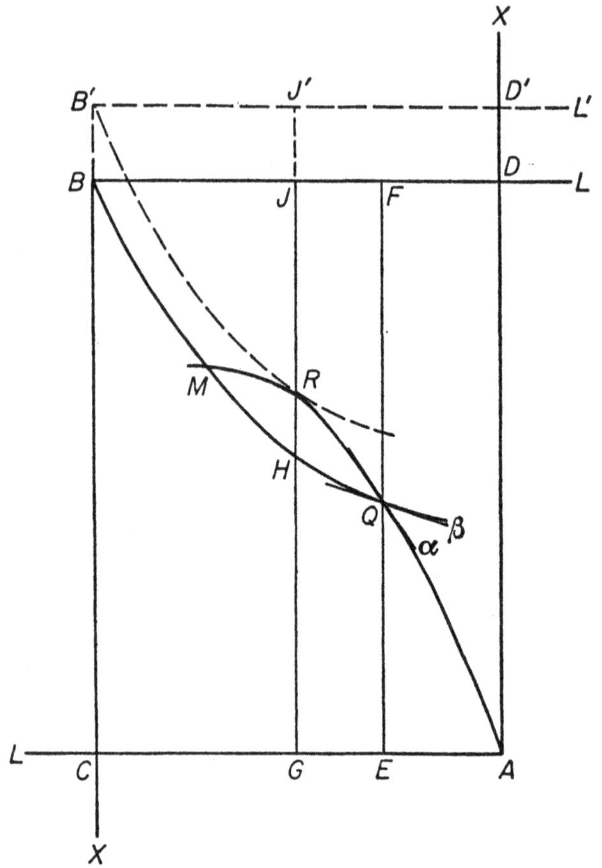

Figure 52

ting the given amount of labour *AC* between the two farms. *AG* should be employed by A and *B'J'* by B.

(ii) In Figure 53 we consider the possibility of increasing the output of *Y* without decreasing the output of *X* by reshuffling the two factors *L* and *N* between the *Y*-industry and the *X*-industry. Figure 53 is constructed on the same general lines as Figures 34, 35, 36 and 37. Horizontally to the left (and vertically upwards) from the point X we measure the amounts of L (and of N) used in the X-industry. Similarly from the point Y to the right (and downwards) we measure the amounts of L (and of N) employed in the Y-industry. At Q X is using CX of L and FX of N, while Y is using YD of L and YE of N. Through Q there passes an X-equi-product

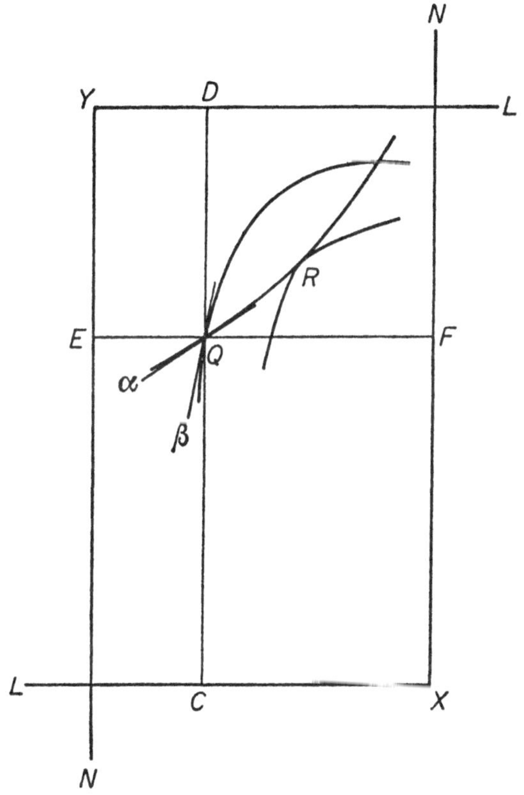

Figure 53

curve with the slope α and a Y-equi-product curve with the slope β. The fact that α is less steep than β indicates that at Q the marginal product of L relatively to the marginal product of N is lower in X than in Y. A shift of L from X to Y and of N from Y to X could bring one to the point R where the output of Y has gone up (the Y-industry is on a higher equi-product curve) while the output of X is unchanged (the X-industry is on the same equi-product curve). Moreover, the point Q would be incompatible with competitive equilibrium, since at that point the value of L relatively to the value of *N* would be lower for the *X*-entrepreneurs than for the *Y*-entrepreneurs.

(iii) Figure 54 represents a case in which it might be possible to increase the output of *Y* without decreasing the output of *X* by rearranging the output programmes of two farms. From the point A we measure to the left (and upwards) the amounts of *X* (and of *Y*) produced with a given amount of resources by farm A; and the curve *CMRQD* represents the farm's production possibility curve

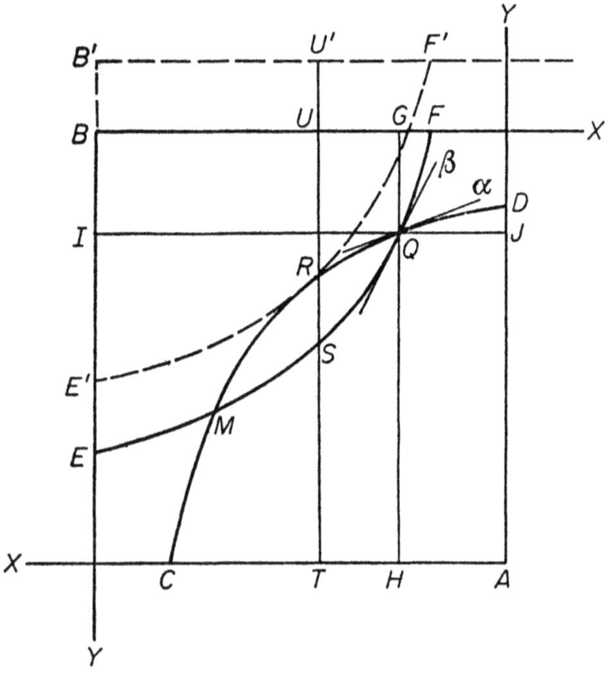

Figure 54

(cf. Figure 39). Similarly for farm B we draw the production possibility curve *EMSQF*, measuring the amounts of *X* (and of *Y*) produced by B to the right (and downwards) from the point *B*. The point *Q* represents a case where A is producing *AH* of *X* and *AJ* of *Y*, while B is producing *BG* of *X* and *BI* of *Y*. At *Q* the marginal cost of *X* relatively to the marginal cost of *Y* is relatively low in A (as shown by the gentle slope of α) and relatively high in B (as shown by the steep slope of β). *Q* is an inefficient point. If A produces *TH* more *X* and B produces *TH* less *X*, the output of *Y* will fall much less in A (from *QH* to *RT*) than it rises in B (from *GQ* to *US*). There is a net increase in *Y* of *RS*.

The point *Q* is incompatible with competitive equilibrium because the marginal cost slope α differs from the marginal cost slope β. They cannot, therefore, both be equal to the ratio of market prices for *X* and *Y*. The distribution of the output of *X* between A and B which will enable the output of *Y* to be maximized can be found by taking the axis *BUF* and raising it until the *B*-production-possibility curve no longer cuts, but just touches the *A*-production-possibility curve. This occurs in Figure 54 when *BUF* has been raised to *B′U′F′*. The output of *Y* has been increased by *BB′*. At *R* the marginal cost ratio is the same for both farms, as is shown by the fact that at this point the slopes of the production possibility curves are the same for A and for B.

(3) *The Optimization of Production*

In Figure 55 we consider the possibility that one consumer, Mrs A, might be made better off without anyone being made worse off if

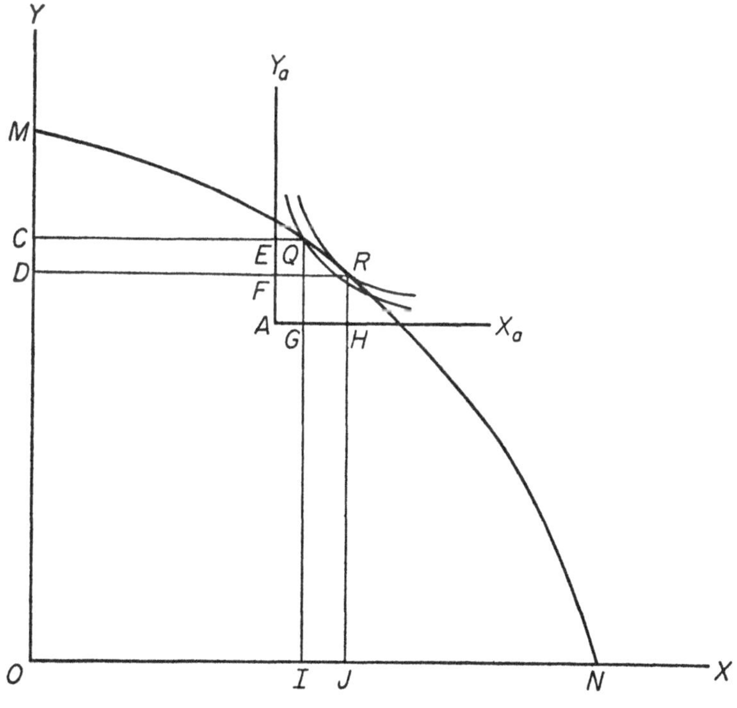

Figure 55

more X and less Y were produced and, at the same time, Mrs A consumed exactly so much more X and so much less Y. From O we measure to the right (and upwards) the total amounts of X (and of Y) produced in the whole economy. We then draw the production possibility curve $MQRN$ for the whole economy. On a separate set of axes, AX_a and AY_a, we measure the amounts of X and of Y consumed by Mrs A. The configuration of the two sets of axes in Figure 55 represents the case where the whole economy is producing at the point Q (i.e. CQ of X and QI of Y), while Mrs A is also consuming at the point Q (i.e. EQ of X and QG of Y). There remains, therefore, for consumption by other citizens CE of X and GI of Y. The slope of Mrs A's indifference curve at Q is steeper than the slope of the community's production possibility curve at Q. If we moved from Q to R Mrs A would be better off (i.e. on a higher indifference curve), while no one else need be worse off, since there remains the same outputs of X and Y ($DF = CE$ units of X and $HJ = GI$ units of Y) for consumption by citizens other than Mrs A. Q is, therefore, an inefficient position. But it could not persist in a competitive equilibrium since the market price of X in terms of Y which would give Mrs A no incentive to alter her consumption of X and Y would be higher than the economy's marginal cost of X in terms of Y.

CHAPTER XIII

THE CENTRALLY PLANNED ECONOMY

(i) THE ORGANIZATION OF CONSUMPTION

We have now considered at length the problem of the allocation of resources to various uses in a completely competitive *laissez-faire* stationary economy. In the three remaining chapters of this volume we will consider how these same problems would present themselves in a completely socialized, centrally planned stationary economy. We maintain all the ten assumptions made in Chapter I (pp. 26–27) except for assumption (3). Assumption (3) stated that the economy was organized on the basis of completely competitive institutions, each individual citizen being free to organize the production of whatever he chose in whatever manner he chose, to hire out his own labour services and the services of his privately owned land to any employer he chose for any use he chose, and to purchase for consumption whatever he chose. We will now start by replacing this extreme *laissez-faire* assumption by another assumption which is equally extreme in the opposite direction. We will assume that there is a single central planning authority which owns all the land (i.e. all the productive resources other than the services of labour), which appoints managers of various firms and farms, which allots to each of these managers the amounts of the various factors of production (various classes of labour and various kinds of land) for his employment, which informs each manager how much of each product he is required to produce with these resources, which directs the individual citizens to the various firms and farms for work, and which allots the finished products to the individual consumers for their enjoyment.

Let us imagine such a system in operation. Certain daily inputs of factors are in fact being used by each manager of a firm or farm and certain daily outputs of products are being produced by each firm or farm; and these products are passing daily into the hands of the individual consumers as each citizen claims his daily ration of each product. The central planning authority would, however, need to consider whether there were any rearrangements of these planned inputs, outputs, and consumers' rations which would represent a more desirable state of affairs. The basic rearrangements which the central authority would have to consider would be the following.

(1) *The problem of the best distribution of real income between the citizens.* Would it be better to give one class of citizens (e.g. the aged) a larger amount to consume at the expense of another class of citizens (e.g. the young)?

(2) *The problem of the optimization of trade in products.* Would it be possible to make some classes of citizens better off without making any worse off by giving to one class of citizens a larger ration of one product and a smaller ration of another product and to another class of citizens a smaller ration of the first and a larger ration of the second product (e.g. by giving the aged more wheel-chairs and less perambulators and by giving the young less wheel-chairs and more perambulators)?

(3) *The problem of the maximization of production.* Would it be possible by reshuffling the resources of land and labour among the various processes in the various firms and farms to increase the community's output of some products without reducing the output of any others?

(4) *The problem of the optimization of production.* Would it be possible to make some citizens better off without making any worse off by altering the output plan for the community (e.g. by allotting less resources to the food industries and more to the clothing industry if there were some classes in the community who were overfed but underclad)?

(5) *The problem of the optimization of trade in occupations.* Would it be possible to make some citizens better off without making any others worse off by altering the distribution of jobs among them (e.g. by directing Mr A to work in plant C rather than plant D and Mr B to work in plant D rather than plant C)?

(6) *The problem of the optimization of effort.* Should hours of work be increased or decreased?

(7) *The problem of the fair distribution of work between the citizens.* Should one class of citizens be asked to relieve another by lengthening the hours of work of the former and shortening those of the latter?

The first and last of these problems are concerned with equity in the distribution of welfare between the citizens—with the distribution of the products of labour (problem 1) and with the distribution of the toil of work itself (problem 7). The other five problems correspond to the five conditions for ensuring efficiency in an economic system which we discussed for a competitive economy in the preceding chapter (pp. 185–88). We will now consider how these seven problems concerning both equity in distribution and efficiency in trade and production may be handled in a centrally planned economy. We will do this by considering in turn three main sectors of the economy. In the remainder of this chapter we will consider the organization of the allocation of consumption goods to consumers (problems 1 and 2). In Chapter XIV we will consider the organization of the processes of production in the State owned firms and farms (problems 3 and 4). Finally, in Chapter XV we will consider the organization of the labour force in the centrally planned economy (problems 5, 6, and 7).

Let us consider first the allocation of consumer goods to the individual citizens. In the extreme type of the planned economy one must imagine that the central authority allots a quantitative ration of each product to each consumer. This would be a most formidable procedure in any modern community with the enormous range of products available for consumption. Each teenage girl would be allotted 100 loaves of bread, 5 lipsticks, 10 nylon stockings, 3 long-playing records of the large size and 2 of the small size, 1 pillow case, 10 cinema tickets, etc., etc., per year; and so on for the rest of the community. The question would then arise whether the citizens would be allowed to organize between themselves a market or markets for the exchange of their products. Would the musical non-smokers be allowed to give up their ration of cigarettes to obtain from the non-musical smokers their ration of concert tickets in exchange?

If such organized exchange were made illegal, that would be the end of the matter. The central authority would be acting as the head of the family does towards the infant members of the family in making for all the decision as to how much each member should have of each available supply.

If, on the other hand, the individual citizens were permitted to organize the exchange between them of the supplies which had been allotted to them, a system of prices would evolve at which the individual citizens would buy or sell particular consumption goods. If there were no official money in our planned economy, some convenient consumption good would probably acquire the status of the *numeraire* in terms of which the market exchange rate between the other products was reckoned. Thus a cigarette might become the measure of value. Those who had long-playing records which they wished to 'sell' in order to 'purchase' additional supplies of note-paper over and above their ration would hand the records over to some dealer for a credit of so many 'cigarettes' and could use this credit of 'cigarettes' to 'spend' on the purchase of so many pads of notepaper. The market prices of records and of notepaper in terms of cigarettes would determine how much notepaper could be obtained for a record.[1]

If this sort of free market for consumption goods were allowed to develop, the allotment of the original rations of each commodity to each class of consumer would deal with problem (1) (p. 200). The central authority would have to decide what it considered was a fair and equitable distribution of real income between the citizens. But the free market for consumption goods would deal with the problem of the optimization of trade in products (problem (2), p. 200). In an organized market there could at any one time be only one cigarette-price ruling for records and only one cigarette-price ruling for notepaper. Any citizens could sell records for notepaper or notepaper for records at this same given rate of exchange. If any two citizens could trade to the advantage of both, they would so trade, the citizen with the high valuation of notepaper in terms of records selling records and buying notepaper and the citizen with the low valuation of notepaper in terms of records selling notepaper and buying records.

Nor would such mutually satisfactory transactions necessarily be bilateral. If citizen A had a specially high valuation of notepaper and low valuation of records, citizen B a high valuation of cinema tickets and a low valuation of notepaper, and citizen C a high valuation of records and a low valuation of cinema tickets, then A could sell records and buy notepaper, B sell notepaper and buy cinema tickets, and C sell cinema tickets and buy records—all transactions taking place with a dealer in terms of cigarettes.

But if this sort of result were desired, it would be much simpler for the central authority to organize the distribution of the supplies of the various consumption goods among the individual citizens by means of a market in the first instance. This could be done in the following manner. The central authority would allot to each citizen each week or each year a certain amount of money (so many $ notes) to be spent during that period on consumption goods. The available supplies of consumption goods would then be sold through State shops to the individual consumers at the highest price which could be obtained for them; the citizens would be competing with each other with their predetermined money incomes for the available

[1] The argument in the text neglects the basic monetary problem of what determines the value of cigarettes themselves when cigarettes are needed for the double purpose of (i) being smoked and (ii) serving as the citizens' stock of money. The absolute level of the cigarette price of other goods is thus left undiscussed. In the text we are concerned solely with showing that some common *numeraire* would be needed in which to measure the values of other goods in terms of each other.

supplies. The issue of the money incomes by the State to the various classes of citizens would in this case determine the distribution of real income between the citizens (problem (1), p. 200); the setting of a single structure of money prices which would clear the market for each consumption good through the competition of the individual citizens would ensure the optimization of trade (problem (2), p. 200).

We have so far discussed the market for consumption goods as if one extreme or the other should be adopted. Either the central authority would decide in a paternalistic manner how much of each product each citizen should consume (a system of rationing with subsequent trading disallowed) or else the authority, having decided in a paternalistic manner what would be a fair distribution of income between citizens, would allow the citizens complete freedom by means of a market to 'optimize trade' between them. But there are in fact many intermediate possibilities. Thus it may well be thought best for a whole range of items (records and notepaper included) to organize distribution through the issue of money incomes to the citizens and the sale of these products through State shops at prices which will clear the market for each product. But it is quite compatible with this (i) that for some goods, e.g. education, the central authority should simply supply a given amount to each citizen, (ii) that for other commodities, e.g. cigarettes, the central authority on paternalistic grounds in order to prevent any one citizen consuming more than was good for him or her should organize the sale of supplies through the State shops but subject to a maximum individual ration, the individuals not being compelled to purchase the whole of their ration but also not being permitted to resell their rationed supplies to other citizens, and (iii) that for still other commodities, e.g. house-room or orange juice, the central authority on paternalistic grounds in order to ensure that each citizen consumed at least as much as his or her health required, should supply a basic ration to each citizen free of charge, which they could not resell to other citizens, but should leave the citizens free to purchase additional supplies through the State shops at whatever price would clear the market for these additional supplies.

In organizing the distribution of goods and services to final consumers in a planned economy some elements of market mechanism and some elements of quantitative allocation are likely to find a place in the system.

CHAPTER XIV

THE CENTRALLY PLANNED ECONOMY (ii) THE ORGANIZATION OF PRODUCTION

Let us turn now to the way in which the Central Authority might cope with problems (3) and (4) on page 200, namely, the maximization and the optimization of production. For this purpose we regard the production system as being composed of a vast set of distinct processes as illustrated in Table XII. Each process is completely

Processes of Production

	I	II	III	IV	etc.
Outputs	Z_1	Z_2	Z_3	Z_4	
	Y_1	Y_2	Y_3	Y_4	
	X_1	X_2	X_3	X_4	
	W_1	W_2	W_3	W_4	
Inputs	N_1	N_2	N_3	N_4	
	M_1	M_2	M_3	M_4	
	L_1	L_2	L_3	L_4	
	K_1	K_2	K_3	K_4	
Scale of Process	S_1	S_2	S_3	S_4	

Table XII

rigid in the sense that the ratio between any one input and any one output is fixed and unchangeable in any one process. Thus in process I in Table XII if Z_1 units of product Z are to be produced, Y_1 units of product Y will necessarily also be produced and N_1 units of factor N will necessarily be employed, and similarly for every other output and input in process I. Each process is thus subject to constant returns to scale in the sense that if each and every input were doubled then each and every output would be doubled. For each process we define arbitrarily a unit for the scale of its operation. Thus, for example, we define a unit of process I as the production of amount Z_1 of Z and thus amounts Y_1X_1 and W_1 of outputs YX and W the use of amounts $N_1M_1L_1$ and K_1 of inputs $NMLK$. Since Z_1

is the output of Z which comes from process I when process I is operated on a unitary scale, the total amount of Z produced by process I is Z_1S_1 where S_1 measures the scale on which process I is operated. For example, if $S_1 = 21$, then the output of Z from process I is 21 times Z_1 and similarly for the other outputs and inputs in process I.

If for practical purposes the whole of the productive possibilities in the economy are to be described by a collection of possible processes of this kind, then we must have not only a different process to describe each industry (dairy farms have one set of inputs and outputs and clothing factories another set of inputs and outputs), but we must have a large collection of processes to describe the possibilities of substitution between inputs and between outputs within any one industry (the dairy farm has one process describing the way in which much butter and little cheese can be produced with much labour and little land, another describing the way in which much butter and little cheese can be produced with little labour and much land, and so on). There are thus groups of processes which describe the possibilities of production within different industries. As we have already argued in Chapter XI, simply by enumerating a sufficient number of slightly different processes for each industry, we can approximate to the situation in which there is a continuous possibility of gradual substitution or transformation between any input or output and any other input or output within an industry.

The Central Authority in the case of extreme centralized quantitative planning of the economy would have to direct the manager of each firm as to which processes to use and on what scale to use each process.[1]

In order that the Central Authority should be able to deal in a satisfactory manner with the organization of this production system it would have to be informed of all the possible processes in all the industries and it would also have to know what were the total available supplies of each factor of production—*KLMN*. Its task would then be to determine on what scale each process should be operated and to allot to each firm that amount of each factor which was necessary to enable it to operate its processes on the planned scales.

Let us consider then how it might set about the solution of the problem of the maximization of production (problem 3 on p. 200). The problem will always present itself in the form of the question whether the existing state of affairs should be modified. At any one

[1] Since the decision not to use process I is simply a decision to use it on a scale equal to zero (i.e. to set $S_1 = 0$), we can describe the whole problem of the Central Authority as that of deciding the values for S_1, S_2, S_3, etc., in Table XII.

time certain inputs will be being used in each firm to produce certain outputs by means of certain processes. The Central Authority knows that the total supplies of the factors available to the community ($K\,L\,M\,N$) are in fact being used to produce certain total outputs of consumption goods—amounts which we will call $\bar{W}\,\bar{X}\,\bar{Y}\,\bar{Z}$. In order to determine whether production is being maximized the Central Authority must ask the following type of question: 'Is it possible to change the scales of the various processes in such a way as to increase the output of, say, Z above the present level $\bar{Z}$ without reducing the other outputs below their existing levels $\bar{W}\,\bar{X}\,\bar{Y}$, etc., and without using more than the total available amounts of factors, $K\,L\,M\,N$, etc.?'

This problem is set out formally in Table XIII. The object is to make the total supply of Z (i.e. $Z_1S_1 + Z_2S_2 + Z_3S_3 + \ldots$) as great as possible without (*a*) reducing any other output below its existing level (for example the output of Y equals $Y_1S_1 + Y_2S_2 + Y_3S_3$ and this must not be reduced below its existing level $\bar{Y}$) or

Problem: to find values of $S_1\; S_2\; S_3$, etc., such that

$$Z = Z_1S_1 + Z_2S_2 + Z_3S_3 + \ldots$$

is maximized, subject to the constraints:—

$$\begin{aligned} (a)\quad & Y_1S_1 + Y_2S_2 + Y_3S_3 + \ldots\ldots \geqslant \bar{Y} \\ & X_1S_1 + X_2S_2 + X_3S_3 + \ldots\ldots \geqslant \bar{X} \\ & \ldots\ldots\ldots\ldots\ldots \\ (b)\quad & N_1S_1 + N_2S_2 + N_3S_3 + \ldots\ldots \leqslant N \\ & M_1S_1 + M_2S_2 + M_3S_3 + \ldots\ldots \leqslant M \\ & \ldots\ldots\ldots\ldots\ldots \\ (c)\quad & S_1 \geqslant 0 \quad S_2 \geqslant 0 \quad S_3 \geqslant 0, \text{ etc.} \end{aligned}$$

Table XIII

(*b*) using any factor in a greater amount than its total available supply (for example, the employment of N is equal to $N_1S_1 + N_2S_2 + N_3S_3 + \ldots$ and this must not be raised above the available supply N) or (*c*) being involved in the nonsense requirement that the scale on which any particular process is operated should be reduced below zero.

The type of problem set out in Table XIII is known as a problem in linear programming. If the values $\bar{Y}\,\bar{X}$, etc., $N\,M$, etc., and the technical coefficients in each process $Z_1\,Y_1X_1 \ldots N_1M_1 \ldots$, etc., are all known, then it is possible to find the values of $S_1 S_2$, etc., which will give the maximum value of Z. We shall not be concerned with the mathematical or computer techniques which are involved in the solution of such problems, but will consider how the answer to the problem could be used by the Central Authority.

If the maximum possible value of Z as reported by the computer is the same as the level of Z actually being produced, then the Central Authority will know that the existing plan is one which maximizes production. But if the maximum possible Z is above the existing level of Z, then the Central Authority will know that the present plan is economically inefficient. It could alter the plan, i.e. alter the scale of the different processes, in such a way as to produce more Z without reducing any other output. In order to do so it would, of course, have to reallocate the available factors between the various firms in order to enable each firm to carry out the new plan. Thus if the computer says that S_4 should be 11, then the Central Authority must allocate to the manager in charge of process IV an amount of factor N equal to 11 times N_4, and similarly for all factors and all processes.

But would the Central Authority necessarily wish to revise the plan in just this way? Suppose the computer told it that the present plan was economically very inefficient in the sense that the greatest possible value of Z was very greatly in excess of the present output of Z. Would the Central Authority wish to take up all the slack by increasing the output of Z alone? Even though Z had been chosen by the Central Authority as a product of great importance of which it appeared particularly desirable to obtain an increased supply, yet the increased supply of Z might be so great that to take up all the productive slack in the system in this particular form might swamp the economy with Z while other products remained relatively scarce.

In other words before the production plan is revised the Central Authority may well wish to consider the optimization of production (problem 4 on p. 200) as well as the maximization of production. To produce all the maximum possible amount of Z will maximize production; but if that were done, it might then well be desirable to optimize production by producing less Z (whose marginal value will be very low because its supply is so great) and more Y or X (whose marginal values will still be relatively high). It would be an obvious waste to reorganize the whole production plan, first, to produce an enormous increase in the output of Z and then, secondly, to produce less Z and more Y or X. Why not take the whole revision at one single step?

If it were possible to set 'demand prices' ($P_x P_y P_z$, etc.) for the products (XYZ, etc.) which properly measured the valuations which should be set on the various products, then it would be possible to set the computer a fresh problem the solution of which would simultaneously deal with the maximization and the optimization of production. This problem is set out formally in Table XIV. The expression $Z_1P_z + Y_1P_y + X_1P_x + \ldots$ measures the value to society of increasing the scale of process I by one unit; it represents

---

Problem: to find values of S_1 S_2 S_3, etc., such that

$$\begin{aligned} &(Z_1P_z + Y_1P_y + X_1P_x + \ldots)S_1 \\ &+(Z_2P_z + Y_2P_y + X_2P_x + \ldots)S_2 \\ &+(Z_3P_z + Y_3P_y + X_3P_x + \ldots)S_3 \\ &+\ldots. \end{aligned}$$

is maximized, subject to the constraints:—

$$\begin{aligned} (a)\ & N_1S_1 + N_2S_2 + N_3S_3 + \ldots \leqslant N \\ & M_1S_1 + M_2S_2 + M_3S_3 + \ldots \leqslant M \\ & \ldots\ldots\ldots\ldots \\ (b)\ & S_1 \geqslant 0 \quad S_2 \geqslant 0 \quad S_3 \geqslant 0, \text{ etc.} \end{aligned}$$

Table XIV

the outputs obtainable from one unit of process I valued at their prices, $P_zP_yP_x$, etc. Production will be maximized and optimized when the sum of these values of every process, each multiplied by its scale of operation, is maximized; for at this point the value of the total output of the whole production system will be maximized, when each individual output (Z Y X, etc.) is valued at its proper value to society ($P_zP_yP_x$, etc.). This value of total output is to be maximized subject to the constraints (*a*) that the total demand for each factor does not exceed the available supply of that factor and (*b*) that no process can be operated at less than a zero level. The computer can solve the problem set in Table XIV; and this will give the scales ($S_1S_2S_3$, etc.) for each process to be used in the revised production plan. The Central Authority can then revise the allocation of resources to the processes accordingly.

The basic difficulty in this solution of the planning problem is the choice of the prices $P_zP_yP_x$, etc. The difficulty is due to the interdependence between the outputs of the products (ZYX) which will be forthcoming in the revised production plan and the prices which would then properly measure their marginal importance to consumers ($P_zP_yP_x$). This problem remains whether (as discussed in the preceding chapter) the Central Authority (i) allows a free market in consumption goods and measures the importance to consumers of additional supplies of the various products by the prices which rule in this market or (ii) on paternalistic grounds itself assesses how much social value should be ascribed to the production of additional supplies of each product. In either case the free market prices or the paternalistic social valuations (the $P_z P_y P_x$, etc.) will depend upon the quantities of the products supplied for consumers. Suppose much Z and little X and Y is being supplied. Then in a free market P_z will be very low (since there is a glut of Z) and P_y and P_x very high (since there are scarcities of Y and X). Similarly if the State is setting paternalistic social valuations of the relative importance of increased supplies of the various products, it also will presumably set a low P_z if Z is very plentiful and a high P_y and P_x if Y and X are very scarce.

For the solution of the problem set in Table XIV the $P_z P_y P_x$, etc., which are relevant are the product prices which would be appropriate when the supplies under the revised plan are produced. But the Central Authority cannot know what these prices are until it knows what quantities will be supplied under the revised plan, and it cannot know what the supplies under the revised plan will be until it has told the computer at what prices the supplies should be valued. The Central Authority might proceed by guessing an appropriate set of product prices for the computer to work on. If it had no reason to believe that the revised plan would greatly alter the relative scarcities of the different products, it might, for example, take the ruling level of product prices as the ones on which the computer should work. But if these prices in fact turned out to be seriously inappropriate, the results might be disastrous.

Suppose, for example, that the existing level of P_z was unduly high, because the existing plan was producing an unduly small amount of Z and making it unduly scarce. Suppose further, simply by way of illustration, that Z was a product which could be produced only by process I and that process I produced only Z. Then, on the basis of the ruling price of Z, the computer might tell the Central Authority that the value of the national product could be maximized by shutting down all processes except process I so that the output of the valuable Z could be maximized regardless of the fact that nothing else at all would be produced.[1]

[1] Incidentally this would involve the partial unemployment of all factors of production except the factor in which process I was most intensive. When all the supplies of this factor had been transferred to process I and when there were employed with it the limited amounts of the other factors which were technically necessary to operate process I, the remaining supplies of these other factors would be unused. They could not be employed to operate any other process because there would not be available for the other processes any supply of the factor for which process I was providing full employment.

If the Central Authority wished to proceed by means of a centrally computed plan rather than by any process of actual trial and error in the market, it would have to cope with this basic problem of the mutual interdependence between the demand prices which are appropriate for the valuation of the outputs of the revised plan and those outputs themselves. In order to do this the Central Authority (i) must know what set of demand prices would be appropriate for every feasible set of outputs $Z\ Y\ X$, etc., and (ii) must modify the problem set to the computer in Table XIV by instructing it to discover the values for $S_1S_2S_3$, etc., which will maximize the value of the national output when the prices at which outputs are valued are those which in fact turn out to be appropriate to the new outputs themselves. On both these counts exclusive reliance on a centrally computed plan without any subsequent adjustments through actual trial and error in the market must probably be ruled out. Even if the information were available under (i), the mathematical problem under (ii) might well be incapable of solution. For there is no reason to believe that the relationships between the demand prices $P_zP_yP_x$ and the supplies $Z\ Y\ X$ would be at all simple in mathematical form. But whether or not the mathematical problem under (ii) could be solved, the problem of information under (i) would certainly be insoluble if the relationship between prices and outputs were to be judged by the free play of a consumers' market and not set solely by paternalistic State decision. For there is really no way of discovering in advance how consumers would value products when they come forward in amounts which consumers have not previously experienced. The solution of the Central Authority's production planning will almost certainly involve some process of actual trial and error in the market.

There are many particular forms which this process of market trial and error might take.[1] We will content ourselves with an outline of the sort of procedure which would be involved. The Central Authority might first calculate a plan for the maximization and optimization of production on the lines of Table XIV, starting with a rather arbitrary set of prices, $P_zP_yP_x$, etc., which on the basis of common-sense guesses and of such partial calculations as it could make seemed reasonable to assume. It could then compare with these prices the resulting quantities of outputs which the calculated

[1] Some of these forms may succeed while others may fail to find an equilibrium solution. This raises the dynamic problems of processes of adjustment which we do not intend to discuss in this volume. But the question is so fundamental in the problem of planning that we have added a Note at the end of this chapter (pp. 220–4) on 'The Stability of Trial-and-Error Planning'. The form of market trial and error described in the text takes account of the basic point made in that Note.

plan would involve. Where the resulting planned quantities seemed to be absurdly low (or high) in relation to the assumed set of demand prices, $P_zP_yP_x$, etc., these prices could be raised (or lowered) slightly. The plan could then be recalculated on the basis of the revised prices. This procedure could be repeated until a set of prices had been found which resulted in a set of planned supplies which seemed reasonably consistent with the demands which might be forthcoming at those prices.

The Central Authority could then set about the implementation of this plan by moving by small gradual degrees the resources which were at present most out of place relatively to the new revised plan. As the new plan was implemented and supplies were gradually changed so as to conform more and more closely to the revised plan, there would be reactions in the markets for consumers' goods and new experiences on which the State could revise its paternalistic views about the needs of the citizens. In the light of these experiences the set of demand prices for outputs which might be expected to rule in the final equilibrium could be again revised. In the light of these revisions of final prices the plan could be recalculated and new very gradual adjustments could be made in the reallocation of resources. Thus by a continuous and gradual process of calculation, allocation of resources, recalculation, reallocation of resources, the Central Authority might hope to reach a final position of equilibrium in which production was maximized and optimized at a set of final prices, $P_zP_yP_x$, which was in fact appropriate to the set of final supplies, $Z\ Y\ X$, coming out of the production system.

So far we have discussed the problem of planning in terms of a completely centralized plan. This, as we have seen (p. 205), involves the Central Authority knowing every single process that every single manager could use in his firm or farm and giving instructions from the centre about the scale on which each manager should use each and every process. But in fact it is impossible to expect the Central Authority to have all the detailed knowledge of the technical possibilities of each industry in each region of the economy. In a planned economy there are for this reason strong arguments for a more decentralized system whereby the Central Authority would make decisions only about the broad allocation of resources among the main industries and/or regions in the economic system. In this case there would be Subordinate Authorities which would possess much more detailed technical knowledge of the specific problems involved in their limited sectors of the economy and who would be responsible for making the best use of the resources which the Central Authority had allocated for use in their sector. Such Subordinate Authorities might be regional authorities, charged with the determination of the whole use of resources within a region, or industrial authorities charged with the determination of the use of all the resources allocated to one industry, or industrial-regional authorities charged with the use of the resources allocated to one industry in one region, or merely managers of firms or farms charged with the use of the resources allocated to one such productive unit.

But whatever may be the best structure for such Subordinate Authorities the problem of principle would be the same. How could the Central and the Subordinate Authorities best divide the responsibilities of planning between them? Here again there is a very large number of possible arrangements and we will illustrate the position by outlining one possible procedure.

The Central Authority might allocate to each Subordinate Authority a given amount of each resource—a given amount of each type of labour and each quality of land—and also inform each Subordinate Authority of the planning prices or social valuations, $P_z P_y P_x$, etc., at which it would value the outputs produced by the Subordinate Authority. It would then be up to each Subordinate Authority with its own special knowledge of the special technical problems of its own branch of the economy to produce the output of the greatest value from the resources allotted to it. Each Subordinate Authority would, in fact, itself be confronted with a problem exactly similar to that illustrated in Table XIV above for the economy as a whole. On the basis of the product prices, $P_z P_y P_x$, announced to it by the Central Authority each Subordinate Authority would maximize and optimize the production which could be achieved by the use of the resources allocated to it by the Central Authority. The Central Authority would take over the outputs produced by the Subordinate Authorities and would dispose of them either through paternalistically determined rations or through market sales to the individual consuming citizens. In the light of its experience in the disposal of supplies to consumers the Central Authority could revise the prices, $P_z P_y P_x$, at which the Subordinate Authorities should value their outputs. By a process of trial and error the Central Authority could thus set a structure of prices which called forth from the Subordinate Authorities a set of supplies of final products which was appropriate to those prices.

But with this system there would still remain the problem of determining whether or not to change the allocation of resources among the Subordinate Authorities. How could the Central Authority decide whether, for the economy as a whole, the social value of total output might not be increased by a reallocation of resources as between the different Subordinate Authorities? For this purpose it is clearly necessary that the information reported by the Subordinate Authorities to the Central Authority should somehow or another enable the Central Authority to determine whether the value of the marginal product of any given resource is in fact greater in the case of one Subordinate Authority than in that of another.

Now it so happens that very closely connected with the calculations which a Subordinate Authority must carry out in order to know how to maximize the value of the output which it can produce with the resources given to it is another set of calculations which will in fact reveal to it what are the values of the marginal products of its various resources when they are used in this optimum fashion. In the jargon of Linear Programming the former set of calculations, concerned with the optimum use of its resources, is called the Primal and the latter set of calculations, concerned with the values of the resources, is called the Dual. In fact each Primal problem in Linear Programming has a Dual associated with it. We will proceed, first, by a simple description of the formal correspondence between a Primal and a Dual problem and, second, by considering the economic meaning of these interconnections for the particular planning problem which we are discussing.[1]

The top half of Table XV repeats from Table XIV the problem of the maximization and optimization of production as it would present itself to a Subordinate Authority. This authority has resources equal to $N\ M$, etc., which it can use in processes I, II, III, etc., on scales $S_1S_2S_3$, etc., to produce outputs. Instead of writing the value of the output from process I as $Z_1P_z + Y_1P_y + X_1P_x +$ ... (as was done in Table XIV), we now write it simply as V_1. This is done solely for convenience, in order to make Table XV less clumsy. V_1, V_2, V_3, etc., are simply measures of the value of the outputs produced by processes I, II, III, etc., when operated on a unitary scale and when the outputs are valued at the given prices $P_zP_yP_x$, etc.

Now the Subordinate Authority could set itself the problem called the Dual and shown in the bottom half of Table XV. Whether there is any economic meaning or sense to be attached to this problem of the Dual is another matter to which we will return shortly. At the moment we are concerned only to describe the Dual problem and to state (without giving any proof of the statements) what are in fact the main formal connections between the Primal problem and its solution, on the one hand, and, on the other hand, the Dual problem and its solution. In the Dual problem the Subordinate Authority sets itself the task of finding certain shadow prices, $P_nP_mP_l$, etc., for the resources $N\ M\ L$, etc. These prices are to be as low as possible

[1] These interconnections are illustrated by a simple example of a Primal and a Dual problem in Note B at the end of this chapter (pp. 224–30 below).

Primal: to find values of $S_1\ S_2\ S_3$, etc., such that

$$V_1S_1 + V_2S_2 + V_3S_3 + \text{etc.}$$

is maximized, subject to the constraints:—

$$(a)\ N_1S_1 + N_2S_2 + N_3S_3 + \ldots\ldots \leqslant N$$

$$M_1S_1 + M_2S_2 + M_3S_3 + \ldots\ldots \leqslant M$$

$$\ldots\ldots\ldots\ldots$$

$$(b)\ S_1 \geqslant 0 \quad S_2 \geqslant 0 \quad S_3 \geqslant 0, \text{ etc.}$$

Dual: to find values of $P_nP_mP_l$, etc., such that

$$NP_n + MP_m + LP_l + \text{etc.} \ldots$$

is minimized, subject to the constraints:—

$$(a)\ N_1P_n + M_1P_m + L_1P_l + \ldots\ldots \geqslant V_1$$

$$N_2P_n + M_2P_m + L_2P_l + \ldots\ldots \geqslant V_2$$

$$\ldots\ldots\ldots\ldots$$

$$(b)\ P_n \geqslant 0 \quad P_m \geqslant 0 \quad P_l \geqslant 0, \text{ etc.}$$

Table XV

in the sense that, valued at these prices, the total cost of all the resources available to the Subordinate Authority is as low as possible. In other words, $NP_n + MP_m + LP_l +$ etc. is to be minimized. But the 'shadow prices' must not be set so low as to leave any one process making a net profit; for example, the cost of operating process I on a unitary scale must not be less than the value of the output of this process. Since N_1 is the amount of N needed to operate process I on a unitary scale and similarly for M_1L_1, etc., the condition that no net profit should be left on process I is that $N_1P_n + M_1P_m + L_1P_l +$etc. (the cost of operation of process I), is at least as great as V_1 (the value of the output produced by process I). Similarly, for the other processes, costs must be at least as high as receipts. Finally, the 'shadow prices' themselves must not be less than zero.

The Dual problem at the bottom half of Table XV is similar in structure to the Primal problem at the top of the tables. The computer can solve the Dual as readily as the Primal.[1] Now it is a

[1] In fact the solution of the Primal can be used very simply to find the solution of the Dual; or the solution of the Dual can be used very simply to find the solution of the Primal. The computer need not do all the sums twice. But we are not concerned here with the mathematical techniques involved.

mathematical fact that there will be certain relationships between the results of the solution of the Primal and the results of the solution of the Dual. We will examine later the important economic meaning of these relationships. At the moment we will merely state them without either mathematical proof of their validity or economic interpretation of their meaning.

It will be observed that if there are, say, 1000 processes whose scale had to be determined in the Primal (S_1S_2, etc., up to S_{1000} to be determined) there are necessarily 1000 of the constraints of type (*a*) in the Dual (costs $\geqslant$ receipts for each of the 1000 processes). It is a mathematical fact that the solution of the Primal will make any one of the *S*'s zero, if in the corresponding constraint in the Dual costs for that process exceed receipts. It is also a mathematical fact that for any one of the *S*'s which the solution of the Primal says should be positive, costs will equal receipts in the corresponding constraint in the Dual.

It will similarly be observed that if there are, say, 400 factors whose shadow prices had to be determined in the Dual ($P_nP_mP_l$, etc., up to P_{400} to be determined) there are necessarily 400 constraints of type (*a*) in the Primal. It is a mathematical fact that the solution of the Dual will make any of the factor prices ($P_nP_mP_l$, etc.) zero, if in the corresponding restraint in the Primal the demand for the factor is less than the available supply. It is also a mathematical fact that for any of the factor prices which the solution of the Dual says should be positive, demand will equal supply for that factor in the corresponding constraint in the Primal.

It is now possible to see the economic meaning of the solution of the Dual. The solution of the Primal tells the Subordinate Authority what processes to use and on what scale to use them in order to get the maximum value of output out of the resources available to it. The Dual finds a set of 'shadow prices' for the resources which have the following properties. Those processes which (according to the Primal) the Subordinate Authority ought to use would just cover their costs, no more and no less, while the Subordinate Authority ought not to use those processes which would in fact make a loss, when the outputs are valued at the prices given by the Central Authority ($P_zP_yP_x$, etc.) and the factors are valued at the shadow prices given by the solution of the Dual ($P_nP_mP_l$, etc.). In other words these 'shadow prices' of the factors correspond to the factor prices which would arise in a perfectly competitive system when production was in equilibrium to meet demands at the given set of selling prices, $P_zP_yP_x$.

The 'shadow price' of a factor would in other words measure the value of the marginal product of that factor to the Subordinate

Authority concerned. This can be seen by a process of reasoning similar to that given above for the competitive system (p. 183). Suppose that a Subordinate Authority were given one more unit of resource N to use. If resource N is already in excess supply to the Subordinate Authority its marginal product will be zero. But in this case, as we have already stated, its shadow price will be zero. But suppose that N is not in excess supply. In order to use the additional unit of N, the Subordinate Authority would have to alter the values of the S's in its plan, expanding the scale of some process which was intensive in N and contracting the scale of some other processes which would release the other factors to go with the N. As a final result of the unit increase in N, the amounts of M L, etc., being unchanged, the inputs and outputs of some processes would be reduced and of others would be increased; the value of the marginal product of N is defined as the price of the outputs that have gone up less the price of any outputs that have gone down; but since the shadow costs of the factors are equal to the values of the outputs in each process that is being used, the value of the net increase of outputs must be equal to the value of the net increase in the inputs; and this is, of course, the shadow price of the additional unit of N. The shadow price of each factor measures the value of the marginal product of that factor to the Subordinate Authority concerned.

We are now in a position to summarize the way in which the Central and Subordinate Authorities might divide the responsibilities of planning between them. The Central Authority would start by allotting certain resources to the Subordinate Authorities and by requiring them to maximize the value of the outputs which could be obtained from these resources, the valuation of the outputs to be carried out at a set of prices determined by the Central Authority. Each Subordinate Authority would plan the use of its resources for this purpose and would report back to the Central Authority the shadow prices or marginal values of the various resources allotted to it. The Central Authority would take over the products produced by the various Subordinate Authorities and in the light of the total supplies thus made available for consumers it could revise the social valuations or demand prices which it set on the various products for the guidance of the Subordinate Authorities. It could also compare the shadow prices quoted by different Subordinate Authorities for the same resource and reallocate the resource in favour of the Subordinate Authorities for whom the value of its marginal product was highest. In the light of the new valuations of outputs and the new allocations of factors, the Subordinate Authorities could recalculate their plans, alter accordingly their outputs, and report back their changed shadow prices. The Central Authority could then react appropriately to these changed outputs and shadow prices, by revising once again the prices which it set for the outputs and the amounts of factors allotted to the various Subordinate Authorities. And so on, until a final equilibrium was achieved in which valuations of outputs were appropriate to the total amounts produced and the shadow price of each factor was the same to each Subordinate Authority. Total production would then be maximized and optimized.

In fact if it were so desired, similar results could be achieved by an even more decentralized process which would approximate very closely to that of a free competitive market mechanism. The Central Authority would announce to the Subordinate Authorities a set of prices ($P_z P_y P_x$, etc.) at which it would take over the products which they produced and a set of factor prices ($P_n P_m P_l$, etc.) at which it would make available to the Subordinate Authorities supplies of the various resources. The Subordinate Authorities would be told to maximize the excess of the values of their outputs over the costs of their inputs (in competitive—economy jargon, to maximize their profits); and for this purpose they would contract any processes which were failing to cover their costs and would expand any processes which were making a profit. The Central Authority would then adjust the prices of the products and of the factors, putting up the price of any product which was in deficient supply, putting down the price of any product in excess supply, putting up the price of any factor for which the demands of the Subordinate Authorities in total exceeded the available supply, and putting down the price of any factor for which the available supply exceeded the sum of the demands.[1] This procedure would also find its equilibrium only in a state in which total production was both maximized and optimized.

The system which we have just outlined is only one degree removed from a completely free competitive market system of the kind which we have examined at length in the first twelve chapters of this volume. The Central Authority could go to the extreme of (i) simply telling its Subordinate Authorities to maximize profits (perhaps giving them an incentive to do so by making their rewards rise or fall according to the total profit or loss they made on their operations), (ii) allowing consumers to compete freely for the available products and thus to determine the price of the products, (iii) allowing labour to move to the employment where it could obtain the best reward, (iv) hiring out the State-owned property of land to the highest bidders among the Subordinate Authorities, and (v) supplementing,

[1] The resources, under this system, would still have to be directly allocated to the various Subordinate Authorities; we will see in the next chapter how even the deployment of labour among its various uses might be decentralized.

on any principle of equity acceptable to the State, the market wages earned by the workers with social dividends paid out of the income received by the State on State-owned property.

But there is in fact an almost infinite variety of possible combinations of quantitative planning and of market mechanism. Simply to illustrate the possibilities we will close this chapter by describing one system whereby some elements in the economy could be subjected to a central quantitative plan while the others could be left to determination by the Subordinate Authorities through a market mechanism. Let us suppose that there are certain products (X and W) and certain factors (L and K) which the Central Authority wishes to plan quantitatively from the centre. Each Subordinate Authority is instructed to produce not less than its appropriate amount of X and of W and to use not more than its allotted amount of L and K. But there are other products (Z and Y) which each Subordinate Authority may produce in whatever quantity it chooses and certain other factors (N and M) which each Subordinate Authority may use in whatever quantities it chooses. The prices (P_z and P_y) at which the Central Authority will take these unplanned products and the prices (P_n and P_m) at which the Central Authority will provide these unplanned factors are announced to the Subordinate Authorities who are told to maximize the excess of their receipts from the production of their unplanned products over the costs of their unplanned factors.

Table XVI shows how this system would look to a single Subordinate Authority. The Primal tells it to choose scales for its different processes so as to maximize the value of its receipts from unplanned products over costs of unplanned factors. But this is subject to the conditions that it chooses scales for its processes that result in (*a*) the production of at least certain stated amounts ($\bar{X}$ and $\bar{W}$) of the planned products and (*b*) the use of not more than certain stated amounts (L and K) of the planned factors. The solution of the Primal will tell it what processes to operate and on what scales.

There is, as always, a Dual to this Primal which is shown in the second half of Table XVI. The Subordinate Authority is to find 'shadow prices' for the planned factors (P_l and P_k) and for the planned outputs (P_x and P_w). This will be done by choosing the lowest possible 'shadow prices' for the planned factors and the highest possible 'shadow prices' for the planned outputs so that the 'shadow loss' on the planned products and factors is minimized, subject to the constraints that for no single process should these 'shadow prices' of factors be so low and for products so high that the process showed a positive sum of 'shadow profits' (on the planned sector) and of 'actual profits' (on the unplanned sector). The 'shadow price' of any planned factor would as before measure the value of the marginal product of that factor to that Subordinate Authority and the 'shadow price' of any planned output would measure the

---

Primal: find values of S_1 S_2 S_3, etc., such that

$$(Z_1P_z + Y_1P_y - N_1P_n - M_1P_m)\,S_1 + (Z_2P_z + Y_2P_y - N_2P_n - M_2P_m)\,S_2 + (Z_3P_z + Y_3P_y - N_3P_n - M_3P_m)\,S_3 + \ldots\ldots$$

is maximized, subject to the constraints:—

(a) $X_1S_1 + X_2S_2 + X_3S_3 + \ldots\ldots \geqslant \bar{X}$

$W_1S_1 + W_2S_2 + W_3S_3 + \ldots\ldots \geqslant \bar{W}$

(b) $L_1S_1 + L_2S_2 + L_3S_3 + \ldots\ldots \leqslant L$

$K_1S_1 + K_2S_2 + K_3S_3 + \ldots\ldots \leqslant K$

(c) $S_1 \geqslant 0 \quad S_2 \geqslant 0 \quad S_3 \geqslant 0$, etc.

Dual: find values of P_x, P_w, P_l and P_k such that

$$LP_l + KP_k - \bar{X}P_x - \bar{W}P_w$$

is minimized, subject to the constraints:—

(a) $L_1P_l + K_1P_k - X_1P_x - W_1P_w \geqslant Z_1P_z + Y_1P_y - N_1P_n - M_1P_m$

$L_2P_l + K_2P_k - X_2P_x - W_2P_w \geqslant Z_2P_z + Y_2P_y - N_2P_n - M_2P_m$

$L_3P_l + K_3P_k - X_3P_x - W_3P_w \geqslant Z_3P_z + Y_3P_y - N_3P_n - M_3P_m$

. . . .

(b) $P_x \geqslant 0 \quad P_w \geqslant 0 \quad P_l \geqslant 0 \quad P_k \geqslant 0.$

Table XVI

marginal cost to that Subordinate Authority of producing more of that product. The Central Authority could then adjust this system (i) by putting up (or down) the prices of any of the unplanned products or factors according as there resulted an excess demand (or supply) of them, (ii) by revising its quantitative plans by shifting the planned factors from Subordinate Authorities in which their shadow prices were low to those where their shadow prices were high and by requiring less output of a planned product from a source where its shadow cost was high and more from a source where its shadow cost was low, and (iii) revising the total quantities of the planned products if there developed a total excess supply or demand for the products concerned. This mixed system also would settle down to rest only in a situation in which production was both maximized and optimized.[1]

Note A to Chapter XIV

THE STABILITY OF TRIAL-AND-ERROR PLANNING

Consider a case in which only two products *X* and *Y* are to be produced by means of the community's given resources. The production-possibility curve is of the kind shown by *LZ* in Figure 56 or Figure 57. The *LZ* curve may approximate to a continuous smooth curve (as is shown in Figures 26, 28 (ii), 39, and 56) or, if the productive system is restricted to a small number of discrete processes, the curve may take the form of a kinked line (as in Figures 25, 42, 43, 44, 46, 49 (i), 50, and 57). The reader is referred back to the discussion of the earlier figures for an explanation why the production-possibility curve takes these forms and, in particular, why the slope of the curve either remains the same (constant costs) or becomes steeper (increasing costs) as we move down it to the right. We will first illustrate the argument of this Note from the continuous curve as shown in Figure 56. As will become clear, the basic features of the argument remain the same if we use the kinked line of Figure 57 instead.

Let us suppose that the planning procedure in our economy is as follows. Certain quantities of *X* and *Y* are put on the market; they are sold for what they will fetch; this gives market prices for *X* and *Y*; on the basis of these market prices (P_x and P_y) and of the known technological possibilities the computer is told to calculate the

[1] In this chapter we have described the use of programming techniques solely in the context of a centrally planned economy. But within a generally *laissez faire* competitive market economy these programming techniques may be of great use to individual firms. Consider a firm with a very complicated choice of combinations of inputs and outputs, but buying and selling in a perfectly competitive (or potentially perfectly competitive) market at given prices for its inputs and outputs. As in the case of a Subordinate Authority described above (pp. 211–16), it can use the technique of linear programming to see (i) (by means of the Primal) whether it is choosing those scales for its different processes which maximize at current market selling prices the value of the output which it can produce by means of its existing level of resources and (ii) (by means of the Dual) what is the value to it of the marginal product of its various resources. It can use (i) to replan its productive processes and (ii) to replan its intake of resources. Economists are apt to assume in discussing the economics of a competitive system that each firm is efficient within itself and that this is solely a question of having good engineers and similar technicians. But there is in fact an economic, as well as a technical-engineering, problem within the firm to decide whether it is using its (technically efficient) processes in the best combinations. The planning techniques described in this chapter thus have their uses in the business economics of the competitive economy.

amounts of X and Y which will maximize the value of the national output $(P_xX + P_yY)$; these amounts are produced and put on the market and sold for what they will fetch; this gives new values for the market prices P_x and P_y; the computer is told to recalculate the quantities of X and Y which will maximize the value of the national output at these new market valuations; and so on. Figure 56 (i) shows a set of conditions in which this crude trial-and-error procedure will fail to find an equilibrium solution of the planning

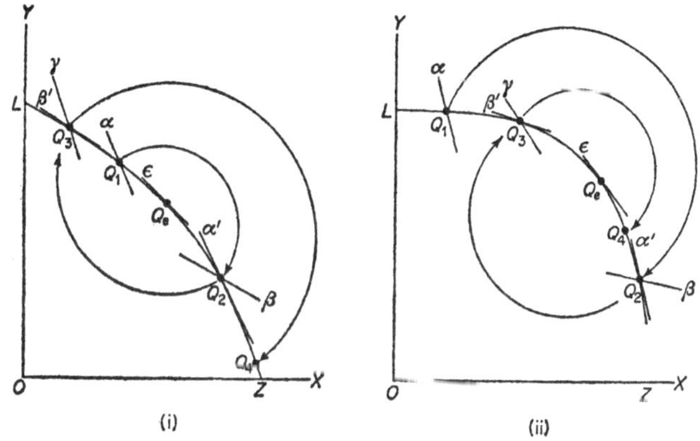

Figure 56

problem, although such an equilibrium does in fact exist. Figure 56 (ii) shows an alternative set of conditions in which this procedure will succeed in finding the equilibrium solution. The explanation of the figure is as follows.

The reader is referred to Chapter VI, Figures 25 and 26 (pp. 91–96) for a proof of the fact that if the computer is given relative prices of X and Y $\left(\frac{P_x}{P_y}\right)$ which correspond to the slope of the line α or α' (α is parallel to α') in Figure 56 (i), it will report that the quantity combination at Q_2 (at which the production-possibility curve has the same slope as the price line α or α') is the one which will maximize the value of total output. Similarly, if the computer is given relative prices of X and Y $\left(\frac{P_x}{P_y}\right)$ which correspond to the slope β or β', it will report that the quantity combination Q_3 is the one which maximizes the value of output. Let us suppose then that we start with the combination Q_1 being produced and sold. Since a relatively large amount of Y is being produced, the price of Y will be relatively low, i.e. the slope of the market demand price line will be rather steep as at α. The computer being given α for its price valuations will decree that the output combination Q_2 be produced and put on the market. Now much X and little Y is produced, so that the demand price line will move to β, where the price of Y is now relatively high. Since, as it happens, the slope of β is less steep than was the slope of the production-possibility curve at the starting-point Q_1, the computer will now decree a production combination, such as Q_3, to the North-West of Q_1. As Q_3 contains more Y and less X than Q_1, the market demand line γ at Q_3 will be more steeply sloped than α at Q_1. The computer will, therefore, now decree that, as at Q_4, more X and less Y be produced than at Q_2 where the less steeply sloped price line α' was the basis of its calculations. Thus although there exists an equilibrium combination Q_e[1] at which the demand prices (ϵ) are the same as the prices used by the computer to plan the output combination Q_e, yet the process of market trial and error swings the planned outputs further and further away from Q_e.

The same process of trial and error in the conditions of Figure 56 (ii) would reach the equilibrium solution at Q_e. We start again at Q_1 with the demand conditions making the price of Y relatively low (slope of α steep). The computer orders a move to Q_2 which gives a market demand price relationship β. But β is in this case more steeply sloped than was the production-possibility curve at the starting-point Q_1, so that the computer now orders a move to Q_3 which is to the South-East of Q_1. And so on. In this case the output combination can be seen to approach the equilibrium point Q_e.

The relevant differences between the conditions which fail—as in Figure 56 (i)—and those which succeed—as in Figure 56 (ii)—in leading this process of trial and error to an equilibrium are twofold. Success is more likely (*a*) the more rigid is the production system and (*b*) the more flexible is the structure of market demands.

(*a*) If the production system is a rigid one, small changes in outputs will cause large changes in relative costs. The production-possibility curve will have a marked curvature as in Figure 56 (ii). Thus, given any initial discrepancy between market prices and the slope of the production-possibility curve as at Q_1,[2] the computer will decree a relatively small change in output from Q_1 to Q_2.

[1] Since at Q_1 the market price line α is more steeply sloped than is the production-possibility curve and at Q_2 the market price line β is less steeply sloped than is the production-possibility curve, there must be some intermediate point, such as Q_e, where the market price line, such as ϵ, has the same slope as the production-possibility curve.

[2] It should be noted that the initial discrepancy is much bigger in Figure 56(ii) than in Figure 56(i).

(*b*) If the demand structure is a flexible one, i.e. if price elasticities of demand are (numerically) large, any given change from Q_1 to Q_2 will cause a relatively small change in the slope of the demand price lines from α to β.

Both reasons (*a*) and (*b*) moderate the change in the price slope between α and β and there is, therefore, a double reason for expecting Q_3 to lie to the South-East of Q_1—as in Figure 56 (ii)—rather than to the North-West of Q_1—as in Figure 56 (i). On the other hand, if a small change in the prices used by the computer causes a violent change in the planned outputs, and if even a small change in the planned outputs causes a violent change in market prices, then one is likely to get the exaggerated swings of Figure 56 (i).

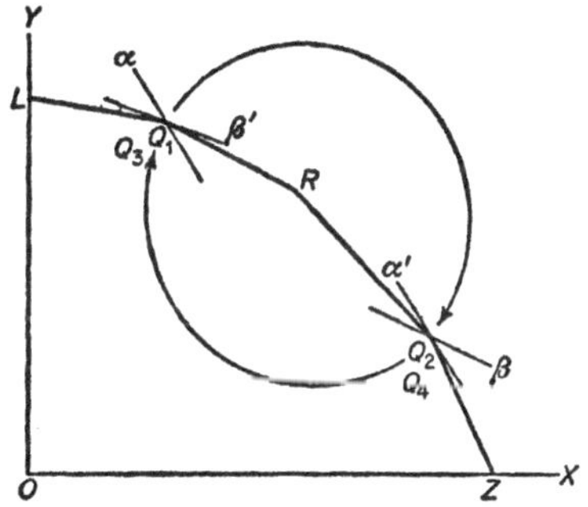

Figure 57

In Figure 56 (i) we have shown a case in which the point Q swings further and further away from the equilibrium point Q_e and in Figure 56 (ii) a case where Q swings nearer and nearer to Q_e. It might conceivably so happen that the slope of the demand line β at Q_2 was neither less steep—as in Figure 56 (i)—nor more steep—as in Figure 56 (ii)—than, but had exactly the same slope as, the production-possibility curve at Q_1. Then Q_3 would coincide with Q_1. The crude trial-and-error procedure would then oscillate from Q_1 to Q_2 to Q_1 to Q_2 and so on.

With a continuous smooth production-possibility curve as *LZ* in Figure 56 the coincidence of Q_1 and Q_3 would be the merest fluke. But with planning on the basis of a small number of discrete processes a kinked production-possibility line would result as in Figure 57. In this case the occurrence of a perpetual oscillation between Q_1 and Q_2 would not involve a mere fluke. Suppose that, as in Figure 57, the demand price line α at the point Q_1 lies somewhere between the slope of RQ_2 and the slope of Q_2Z, and that the demand price line β at the point Q_2 lies somewhere between the slope of LQ_1 and the slope of Q_1R. This constellation of demand and supply conditions covers not one single fluke occurrence, but quite a large range of cases. Then, as can be seen from Figure 57, on the basis of the analysis already applied to Figure 56, there will be a perpetual oscillation from Q_1 to Q_2 to Q_1 to Q_2 and so on.[1]

There is one broad moral to be learned from this analysis. If a market process of trial and error is adopted, the changes in the amounts put on the market should be small and gradual in order to try out the degree of change required. In terms of Figure 56 (i) or Figure 57 the fault lies in allowing the market price line α to induce the planners at one fell swoop to change the planned quantities from Q_1 to Q_2 rather than to use the price line α merely as an indication that some moderate move from Q_1 in the general direction of Q_2 should be tried out.

Note B to Chapter XIV

A SIMPLE EXAMPLE OF THE PRIMAL AND DUAL PROBLEMS

The relationships between the Primal and Dual problems discussed on pages 213–15 above may become clearer if we apply the analysis to a very simple case. For this purpose we take the case examined on pages 160–5 in Chapter XI, which has already been illustrated in Table VI and Figure 42. We have two factors, L and N, used in fixed proportions in either of two processes; the first process produces only X, using 1 unit of L and 2 units of N to produce 1 unit of X; and the second process produces only Z, using 2 units of L and 1 unit of N to produce 1 unit of Z. We can describe these two processes (cf. Table XII) in the following way:

		Processes I	II
Outputs of	X	1	0
	Z	0	1
Inputs of	L	1	2
	N	2	1
Scale[2]	S	X	Z

[1] This case is essentially similar to the possible oscillation between points R and S on Figure 25 discussed in Chapter VI (pp. 93–94).

[2] A unit scale for Process I is defined as one which produces 1 unit of X. Since X is produced only by Process I, the number of units of X produced measures the scale on which Process I is operated. Similarly the number of units of Z produced measures S for Process II.

If in addition we know how much L and how much N are available in the economy as a whole, we can in this simple case describe the production possibilities by a simple diagram of the kind shown already in Figure 42, the basic features of which are reproduced here in Figure 58. The line AE represents the constraint on the

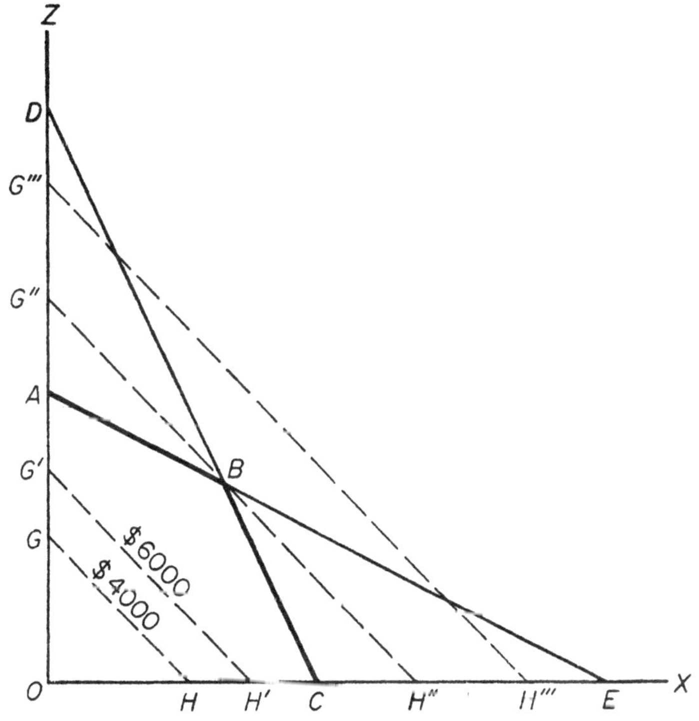

Figure 58

production of X and Z imposed by the limited supply of the factor L, and the line DC represents the constraint on the production of X and Z imposed by the limited supply of the factor N. The kinked line ABC then represents the production possibilities.

If we then know the prices of the products X and Z, we can draw a series of equi-revenue lines GH, $G'H'$, etc., each of which represents the combinations of X and Z which would sell for a given total revenue (cf. Figure 39 and pp. 129–30 above). The slope of these lines measures the price of Z relatively to the price of X or the amount of Z which would exchange for a unit of X at the current market prices, P_x and P_z.

P

The discussion on pages 162–5 can be used to show how the forces of competition will cause a movement of output along the *ABC* kinked line until the highest *GH* line is reached. The same problem, instead of being put for solution to the competitive market, could be set by a planning authority as a programming problem to a computer, who would be instructed to discover quantities for X and Z on the highest possible *GH* line subject to (1) not going North East of the line *AE* (i.e. not using more than the available supply of the factor L), (2) not going North East of the line *CD* (i.e. not using more than the available supply of the factor N), and (3) not going West or South of the axes *ZOX* (i.e. not producing a negative quantity of X or Z). This is, of course, the Primal problem corresponding to the simple competitive case discussed on pages 160–6. It can be expressed as:

Find values of X and Z such that $P_xX + P_zZ$ is maximized, subject to:

(i) $1X + 2Z \leqslant L$
(ii) $2X + 1Z \leqslant N$
(iii) $X \geqslant O$
(iv) $Z \geqslant O$

Now it is clear from the discussion of this case on pages 160–6 that the competitive process which adjusts the outputs X and Z to the demand prices P_x and P_z will in fact also determine the competitive market prices of the two factors, P_l and P_n. These prices are not directly shown on Figures 42 or 58; and they are not directly produced by the computer in the solution of the corresponding Primal programming problem. But as is shown on page 164 the factor prices P_l and P_n do in fact lie hidden behind Figure 42; and in a similar way certain corresponding 'shadow prices' lie hidden in the solution of the Primal problem.

In the geometric description of the competitive process we could have started at the price end rather than the quantity end of the problem. We can enquire directly how the factor prices (P_l and P_n) are determined by the demand prices for the products (P_x and P_z), given the technical co-efficients in the two production processes and given the total supplies of the two factors available to the economy as a whole. The Dual programming problem corresponds to this direct enquiry into the determination of the factor prices (P_l and P_n) by the market forces of competition.

Let us consider then how we could show geometrically the determination of the factor prices (P_l and P_n) in the competitive conditions discussed on pages 160–5. In Figure 59 we measure P_l along the horizontal axis and P_n up the vertical axis. Since the production of 1 unit of X requires 1 unit of L and 2 units of N, the cost of production of a unit of X is $1P_l + 2P_n$. In competition the cost of X must be equal to the price of X, if X is produced. Suppose the price of X is \$2. Then if X is produced, we have

$$1P_l + 2P_n = \$2.$$

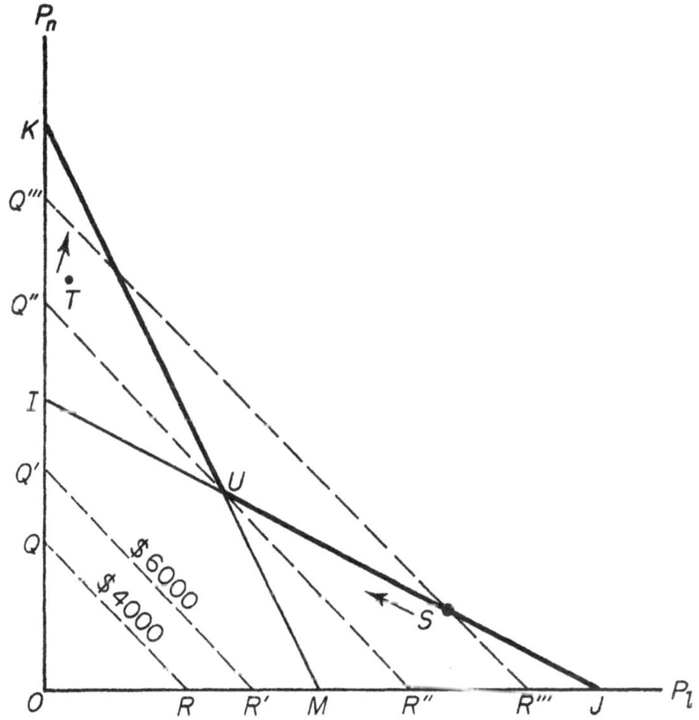

Figure 59

We can represent this by the line IJ which shows the combinations of P_l and P_n which will make the cost of X equal to \$2. For every fall of one cent in P_n we can have a rise of two cents in P_l, since X uses 2 units of N to every 1 unit of L. The slope of IJ thus measures the ratio L_x/N_x, i.e., the fixed ratio L to N needed in the production of X. If P_x falls, then the line IJ falls; but its slope remains unchanged because it depends solely on the fixed ratio L_x/N_x.

Similarly one can draw a line KM which represents the equality between cost and price for product Z, namely:

$$2P_l + 1P_n = P_z.$$

The slope of this line will be steeper than that of the line *IJ* because the production of *Z* takes 2 units of *L* to 1 unit of *N*, so that we can now have for each fall of one cent in P_n an increase of only ½ cent in P_l to keep the cost of *Z* constant.

Competition will ensure that P_l and P_n are combined together only at points on the kinked line *KUJ*. If P_l and P_n were at the point *T* to the South-West of the line *KM*, the production of *Z* would show a profit over and above its cost. P_l and P_n would both be driven up by the competition of employers to obtain more factors to expand the profitable *Z*-production. *T* would move in the direction of the arrow. At *T* which is North-East of the line *IJ*, no *X* would be produced because the combined cost of the factors would be greater than the selling price of the product. If the point *T* were North-East of both *KM* and *IJ*, both products would be unprofitable. All production would be damped down, and the prices of both factors would fall as the demand for them declined. Thus competition would keep the prices of the factors on the kinked line *KUJ*. Between *K* and *U* P_n is so high relatively to P_l that only the *L*-intensive product *Z* will be produced. Between *U* and *J* only the *N*-intensive product *X* will be produced. At *U* both products cover their costs.

Figure 59 shows clearly certain relationships between the prices of the products and of the factors. Suppose that the demand price for *X* (P_x) falls. Then, as we have seen, the line *IJ* falls, maintaining the same slope. Thus the point *U* at which both industries cover their costs moves South-East. The fall in the demand for the *N*-intensive product *X* would have caused the price of *N* to fall; but the price of *L* would be driven up because of the increased demand for *L* to produce the *L*-intensive product *Z*. If P_x falls so low that *J* moves to the left of *M*, then no *X* will be produced, because there is now no combination of factor prices sufficiently low both to make *X* profitable and also not to leave a supernormal profit on *Z*—with the consequence that the *Z*-producers would bid up the factor prices and make *X* unprofitable. (This case is the same as the case of the price line α in Figure 42, where P_x is so low relatively to P_y that no *X* will be produced.)

We can now complete Figure 59 by considering the total amounts of the factors which are available in the community. We have seen that the slopes of *IJ* (and of *KM*) measure L_x/N_x (and L_z/N_z), the fixed ratios of *L* to *N* needed in the two industries. Draw a series of parallel lines *QR*, *Q′R′*, etc., the slope of which measures L/N, the ratio of *L* to *N* in the total factor supplies available to the community. Consider any point such as *S* on the kinked line *KUJ*. At *S* the production of *Z* is unprofitable. Only *X* is produced. But the ratio of L_x/N_x (the slope of *UJ*) is less than the ratio L/N (the slope of $Q'''R'''$). There will, therefore, be unemployed *L*, since the ratio of *L* to *N* available in the economy is greater than the ratio of *L* to *N* used in the only profitable industry *X*. Competition among the factors will, therefore, cause P_l to fall and P_n to rise. *S* will move along *JU* towards *U*, as shown by the arrow. Alternatively, if the *QR* lines were more gently sloped than the line *UJ* (and *a fortiori* more gently sloped than the *KU* line), this would represent the case in which the ratio of *L* to *N* available in the community were less than the ratio of *L* to *N* needed in the least *L*-intensive industry *X*. There would necessarily be some unemployed *N*. The point *S* where-ever it might start on *KUJ* would move down *KUJ* to *J*. *N* would become a free good and P_n would become zero. (This is the same case as that shown on Figure 42 by the line *A′E′* which represents the case where *N* is so plentiful relatively to *L*, that it is only the factor *L* which acts as a constraint on production.)

It is clear from Figure 59 that competition (i) will keep P_l and P_n in relation to each other so that they remain on the kinked line *KUJ* and (ii) will make the equilibrium point move down from *K* towards *J* (or up from *J* towards *K*) according as the slope of the *QR* lines is less (or more) steep than that of the relevant section of the *KUJ* line. In other words, we move along the *KUJ* line until we reach the lowest possible *QR* line.

Now it is to be observed that the *QR* lines in fact represent lines of equal total factor costs for the economy as a whole. Suppose, for example, that in the economy as a whole $L = 2000$ and $N = 1000$. We have drawn the *QR* lines so that their slope measures L/N or, in our example, 2000/1000. In other words $OQ/OR = 2$. Suppose the distance *OR* measures a wage rate (P_l) of \$2. Then the distance *OQ* measures a rate of rent (P_n) of \$4, because $OQ/OR = 2$ so that $OQ = 2 \times \$2$. At the point *R* $P_l = \$2$ and $P_n = \$0$, so that total factor costs $= 2000 \times \$2 + 1000 \times \$0 = \$4{,}000$. At the point *Q* $P_l = \$0$ and $P_n = \$4$, so that factor costs equal $2000 \times \$0 + 1000 \times \$4 = \$4{,}000$. As we move up from *R* to *Q*, P_n rises by 2 cents for each fall of 1 cent in P_l. Since there is twice as much *L* as *N*, total factor costs remain constant at \$4,000. *QR* thus represents the combinations of P_l and P_n which will give total factor costs of \$4,000. If *OQ′* is $1\frac{1}{2}$ times *OQ* and *OR′* is $1\frac{1}{2}$ times *OR*, then the line *Q′R′* represents combinations of P_l and P_n which will give total factor costs of \$6,000 for the same given total amounts of the factors; and so on for *Q″R″*, etc.

If we now want our computer to tell the planning authority what the prices of the factors would be if they were submitted to this competitive process, we could set it the following exercise. Find values for P_l and P_n on the lowest possible QR line (i.e., the lowest total of factor costs) which is compatible with (1) not moving South-West of the line KM (i.e., not allowing an excess profit in Z-production), (2) not moving South-West of the line IJ (i.e., not allowing an excess profit in X-production), and (3) not moving South or West of the axes P_nOP_l (i.e., not fixing minus quantities for the wage rate or the rate of rent). This is, of course, the Dual of our previous Primal programming problem. It can be expressed in the following way:

Find values of P_l and P_n such that $LP_l + NP_n$ is minimized, subject to:

$$
\begin{aligned}
&\text{(i)}\ \ 1P_l + 2P_n \geqslant P_x \\
&\text{(ii)}\ \ 2P_l + 1P_n \geqslant P_z \\
&\text{(iii)}\ \ P_l \qquad\quad \geqslant 0 \\
&\text{(iv)}\ \ P_n \qquad\quad \geqslant 0
\end{aligned}
$$

The mathematicians reassure the economists that the solutions of the Primal and Dual reached by a good computer will display the following connections. If in the Primal the computer says that some X should be produced ($X > 0$), then in the Dual it will say that the 'shadow' cost of X will be equal to the price of X ($1P_l + 2P_n = P_x$). But if in the Dual, it says that the 'shadow' cost of X will exceed its price ($1P_l + 2P_n > P_x$), then in the Primal it will say that no X should be produced ($X = 0$). Conversely, if in the Dual it says that the 'shadow' price of L should be positive ($P_l > 0$), then in the Primal it will say that L should be fully employed ($1X + 2Z = L$). But if in the Primal it says that some L should remain unemployed ($1X + 2Z < L$), then in the Dual it will say that the 'shadow' price of L should be zero ($P_l = 0$). And similarly for the other products and factors and for their costs and prices. The computer will also declare that the maximum value of the total output calculated in the Primal equals the minimum value of the total factor costs calculated in the Dual. Total receipts will be equal to total 'shadow' costs as in the competitive process. In fact the Primal and the Dual in the programming computation correspond exactly to the determination of quantities and of prices respectively in the perfectly competitive process.

CHAPTER XV

THE CENTRALLY PLANNED ECONOMY (iii) THE DEPLOYMENT OF LABOUR—CONCLUSION

We must turn now to a discussion of problems 5, 6, and 7 on page 200 above. The planning procedures which have been discussed in the previous chapter have all been based upon the assumption that the Central Authority will allot the factors of production to their various employments. In the case of labour this involves the direction of the citizens to their appropriate tasks in the community. This raises a number of special issues which we will consider in the present chapter.

In directing workers to their tasks the Central Authority would have to consider the following five issues:

(i) Labour is not a homogeneous factor. The aptitudes of the young are not the same as those of the old, and those of women are not the same as those of men; some workers are more intelligent than others, some stronger physically than others, some are more nimble with their fingers than others, and so on for a wide range of differences. There is a very large number of possible combinations of abilities and disabilities; and each type of worker should be treated as a different factor of production. The shadow prices which the Subordinate Authorities would quote to the Central Authority, should, therefore, refer separately to each type of labour. To achieve full efficiency in its plan the Central Authority would have to know separately the available supply of every type of labour.

(ii) Not only do workers differ in their aptitudes; jobs also differ in their pleasantness. To achieve full economic efficiency the Central Authority should not always shift workers of a given grade from a task for which the shadow price was low to one in which it was high. It should do so only if the job with the high shadow price was not so much more unpleasant than the job with the low shadow price that the worker would prefer the latter job with the low reward to the former job with the high reward. (See the analysis on pages 187–8 above.) In the absence of anything corresponding to a free labour market, the Central Authority would have to form its own paternalistic view as to whether the differences in shadow prices for any one grade of labour did or did not correspond to differences in the pleasantness of the tasks.

(iii) Moreover, different men may have different attitudes to the same jobs. One man may prefer outdoor work and another indoor work. One may prefer work in one locality and another work in another locality. Thus workers of the same grade may gain without anyone else losing if they are able to exchange jobs. (See the analysis on p. 188 above.) In the absence of anything like a free labour market the Central Authority would have to try by direct enquiry from the workers to direct each worker to the types of work for which the worker expressed a preference; but in doing so it would have, by its own paternalistic judgment, to weigh the importance of the workers' preference against the relative importance to the community of different tasks as measured by their shadow prices.

(iv) The Central Authority would also have to decide how long hours each group of workers should work. This raises a problem of economic efficiency. Would a group of workers prefer an extra hour's leisure or the extra output of an additional hour's work? In the absence of anything corresponding to a labour market the Central Authority would have to make this decision on the workers' behalf.

(v) The decision about hours of work for various workers would raise for the Central Authority not only the question whether by working more or less one group of workers could be made better off without anyone being made worse off, but also the question whether the burden of work was fairly distributed among the various workers.

It is apparent merely from this enumeration of the issues involved that something corresponding to a labour market would enormously simplify the task of the Central Authority. Let us consider one possible set of institutional arrangements to see how the system might work. Suppose then that the State pays to its citizens social dividends or benefits out of the income received on State Property, these social dividends or benefits being based on such criteria of needs as age, health, and the like, but not being adjusted at all to take account of the family's income from wages. Suppose further that a wage income is paid to each worker in each job which is equal to the shadow price of that work in that job. For this purpose the Subordinate Authorities in charge of each process might be given considerable responsibility in determining the actual grade of labour in which each particular worker should be included. Suppose finally that the incomes received from social benefits and from wages can be spent in a free consumers' market on the products of the various firms and farms. The essential features of this arrangement are (i) that the worker's real wage varies directly with the value of the marginal product of his current work and (ii) that this is not offset by counteracting variations in the social benefits received by him and his family.

With such a system the problems which the Central Authority would have to face in directing labour in an efficient manner would be greatly simplified. The wage earner's real income in various employments would correspond to the value of his marginal product in those occupations. He could indicate to the Central Authority in which particular jobs he would prefer employment in view both of the pleasantness or unpleasantness of the task to him and also of the real wage which he could earn in it. The Central Authority could shift the labour from the less to the more preferred tasks.

Similarly it would be possible for the individual worker to indicate to the Central Authority whether at the real wage per hour which he was receiving (and which would correspond to the value of his marginal product) he preferred more work or more leisure. To the extent to which it was administratively possible the Central Authority could then adjust the hours worked in the desired direction.[1]

As labour was redirected to the employments of its own choice and as hours of work in different processes were adjusted, so the various production plans of the Subordinate Authorities could be revised on the principles discussed in the last chapter. Thus the shadow prices of labour would be raised in those jobs to which less labour had been directed or in which hours of work had been cut and would be reduced in those jobs to which more labour had been directed or in which hours of work had been increased. Finally an equilibrium might be reached in which (i) each worker received a wage equal to the value of his marginal product in the job in which he was employed, (ii) each worker of any given grade preferred at this wage his current job to any other available to him, and (iii) no worker wished to vary his hours of work at the real wage which he was receiving. On the basis of this analysis already applied to the competitive economy (see pp. 186–8 above) it can be seen that this would represent an efficient deployment of the labour force.

But would the distribution of income be an equitable one? An essential feature of the above arrangements for achieving an efficient deployment of labour is that the incomes received as social dividends or social benefits should not be adjusted to take into account dif-

[1] Even if it is impossible to allow each worker independently to choose in any one given firm how many hours work he shall do a day, considerable adjustment is possible in two ways. First, the hours of work for a whole group of workers can be lengthened or shortened if there is a general desire for a change at the current hourly real wage rate. Second, it is possible to organize different lengths of shift in the same or in different firms (e.g. either two shifts of 6 hours each or three shifts of 4 hours each) and to allow workers to express a preference to join the one shift or the other.

ferences in wage earnings. The reason for this is clear. A man considering a move, say, from a pleasant low-paid job to an unpleasant high-paid job would reach the correct decision if both of two conditions are fulfilled: (i) the two wages reflect the different marginal products of the jobs and (ii) the wage earner keeps the whole (no more and no less) of the increase in the wage income if he moves. But if a man's social dividend or social benefits are reduced when his wage income goes up, the worker will not feel the whole of the incentive which he should feel on moving from a job with a low marginal product to one with a high marginal product. For an efficient solution then (i) wage rates must be equal to marginal products and (ii) social dividends and social benefits must be fixed independently of wage earnings.

This means, however, that there will be considerable inequalities of income so long as the distribution of abilities relatively to requirements in jobs is unequal. Those workers who have the scarce abilities may earn much more than those who have only the commoner abilities. The basic conditions in the economy may be such that wage earnings make up a much larger proportion of the national income than do the social dividends and benefits paid out of income from property.[1] If in addition there were great disparities in human abilities, the system might be one in which there were great inequalities of income. If it was desired to offset these inequalities, there would be a basic clash between efficiency and equity in distribution. The progressive taxation of high wage earnings to supplement the social benefits of the poor would reduce inequalities of income but would blunt the incentives for efficiency which depend upon variations in retained earnings corresponding to variations in the marginal products of the work done.

We have in this and the last two chapters considered briefly the way in which a centrally planned economy would have to cope with the problems previously discussed (Chapters I to XII) in the framework of a fully competitive *laissez-faire* economy. On the strict assumptions made in Chapter I and which have been maintained throughout this volume, there would seem to be little to recommend the replacement of a *laissez faire* competitive economy with a centrally planned economy, except in so far as the income from property would accrue to the State and could be distributed by the State in social dividends on some planned equitable basis. Otherwise everything would pro-

[1] This will depend upon the relative marginal products of labour and of land of various qualities resulting from the relative scarcity of the two types of factor and the nature of consumers' preferences as between labour-intensive and land-intensive products.

ceed efficiently as in a completely *laissez faire* competitive economy. Consumers would receive incomes from wages and social dividends. These they would spend in competition in the Shops on the goods produced by private-enterprise competing Firms and Farms. The entrepreneurs would produce what was most profitable in view of the selling prices of the products; and they would bid up the rewards to the factors to a level equal to the value of the marginal product of each factor in each occupation. As far as labour was concerned, the workers would compete for the jobs at the wage rates offered by the employers. As far as the rents of land were concerned, the State would mimic a competitive market, letting out each acre of land to that employer who offered the best price for it. This system would be an economically efficient one. Whether the distribution of income would be acceptable or not would depend upon the extent of the resulting inequalities in wage-earnings. To correct any such remaining undesirable inequities in income distribution would then involve some clash between setting the incentives desired for economic efficiency and obtaining the desired distribution of income.

But the fact that on the assumptions of the present volume there is little case for a central economic plan should not be supposed to beg the question for the choice of institutions in the world of reality. As we have tried to show in the closing chapters of this volume, there are a large number of different institutional settings in which elements of the market mechanism can be combined with elements of a central plan. Many features of the real world which are particularly relevant to the choice of the best institutional mixture have been assumed away throughout this volume. Any final judgment about economic institutions must be left to a much later stage in this work when these relevant conditions of the real world have been brought back into the picture. We will close this volume merely by enumerating the most important of them.

(i) So far we have neglected the fact that capital goods and raw materials exist and that the production system includes these intermediate products which are both outputs of some processes and the inputs of others. This introduces many considerations some in favour of a free market mechanism and some in favour of a central plan.

(ii) We have not yet allowed for continuous change in our economy due to population growth, capital accumulation, and technical progress. The process of adjustment of the economy to continuous change, its reactions to uncertainty and mistakes, and the stability of its development are considerations of the utmost importance for the choice between free markets and central control. Once again these considerations do not point unequivocally to the one solution or the other.

(iii) In this volume we have said little about the motives of those who are in charge of economic processes. Whether they respond more effectively to the search for private profit or for the performance of a sound professional task is a basic psychological issue. But a still broader question arises when the assumptions made in this volume are modified, namely whether the market will always give to private entrepreneurs the private incentives to do what is socially desirable. One particularly important instance of this is the problem of setting the right incentives for research, invention, and innovation. Once again the answer is not at all clear cut.

(iv) So far we have assumed constant returns to scale throughout industry. Later we shall have to allow for the fact that in many cases there will be increasing returns to scale and that for this reason there will be inevitable elements of monopoly in many markets. This set of considerations can very greatly affect one's attitude towards the workings of the free market mechanism and introduces a number of new reasons for considering favourably some elements of central control.

(v) Moreover, we have so far assumed that there are no external economies or diseconomies in the economy and—as an extreme result of this—that there are no objects of communal as opposed to individual consumption, such as justice, defence, public education and the like. We have also assumed that individual's preferences are consistent, rational, and independent of other people's actions, which involves—*inter alia*—the assumption that no one is susceptible to the persuasions of the advertisers. Clearly the modification of these assumptions will greatly strengthen the case for certain forms of economic action by the State.

In fact the particular model discussed at great length in this volume is peculiarly well adapted to show some of the strongest virtues of the free competitive market economy. It will have served its purpose if, in addition to providing a training in certain techniques of analysis which will still find their use in later volumes, it has demonstrated the basic case for the use of a price mechanism of some sort. But it must not be thought to provide the basis for a fair assessment of the great issue between *laissez faire* and socialism. Before that judgment can be passed there is much more to be considered.

INDEX

For Product Safety Concerns and Information please contact our EU representative GPSR@taylorandfrancis.com
Taylor & Francis Verlag GmbH, Kaufingerstraße 24, 80331 München, Germany

www.ingramcontent.com/pod-product-compliance
Lightning Source LLC
LaVergne TN
LVHW011126300926
849160LV00008B/536

* 9 7 8 0 4 1 5 6 2 1 7 4 8 *